CONCENTRATE Q&A
FAMILY LAW

CONCENTRATE
Q&A
FAMILY LAW

Ruth Gaffney-Rhys

Reader in Law
University of South Wales

OXFORD
UNIVERSITY PRESS

OXFORD
UNIVERSITY PRESS

Great Clarendon Street, Oxford, OX2 6DP,
United Kingdom

Oxford University Press is a department of the University of Oxford.
It furthers the University's objective of excellence in research, scholarship,
and education by publishing worldwide. Oxford is a registered trade mark of
Oxford University Press in the UK and in certain other countries

Public sector information reproduced under Open Government Licence v3.0
(http://www.nationalarchives.gov.uk/doc/open-government-licence/open-government-licence.htm)

Published in the United States of America by Oxford University Press
198 Madison Avenue, New York, NY 10016, United States of America

British Library Cataloguing in Publication Data
Data available

Library of Congress Control Number: 2016942460

ISBN 978–0–19–871575–7

Printed in Great Britain by
Bell & Bain Ltd., Glasgow

Contents

Editor's acknowledgements

The brand-new Concentrate Q&A series from Oxford University Press has been developed alongside hundreds of students and lecturers from a range of universities across the UK.

I'd like to take this opportunity to thank all those law students who've filled in questionnaires, completed in-depth reviews of sample materials, attended focus groups, and provided us with the insight and feedback we needed to shape a series relevant for today's law students.

Also to the lecturers the length and breadth of the UK who have given so generously of their time by being heavily involved in our lengthy review process; their inside information gained from experience as teachers and examiners has been vital in the shaping of this new series.

You told us that you wanted a Q&A book that:

- gives you tips to help you understand exactly what the question is asking
- offers focused guidance on how to structure your answer and develop your arguments
- uses clear and simple diagrams to help you see how to structure your answers at a glance
- highlights key debates and extra points for you to add to your answers to get the highest marks
- flags common mistakes to avoid when answering questions
- offers detailed advice on coursework assignments as well as exams
- provides focused reading suggestions to help you develop in-depth knowledge for when you are looking for the highest marks
- is accompanied by a great range of online support

We listened and we have delivered.

We are confident that because they provide exactly what you told us you need, the Concentrate Q&As offer you better support and a greater chance for succeeding than any competing series.

We wish you all the best throughout your law course and in your exams and hope that these guides give you the confidence to tackle any question that you encounter, and give you the skills you need to excel during your studies and beyond.

Good luck
Carol Barber, Senior Publishing Editor

This is what you said:

'The content is exceptional; the best Q&A books that I've read'

Wendy Chinenye Akaigwe, law student, London Metropolitan University

'Since I started using the OUP Q&A guides my grades have dramatically improved'

Glen Sylvester, law student, Bournemouth University

'A sure-fire way to get a 1st class result'

Naomi M, law student, Coventry University

'100% would recommend. Makes you feel like you will pass with flying colours'

Elysia Marie Vaughan, law student, University of Hertfordshire

'Excellent. Very detailed which makes a change from the brief answers in other Q&A books . . . fantastic'

Frances Easton, law student, University of Birmingham

This is what your lecturers said:

'Much more substantial and less superficial than competitor Q&As. Some guides are rather too simplistic but the OUP guides are much better than the norm'

Dr Tony Harvey, Principal law lecturer, Liverpool John Moores University

'Cleverly and carefully put together. Every bit as good as one would expect from OUP, you really have cornered the market in the revision guides sector. I am also a huge fan of the OUP Concentrate series and I think that these books sit neatly alongside this'

Alice Blythe, law lecturer, University of Bolton

'I think Q&A guides are crucial and advise my students to buy early on'

Loretta Trickett, law lecturer, Nottingham Trent University

'Students often lack experience in writing full answers but seeing suggested answers like this provides them with confidence and structure. I will be recommending this book to my students not just for revision purposes but for the duration of the unit'

Nick Longworth, law lecturer, Manchester Metropolitan University

Guide to the book

Every book in the Concentrate Q&A series contains the following features:

ARE YOU READY?

Are you ready to face the exam? This box at the start of each chapter identifies the key topics and cases that you need to have learned, revised, and understood before tackling the questions in each chapter.

DIAGRAM ANSWER PLANS

Not sure where to begin? Clear diagram answer plans at the start of each question help you see how to structure your answer at a glance, and take you through each point step-by-step.

KEY DEBATES

Demonstrating your knowledge of the crucial debates is a sure-fire way to impress examiners. These at-a-glance boxes help remind you of the key debates relevant to each topic, which you should discuss in your answers to get the highest marks.

SUGGESTED ANSWER

What makes a great answer great? Our authors show you the thought process behind their own answers, and how you can do the same in your exam. Key sentences are highlighted and advice is given on how to structure your answer well and develop your arguments.

QUESTION

Each question represents a typical essay or problem question so that you know exactly what to expect in your exam.

LOOKING FOR EXTRA MARKS?

Don't settle for a good answer—make it great! This feature gives you extra points to include in the exam if you want to gain more marks and make your answer stand out.

CAUTION!

Don't fall into any traps! This feature points out common mistakes that students make, and which you need to avoid when answering each question.

TAKING THINGS FURTHER

Really push yourself and impress your examiner by going beyond what is expected. Focused further reading suggestions allow you to develop in-depth knowledge of the subject for when you are looking for the highest marks.

Guide to the Online Resource Centre

Every book in the Concentrate Q&A series is supported by additional online materials to aid your study and revision: www.oxfordtextbooks.co.uk/orc/qanda

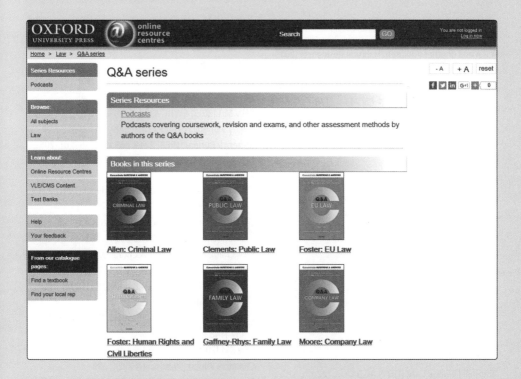

- Extra essay and problem questions.

- Bonus questions to help you practise and refine your technique. Questions are annotated, highlighting key terms and legal issues to help you plan your own answers. An indication of what your answers should cover is also provided.

- Online versions of the diagram answer plans.

- Video guidance on how to put an answer plan together.

- Flashcard glossaries of key terms.

- Audio advice on revision and exam technique from Nigel Foster.

- Audio advice on coursework technique.

- Audio advice on other assessment methods, for example MCQs, presentations, or mooting.

Table of cases

European Court of Human Rights cases

Table of legislation

UK bills

Australian legislation

UK statutory instruments

Exam Skills for Success in Family Law

1

Techniques for Examinations and Assignments

Examination and assignment questions can take the form of essays or problem scenarios.

Essay questions

- **Essay questions** often appear easier than problem questions because you do not have to work out what the questions are about. But, do not underestimate their difficulty: they often require candidates to demonstrate higher-level skills, for example critical analysis.

- In addition, essay questions are more likely to require students to cite academic opinion and sources such as Law Commission reports.

- Ensure that you address the specific question that has been set. Do not write everything you know about the topic and do not answer the question you wish had been set.

- When answering an essay question it useful to adopt the **PEA** method: **P**oint, **E**vidence, **A**nalysis.

- Each paragraph should make a specific **p**oint and should provide **e**vidence to support the point being made. The paragraph should end with your own **a**nalysis, with specific links being made to the question set.

- Utilising this method will ensure that your essay follows a logical structure and demonstrates the higher-level skills required by second, third or fourth year students.

Problem questions

- These may appear more difficult than essay questions because it is not immediately obvious what the question is about.

- Do not attempt a problem question in an examination unless you are sure that you have identified the relevant issue or issues.

- Ensure that you read problem questions very carefully, otherwise you might miss crucial facts, which could fundamentally affect the quality of your answer.

- Problem questions rarely contain superfluous information. If the scenario contains facts that you have not discussed, you have probably missed something.

- When answering a problem question, you should adopt the **IRAC** method: **I**ssue, **R**elevant Law, **A**pplication, **C**onclusion.

- Begin by identifying the legal issues raised in the problem question and then explain the relevant law. Next, you should apply the relevant law to the facts of the scenario and finally you should reach a conclusion, i.e. provide the advice required by the question.

- Check the instruction at the end of the factual scenario—are you required to explain the legal position in this case or are you asked to advise one specific party?

- Do not panic if you cannot reach a definite conclusion. This may be due to the fact that the examiner has deliberately omitted crucial facts or because the law itself is unclear. You are expected to raise and discuss these issues.

Family Law Assignments

Family law modules increasingly utilise in-course assignments or coursework as a means to formally assess students. Given the time that students have to complete an assignment, the lecturer will be far more stringent when assessing coursework than he or she is when marking examination papers (see chapter 12).

The questions included in this textbook could be set as assignment or examination questions. The suggested answers are likely to be shorter than you would be expected to produce for an assignment and will contain fewer academic references and references to Government reports etc. than a marker would expect in an assignment to achieve a good mark. You would also be expected to produce more in-depth conclusions than the brief ones included in this textbook.

The 'Looking for Extra Marks' feature that accompanies each question in this textbook and the comments attached to the suggested answer will provide guidance as to how to supplement the suggested answer, if the question is set as an assignment task. In addition, the 'Taking Things Further' section at the end of the chapter will direct you to sources that you may be able to utilise when completing coursework.

NB. The answers in this book are not accompanied by a bibliography or tables of cases and statutes, which are expected when you produce an assignment. In addition, the information in the answers is not referenced in accordance with a particular academic referencing system such as OSCOLA, which is commonly recommended by Law Schools (see chapter 12).

Examination Preparation

- Make sure that you attend any formal revision sessions offered by your tutor. If you do not do so, you may miss out on several useful hints and tips.

- Ensure that you know where and when the examination will take place. Check and double-check this information and do not rely on your fellow students. If the examination is to take place in a room or building that you have not been to before, find it at least one day prior to the examination.

- If you are entitled to special provision, for example a scribe, a word processor, extra time or a private room, ensure that your tutor or the student support services have arranged it. They will not assume that you require such provision—you must request it.

● Make sure that you know the format of the examination, i.e. How long is it? How many questions are you expected to answer? What degree of choice do you have? Are any of the questions compulsory? How are the marks awarded? Is it an open-book examination? If not, are statute books permitted? What style of questions will be used? Each of these will impact upon your examination preparation.

● Start your examination preparation early and make sure that you do enough work. You may be able to scrape a bare pass with little revision, but will not be able to achieve an upper second or first class honours unless you devote a considerable amount of time to examination preparation.

● Solid revision will not only ensure that you have the knowledge required to pass the examination; it will also help to ensure that you enter the examination room in a confident state of mind, which can clearly affect your performance on the day.

● An open-book examination does not mean that you do not need to revise. You need to be able to recount basic information without having to look for it in your notes or textbooks, as you won't have time to do so in the examination itself. In addition, the examiner will expect more of you in terms of detail and analysis if the examination is open-book, which means that your preparation should be different rather than non-existent.

● It is worth looking at past paper questions, particularly if the person setting your examination has written the papers in previous years. You will then become familiar with the examiner's style and may be able to 'guess' which topics are likely to appear in your examination.

● It is also worth practising past paper questions, if possible under examination conditions. I for one am always happy to mark practice papers that my students have completed in their own time. It may therefore be worth asking your tutor to assess your work. Even if he or she is unwilling to do so (university lecturers are very busy!), practising past papers is still a valuable exercise, as it shows you how much you can write in a limited period of time and how much you know.

● If you believe that your examination techniques are weak, seek advice from the support services available at your university.

At the Start of the Examination

● If you have not done so beforehand, work out the time at which you should be starting the second question, third question etc. and write it at the top of your examination paper/answer booklet once you have been given permission to start writing.

● If you have been given reading time use it effectively. Candidates are not normally permitted to start writing in their answer booklets during the reading time but may be able to highlight or underline the question paper.

● Begin by reading the instructions on the front page to ensure that your beliefs regarding the examination format, for example the number of questions that you must answer, are correct.

● During the reading time (or at the beginning of the examination if you have not been given reading time), read the entire paper in order to determine which questions you can and will answer.

● Read each question all the way through because questions that are divided into parts and lengthy problem questions may involve more than one topic. If your decision to answer a question was based on reading the first few lines, you may discover, part way through your answer, that you cannot actually complete it.

● Do not panic if you cannot immediately determine what a problem question is about. Reread it and mentally run through the topics you covered during the course. It would be a shame to miss the opportunity to address a topic that you know well, simply because you didn't read the problem question carefully or because you rushed your question selection.

● If you are genuinely unsure what a problem question is about, do not attempt to answer it, unless you feel even less confident about the remaining questions.

● Do not rush your question selection! Do not feel under pressure to begin writing simply because those around you have done so.

● If your examination is open-book or if statute books are permitted, use the reading time (or the first few minutes of the examination) to find the sources that you will need, at least for the first question.

● Students may find it useful to construct an essay plan for each question before beginning the answer. Use the reading time to do this, if you have permission to write. Strike through anything that you do not want the examiner to mark.

Answering Examination Questions

● When answering the examination questions use the PEA and IRAC methods discussed earlier.

● You should use full sentences: do not use note form unless you are desperate for time.

● Although tutors will be more lenient in terms of literacy when marking examination papers than they will be when marking coursework, candidates should be able to spell basic words correctly, use correct punctuation and construct a clear sentence.

● Support the points you make with a legal authority.

● In terms of case law, the correct name and date is expected if the examination is open-book. If it is not, the basic facts, the decision and the principle of the case are most important. Cite the name if you can remember it, and part of the case name is better than nothing, for example *Kernott*. If you cannot recall the name, utilise phrases such as: 'in a decided case' or 'the Supreme Court recently held'. The date is the least significant part of the case, although you would be expected to know if a decision is very recent. If you have time, underline the case name (if cited).

● You are expected to cite the full name and date of the most important family law statutes, even in closed-book examinations, for example **The Matrimonial Causes Act 1973**, **the Children Act 1989**. Once you have cited a statute correctly, you can abbreviate it thereafter, for example **MCA 1973**.

● In an open-book examination or an examination that permits you to use a statute book, you will be expected to cite the relevant section numbers precisely. In a closed-book examination that does not even permit statute books, the marker will be more lenient, but will expect to see the basics, for example **s.8 of the Children Act 1989**.

● Start a new page when you begin a new question and leave a blank page between questions so that you can return to them and add to them later in the examination.

● Once you have finished answering all the questions that you are required to complete, read through your answers if you have time. Correct any spelling and grammatical errors that you spot and underline case names. Often, when you read your answers, additional points will come to mind, and if you left a page between questions you will be able to add them easily.

Tips for Family Law Examinations (and Assignments)

● Family law is a very dynamic subject, which means that examiners expect (or are hoping) to see recent case law and proposals for reform. An examiner will be particularly impressed if you cite a case that has been decided since the topic was covered in class. It is therefore useful to spend some revision time checking the most recent law reports. A free online resource is www.familylawweek. co.uk, which contains recent judgements, as well as brief articles on contemporary issues.

● Be prepared to cite some statistics, for example the number of marriages, civil partnerships, co-habiting couples, children born outside of marriage etc., particularly in essay questions. To do so demonstrates awareness of context and can sometimes support an argument that you are making in terms of reforming the law.

● Include reference to **the European Convention on Human Rights 1950 (ECHR)** and **the UN Convention on the Rights of the Child 1989 (UNCRC)** wherever possible and be aware of the status that each has under English law. If you are answering a question on international child abduction, detailed knowledge of **the Hague Convention on Civil Aspects of Child Abduction 1980** and possibly the EU Regulations that impact upon abduction, would be required.

● Mixed topic questions are common in family law assessments, because they reflect life in the real world. A client may request a divorce, financial relief, an order relating to children and protection from domestic violence and as a consequence, the characters in problem questions may also do so. Chapter 11 of this book contains examples of questions involving more than one family law topic.

● Family law problem questions usually (but not always) involve an adult couple that have separated (or are about to separate) and are in dispute regarding their finances, property, children or the formal termination of their relationship. The first thing you need to do is to determine if they are married, civil partners or (former) cohabitants.

● In family law problem questions dates and ages are very significant. For example, the duration of a marriage can affect the ability to petition for an annulment and can influence financial orders granted by the courts. The age of a spouse can affect her earning capacity and needs, whilst the age of a child is relevant in relation to financial relief and child support, but also in terms of how much weight to attach to his or her opinion in residence or contact disputes.

● Do not make basic mistakes. A well-prepared candidate would never refer to the Children's Act or Matrimonial Clauses Act! This will not impress the examiner.

The Answers in this Book

The answers in this book are 'suggested' answers, rather than 'model' answers. They show you how you can apply the law to a problem scenario and how you can tackle an essay question. The law is explained in such as way as to ensure that the information is clear: you may be able to describe the law more concisely in an examination. You may include different cases in your answers and may include additional sources to those contained in the suggested answers. You may cite more academic opinion and evaluation and may structure your answer differently.

TAKING THINGS FURTHER

■ Gilmore, S. and Glennon, L. *Hayes & Williams' Family Law* (2016) 5th edn, Oxford University Press.

■ Lowe, N. and Douglas, G. *Bromley's Family Law* (2015) 11th edn, Oxford University Press.

■ Oldham, M. *Blackstone's Statutes on Family Law* (2015–2016) 24th edn, Oxford University Press.

The Formation and Recognition of Adult Relationships: Marriage, Civil Partnerships and Cohabitation

ARE YOU READY?

In order to attempt the four questions in this chapter you will need to have covered the following topics:

- the right to marry contained in **the European Convention on Human Rights**;
- the impact of **the Human Rights Act 1998**;
- the definition of forced marriage and the protection provided by the law;
- the similarities and differences between opposite-sex marriage, same-sex marriage and civil partnerships;
- the rights of cohabiting couples, compared with the rights of spouses and civil partners.

KEY DEBATES

Debate: Modernising marriage law

It can be argued that individuals should have a greater degree of choice in terms of how and where they marry. The Law Commission is currently reviewing the law in this area and so we may witness change in the future.

Debate: What is the future for civil partnerships in England and Wales?

The Marriage (Same Sex Couples) Act 2013 allows same-sex couples to marry but did not abolish civil partnerships. Do we still need civil partnerships, given that they were a stepping-stone to the introduction of same-sex marriage? I have argued that if they are retained they should be extended to opposite-sex couples to ensure fairness and to protect transgender civil partners.

Debate: The rights of cohabitants

It is often argued that cohabitants should be granted similar rights to spouses and civil partners in relation to separation and death. Is the protection of vulnerable people more important than respecting individual autonomy? If a statutory scheme is introduced to provide cohabitants with rights similar to spouses and civil partners, should it be an opt-in or an opt-out scheme?

QUESTION | 1

Article 12 of the **European Convention on Human Rights 1950** provides that 'men and women of marriageable age have the right to marry and to found a family in accordance with national laws governing the exercise of this right'.

Analyse the scope of the 'right to marry'.

! CAUTION!

- Make sure that you read the question properly—it asks you analyse the scope of the right to marry, not the right to found a family. However, you may discuss procreation issues if they directly relate to the right to marry.

- You need to be able to discuss the legitimate restrictions that contracting states can place on the right to marry.

☐ DIAGRAM ANSWER PLAN

> Provide background information on the European Convention on Human Rights

> Explain the meaning of men and women

> Explain the meaning of marriageable age

> Consider the right to divorce and remarry

> Discuss cases where the right to marry was infringed

> Conclusion

SUGGESTED ANSWER

[1] You can begin by briefly explaining the Convention and its incorporation into UK law. This shows that you understand why article 12 is relevant to English family law.

The European Convention on Human Rights[1] was adopted by the Council of Europe in 1950 and has been ratified by over 40 states. The United Kingdom incorporated the Convention into national law by enacting the **Human Rights Act 1998. Section 2** requires the courts to take into account the jurisprudence of the European Court of Human Rights, whilst **s.3** provides that, so far as is possible legislation must be interpreted in a way which is compatible with Convention rights. If it is not possible, the courts should make a declaration of incompatibility under **s.4**.

Article 12 of the **European Convention** provides that 'men and women of marriageable age have the right to marry and to found a family in accordance with national laws governing the exercise of this right'. In order to determine the scope of the right to marry it is necessary to discuss the terms 'men and women', 'marriageable age' and the 'national laws' that contracting states are permitted to enact.

Men and Women

[2] The point being made in this paragraph is whether post-operative transsexuals have the right to marry in their acquired sex.

The meaning of the words 'men and women' has been considered in several cases concerning post-operative transsexuals.[2] In the UK, a person's sex was defined at birth and his or her birth certificate would not be changed following gender reassignment. This was challenged in *Rees v UK* **[1986] 9 EHRR 56** and *Cossey v UK* **[1990] 13 EHRR 622**. The European Court of Human Rights rejected the applications because contracting states are allowed to regulate the right to marry by enacting national laws, as **art. 12** makes clear. Refusing to recognise the post-operative sex of the applicants for the purpose of capacity to marry fell within the state's margin of appreciation.

Over a decade later, UK law was again challenged in *Goodwin v UK* **[2002] 35 EHRR 18**, but the application was upheld because of the social, scientific and medical changes that had occurred since *Cossey*. The Court indicated that states could no longer justify barring transsexuals from enjoying the right to marry. It also pointed out that the inability to procreate naturally was not a pre-condition of the exercise of the right to marry.[3] Van der Sloot argues that from 2000 the Court of Human Rights began to adopt a more liberal approach to **art. 12**, as *Goodwin* demonstrates, whereas prior to that, the approach was conservative (2014).

[3] Analysis—this point demonstrates awareness of the scope of the right to marry as the question requires.

The use of the term 'men and women' also impacts on the rights of gay couples to marry. In *Parry v UK* **[2006] App. No. 42971/05** this issue was indirectly considered. The case concerned a married man who underwent gender reassignment surgery but could not obtain a full gender recognition certificate because he was married. Parry complained that the requirement to obtain a decree of nullity infringed his right to private and family life under **art. 8** and the right to marry contained in **art. 12**. The Court rejected these contentions, which indicates that signatory states are permitted to restrict marriage to heterosexual couples. In the same year, the High Court in England and Wales stated that the law was not obliged to recognise same-sex marriages formed in jurisdictions that permit such unions. In *Wilkinson v Kitzinger and HM Attorney General* **[2006] EWHC 2022** the High Court declared that a same-sex wedding celebrated in Canada could only confer civil partnership status on the parties in the UK and that this did not infringe the rights of the parties to marry. In 2010, the European Court of Human Rights confirmed that contracting states are not required to allow same-sex couples to marry (*Schalke and Kopf v Austria* **[2010] ECHR 995**). The introduction of same-sex marriage in England and Wales by **the Marriage (Same Sex Couples) Act 2013** was not, therefore, the result of an obligation under the European Convention.

Marriageable Age

The term 'marriageable age' is not defined in the European Convention, which indicates that the age for marriage can be determined by the signatories. However, the use of the words 'men' and 'women' rather than 'male and female' suggests that the draftsmen intended to provide 'adults' with a right to marry.[4] In all UK jurisdictions the minimum age for marriage is 16 and in *Khan v UK* **(1986) 48 DR 253** the refusal to allow a Muslim man to marry a 14-year-old girl did not contravene **art. 12**. The case indicates that certain restrictions on capacity to marry are justifiable and implies that states are not required to recognise all marital customs practised in other jurisdictions. As a consequence, it is suggested that the ban on polygamous marriages contained in **the Matrimonial Causes Act 1973** does not infringe **art. 12**.

[4] You might refer to the UN Convention on the Elimination of all Forms of Discrimination Against Women 1979, which prohibits child marriage, particularly in a coursework question.

The Right to Divorce and Remarry

In *Johnston v Ireland* **[1986] 9 EHRR 203** the Court of Human Rights stated that the right to marry does not imply a right to divorce, in order to remarry. As all contracting states now permit divorce, this decision is no longer of practical relevance. *F v Switzerland* **[1987] 10 EHRR 411** also concerned the right to remarry. The applicant in this case had been married and divorced three times in a relatively short period of time. Because the applicant was held responsible for the breakdown of the marriages, the court that granted the third divorce placed a ban on him remarrying for a three-year period. The European

[5] You could consider whether a shorter ban could have been justified.

Court of Human Rights accepted that states could enact measures to protect marital stability, but held that the three-year ban on remarriage was disproportionate.[5]

Violations of Article 12

Although contracting states are permitted to enact laws regulating the right to marry, it is evident that certain restrictions on capacity to marry violate **art. 12**, as *Goodwin v UK* and *F v Switzerland* demonstrate. In *B and L v UK* **[2006] 1 FLR 35**, the law relating to marriage between a man and his former daughter-in-law (or a woman and her former son-in-law) was challenged. At that time, **Schedule 1** to **the Marriage Act 1949** indicated that a man could only marry his former daughter-in-law if both parties were over 21 and the former spouses of both parties were deceased. B could not marry his former daughter-in-law (L) because his son was still living. The UK attempted to justify restrictions on marriage between in-laws on the basis that it preserved the integrity of the family. However, the Court of Human Rights declared that the law was illogical because the couple could legitimately cohabit: the legislation merely prevented them from obtaining legal and social recognition of their relationship. Furthermore, the Act did not ban such couples from marrying: they could do so if both former spouses were deceased or if they obtained a private Act of Parliament. As a consequence of this decision the restriction was removed from **the Marriage Act 1949** (by **the Marriage Act 1949 (Remedial) Order 2007).**[6]

[6] You might consider whether the remaining restrictions based on affinity breach article 12.

Procedural rules and formal requirements relating to marriage can also breach **art. 12** of the Convention. For example, in *Hamer v UK* **[1979] 4 EHRR 139** the UK's refusal to make arrangements to allow a prisoner to marry violated **art. 12**. *R (Baiai) v Secretary of State for the Home Department* **[2008] UKHL 53** concerned the scheme created by **s.19** of **the Asylum and Immigration (Treatment of Claimants etc.) Act 2004**, which required those subject to immigration control to obtain permission to marry from the Secretary of State.[7] The legislation was introduced to prevent sham marriages, but did not apply to marriages celebrated in Anglican churches. The scheme was thus discriminatory and in addition, the fee that had to be paid might deter couples from making an application. The European Court of Human Rights therefore held that the legislation infringed **art. 12**. However, it is unlikely that standard formal requirements will violate **art. 12** of the Convention. In *Mundoz Diaz v Spain* **[2010] 1 FLR 1421**, the non-recognition of a traditional Roma marriage which did not comply with the formalities established by Spanish law did not breach the right to marry. The non-recognition of religious marriages that do not comply with the formalities established in **the Marriage**

[7] You could also consider *R (OTA Quila and anor) v Secretary of State for the Home Department* [2011] UKSC 45.

Act 1949 will not therefore infringe **art. 12**. It is thus clear that there is no right to marry in accordance with a minority culture.

Procedural matters were also considered by the Court of Appeal in ***Rota CPS v Registrar General of Births, Deaths and Marriages*** **[2002] EWCA Civ 1661**. In this case, the CPS attempted to prevent the Registrar General from authorising the marriage between a man facing a murder charge and a woman who was supposed to act as the main prosecution witness. If the couple married, the wife could not be compelled to give evidence against her husband. The CPS failed in its application because the right of the parties to marry could not be violated.[8]

[8] See *Frasik v Poland* Application No. 22933/02 for the Court of Human Rights' perspective on this type of situation.

Conclusion.[9]

[9] This short conclusion sums up the answer to the question set. In a coursework question your conclusion is likely to be longer.

The discussion above has demonstrated that the right to marry is a fundamental right provided by the European Convention on Human Rights. Although contracting states are permitted to enact national laws that regulate the right to marry, restrictions placed on it must be justified and proportionate.

LOOKING FOR EXTRA MARKS?

- Utilise the PEA method (see chapter 1) to ensure that your answer is logically structured and contains sufficient analysis.

- Do not just write about the jurisprudence of the European Court of Human Rights—you can also discuss the case law of the English courts.

- Gain extra marks by considering whether the law in England and Wales infringes the right to marry.

QUESTION | 2

Discuss why the Forced Marriage (Civil Protection) Act 2007 was adopted and consider whether it provides adequate protection for adults at risk of being forced to marry.

CAUTION!

- In order to answer this question, you should be able to define a forced marriage and distinguish it from an arranged marriage.

- Read the question carefully—it refers to protecting *adults*, not *children*.

- You should focus on protection from forced marriage, rather than nullity, which is available to those who actually have been forced to wed.

DIAGRAM ANSWER PLAN

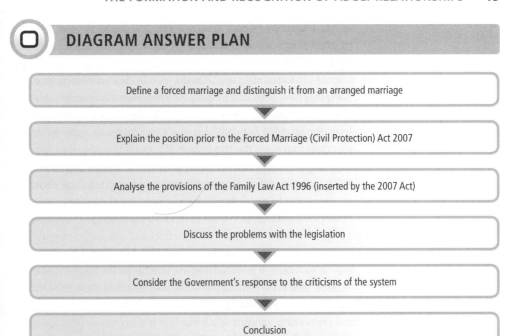

Define a forced marriage and distinguish it from an arranged marriage

▼

Explain the position prior to the Forced Marriage (Civil Protection) Act 2007

▼

Analyse the provisions of the Family Law Act 1996 (inserted by the 2007 Act)

▼

Discuss the problems with the legislation

▼

Consider the Government's response to the criticisms of the system

▼

Conclusion

A SUGGESTED ANSWER

The Consultation Paper Forced Marriage: A Wrong not a Right (FCO/ Home Office, 2005) defined a forced marriage as one 'conducted without the valid consent of one or both parties where duress is a factor' (p. 1). It must be distinguished from an arranged marriage, which is one where the families of one or both parties take a leading role in choosing the spouse, but the bride and groom provide free and full consent. The Forced Marriage Unit (which is run by the Foreign and Commonwealth Office and the Home Office) was established to provide assistance for those at risk of being forced to marry in the UK and overseas. In 2014, the Unit provided advice and support in 1,267 cases (www.gov.uk/forced-marriage).[1] However, it should be noted that many victims of forced marriage do not actually report the matter.

[1] The statistics show why **the Forced Marriage (Civil Protection) Act 2007** was required.

Why was the Legislation Necessary?

Prior to the adoption of **the Forced Marriage (Civil Protection) Act 2007**, the family courts could utilise a range of non-specific powers to protect an adult at risk of being forced into a marriage.[2] First, the High Court could use its inherent jurisdiction, which means the automatic, non-statutory powers that the Court can exercise on behalf of the Crown. For example, in *Re SK (Proposed Plaintiff)(An Adult by Way*

[2] This paragraph explains the law utilised prior to the 2007 Act and the problems with it, in order to explain why the 2007 Act was necessary.

of her Litigation Friend) **[2005] 2 FLR 230** the High Court used its inherent jurisdiction to secure the return to the UK of an adult female who was believed to have been taken to Bangladesh for the purpose of a forced marriage. Secondly, an individual under pressure to marry may have been able to apply for a non-molestation order under **the Family Law Act 1996** or an injunction under **the Protection from Harassment Act 1997.**[3] It was also possible to apply for an injunction to prevent the commission of a tort (e.g. battery and false imprisonment) under **s.37** of (what is now) **the Senior Courts Act 1981**. However, victims or potential victims of forced marriage would not necessarily be aware that they could make use of these provisions, as they were not created in order to tackle forced marriage. In addition, it should be noted that the activities associated with forced marriage can involve the commission of a criminal offence (e.g. assault and kidnap). In such cases, it was (and remains) possible for the perpetrators to be prosecuted in the criminal courts. The laws described above were not created with forced marriage in mind and did not therefore make it clear that pressurising someone into a marriage is unacceptable. Parliament thus enacted **the Forced Marriage (Civil Protection) Act 2007** in order to make this explicit and to provide more practical remedies.[4]

[3] You could discuss specific problems relating to this legislation: harassment requires conduct on at least two occasions.

[4] Analysis—the paragraph ends by summarising the problems with the law and explaining why the 2007 Act was necessary.

The Provisions of the Forced Marriage (Civil Protection) Act 2007

The Forced Marriage (Civil Protection) Act inserted 19 provisions into **the Family Law Act 1996** and therefore amalgamated the new provisions on forced marriage and those that already existed to protect the victims of domestic violence.[5] **Section 63A** of **the Family Law Act 1996** provides that the Court can make an order for the purpose of protecting a person from being forced into a marriage or for the purpose of protecting a person who has been forced into a marriage. Force includes coercion 'by threats or other psychological means' **(s.63A(6))** which reflects the fact that threats of social exclusion are common in forced marriage cases (see, for example *Hirani v Hirani* **[1983] 4 FLR 232**). The conduct that forces (or attempts to force) an individual to marry may be directed at the victim him- or herself, the perpetrator him- or herself or another person **(s.64A(5))**. This provision was included because the perpetrators of forced marriage may threaten to harm themselves or other family members rather than the victim. For example, in *NS v MI* **[2007] 1 FLR 444** the victim's parents threatened to kill themselves if NS did not marry MI.

[5] This emphasises that forced marriage is considered a form of domestic violence.

Section 63C(2) of the Act provides that an application can be made by the person to be protected or a relevant third party without the need for leave of the court. **The Family Law Act 1996 (Forced Marriage) (Relevant Third Party) Order 2009** designates local authorities as relevant third parties, which is appropriate given their expertise in child abuse cases and the protection of vulnerable adults. Any other interested person, such as friends, teachers and relatives, will require leave to apply for an order. It is essential that third parties can make an application because the victim may be too vulnerable to act for him- or herself, unwilling to instigate proceedings for fear of reprisals or physically unable to make an application if he or she is being held against his or her will (as *Re S K* demonstrates).[6]

[6] This is an example of a provision that ensures the best possible protection for victims.

The order can be made against those who force, attempt to force or may force a person to marry (**s.63B(2)**) and those who encourage or assist them (**s.63B(3)**). Where necessary, the application can be made without notice [7] (**s.63D**). The order itself may contain 'any such prohibitions, restrictions or requirements and such other terms as the court considers appropriate' (**s.63B(1)**). For example, an order might prohibit the respondents from organising a marriage for the victim and oblige them to surrender the victim's passport to the court. If the victim has been removed from the jurisdiction, the order can require the respondent to allow the victim to attend the British High Commission. This obligation was imposed by the High Court in the much-publicised case of Dr Humayra Abedin, who was held captive by her family in Bangladesh. Following the order, Dr Abedin was released into the custody of the British High Commission and returned to the UK.

[7] You should explain why this may be necessary.

Failure to comply with a protection order constitutes contempt of court,[8] which is punishable by up to two years in prison (**s.63O**). This was designed to ensure that orders are taken seriously, but not deter those at risk from coming forward, as their relatives will not automatically be prosecuted.

[8] You could discuss the problems associated with enforcement by contempt of court proceedings.

Was the Legislation Adequate?[9]

[9] This whole paragraph addresses the question about the adequacy of the legislation.

The provisions of **the Forced Marriage (Civil Protection) Act 2007** were appropriate to assist victims and potential victims of forced marriage: as Gill and Van Engelend point out, the approach adopted was 'victim-based' (2014, p. 242). But according to the Forced Marriage Unit, the legislation was not being utilised to full effect due to, amongst other things, a lack of commitment amongst Government agencies to tackle forced marriage and inconsistent training of professionals (Report on the Implementation of Multi-Agency Statutory Guidance for Dealing with Forced Marriage, 2008). In addition, in 2011 the Home Affairs Select Committee pointed to a lack of awareness of the legislation amongst frontline professionals and identified problems with the monitoring and enforcement of orders. It should be noted that breach of a non-molestation order, which is the primary remedy for domestic violence, constitutes a specific criminal offence punishable by up to five years in prison. Failing to treat breach of a forced marriage protection order with the same degree of severity might imply that it was considered a less serious form of domestic violence. This issue was addressed by **s.120(1)** of **the Anti-social Behaviour, Crime and Policing Act 2014**, which makes breach of a forced marriage protection order a specific criminal offence punishable by up to five years in prison.

Criminalisation

Following a consultation conducted in 2011, the Government announced its intention to create a specific offence of forcing someone to marry (Home Office, Forced Marriage—A Consultation—Summary of Responses, 2012, p.7).[10] The purpose of criminalisation is: to send a powerful message that forced marriage is unacceptable; to deter those who may force another person into marriage; and to provide proper punishment for those who force another to wed. The Government's proposal was implemented by **s.121(1)** of **the Anti-social Behaviour, Crime and Policing Act 2014**, which creates a specific offence of forcing someone to marry, whilst **s.121(3)** makes it an offence to practise deception with the intention of causing another person to leave the UK for the purpose of forced marriage. Both offences are punishable by up to seven years in prison. Gill and Van Engelend indicate that there are 'concerns that such measures will do more harm than good' (2014, p. 255). Criminalisation may drive the practice of forced marriage underground and victims or potential victims may not seek help for fear that their family members will be prosecuted. However, the number of forced marriage protection orders has increased since criminalisation in 2014 (Family Court Statistics Quarterly: April to June 2014).

[10] You would not necessarily be expected to remember the full titles of official documents in an examination, but you would be expected to know that a consultation took place.

Conclusion

The Forced Marriage (Civil Protection) Act 2007 was adopted to protect those at risk of being forced to marry (and those who have been forced to wed) and to emphasise that pressurising someone to marry is unacceptable. The powers granted to the courts can only be exercised if those at risk (or persons acting on their behalf) are willing to come forward. It is therefore essential that those at risk and frontline professionals are more aware of the protection available, for the actual number of victims is thought to far exceed the number of reported cases. Criminalisation does not seem to have had a negative impact, but whether this continues remains to be seen.

LOOKING FOR EXTRA MARKS?

- Refer to Government Reports such as the Forced Marriage Unit Report on the Implementation of Multi-agency Statutory Guidance for Dealing with Forced Marriage (2008).
- Refer to **the Anti-social Behaviour, Crime and Policing Act 2014**, which made forcing someone to marry a criminal offence. Does it suggest that **the Forced Marriage (Civil Protection) Act 2007** was inadequate?

QUESTION 3

Analyse the similarities and differences between opposite-sex marriage, same-sex marriage and civil partnerships.

CAUTION!

- Do not assume that opposite-sex and same-sex marriages are treated in exactly the same way.
- As you have to compare three forms of relationship, there is a risk that your answer will lack structure. It is advisable to compare each relationship in terms of capacity, formalities etc.
- Your explanation of the law will need to be concise as you have a lot to cover.

DIAGRAM ANSWER PLAN

Introduction

↓

Explain the rules relating to capacity to form each relationship

↓

Discuss the formal requirements for creating each relationship

↓

Consider the rights of opposite-sex spouses, same-sex spouses and civil partners

↓

Discuss the rules relating to the dissolution and annulment of the relationships

↓

Conclusion

This essay considers the similarities and differences between opposite-sex marriage, same-sex marriage and civil partnerships. **The Civil Partnership Act 2004** was enacted to enable same-sex couples to formalise their relationship via a statutory procedure. It constituted a stepping-stone towards same-sex marriage, which was introduced by **the Marriage (Same Sex Couples) Act 2013**.

Capacity[1]

[1] The point of this paragraph is to compare the rules on eligibility. The evidence is contained in **the Matrimonial Causes Act 1973** and **the Civil Partnership Act 2004**.

In order to create a valid marriage or civil partnership, the parties must have capacity (or be eligible) to form the relationship. Following **the Marriage (Same Sex Couples) Act 2013**, a couple have capacity to marry one another if they are both over the age of 16, neither party is already married or in a civil partnership and they are not related within prohibited degrees. If the couple marry in contravention of these requirements, the marriage is void under **s.11** of **the Matrimonial Causes Act 1973**. The eligibility requirements under **s.3** of the **Civil Partnership Act 2004** are identical to those that apply to marriage except that the parties must be the same sex (**s.1(1)** and **s.1(3)(a) CPA**). If the parties are ineligible to register, the partnership is void under **s.49** of the Act. It is therefore clear that both relationships involve two unmarried or unregistered persons over the age of 16, who are not closely related. The main difference between them is that a marriage can be formed by an opposite-sex or same-sex couple, whereas a civil partnership cannot be registered by a mixed-sex couple.[2] This has consequences for those who change gender. If a spouse changes gender and wishes to obtain a full-gender recognition certificate under **the Gender Recognition Act 2004**, he or she can remain married, provided that the other spouse consents. But if a civil partner changes gender, a full-gender recognition certificate can only be obtained if the partnership is annulled, dissolved or converted into a marriage (see Gaffney-Rhys, 2014a, p.178).

[2] The paragraph concludes that marriage and civil partnerships are very similar in terms of eligibility, but the key difference between them has important consequences for some people.

Formalities[3]

[3] It is worth pointing out that the Law Commission is currently reviewing how and where people can marry, which may result in a change to the law relating to formalities.

In order to create a lawful marriage or civil partnership, certain formalities must be complied with. If the parties knowingly and wilfully disregard certain formal requirements the marriage or civil partnership will be void under **s.11(a)(iii)** of **the Matrimonial Causes Act 1973** and **s.49(b)** of **the Civil Partnership Act 2004**, respectively.

First, the couple must publicise their intention to marry or form a civil partnership. The marriage of a man and a woman can be preceded by Anglican preliminaries, for example publishing the banns of matrimony, or by civil preliminaries, which usually involve giving notice to the superintendent registrar of the district where the parties have resided for at least seven days. The parties' details will be displayed in the marriage notice book and the couple can marry 28 days later.[4] This civil process is also used to publicise same-sex marriages: unlike opposite-sex marriages, they cannot be authorised by the Anglican Church. The standard procedure for publicising intention to register a civil partnership is almost identical to the civil preliminaries for marriage described above (**ss.8–17 CPA 2004**). It is thus clear that the parties to a marriage *and* the parties to a civil partnership must publicise their intention to form the relationship. This ensures that the parties have capacity and that persons can object to either union.

Opposite-sex marriage ceremonies can take place in Anglican places of worship, other religious buildings that have been registered for the purpose of marriage, register offices and approved premises.[5] In contrast, same-sex marriage ceremonies cannot take place in Anglican Churches (**s.1(2)–(5) Marriage (Same Sex Couples) Act 2013**) and can only be celebrated in other religious buildings if the Governing Body of the relevant organisation has opted in (**ss.4–5 Marriage (Same Sex Couples) Act 2013**). Initially, a civil partnership could not be formed in a religious building, which reflected the fact that registered partnerships were introduced by statute to give same-sex couples civil status, whereas marriage was historically linked to Christian practice and is still regarded by many as a religious institution. **The Equality Act 2010** removed the prohibition and following **the Marriages and Civil Partnerships (Approved Premises) (Amendment) Regulations 2011,** religious premises can be approved for the formation of civil partnerships.

Opposite-sex marriage ceremonies that take place in Anglican Churches will follow one of the forms of service authorised by the church. All other marriage ceremonies, civil or religious, same-sex or opposite-sex, must incorporate the prescribed words contained in **s.44** of **the Marriage Act 1949**. In all cases, the ceremony must be conducted before two or more witnesses and in most cases, in a building that is open to the public. The marriage comes into existence once the parties have exchanged vows, not at the point of registration, although the latter is required under **Part IV** of **the Marriage Act 1949**. Apart from the fact that same-sex marriages cannot be solemnised in Anglican Churches, there is little difference between same-sex and opposite-sex marriage ceremonies. Civil partnerships must also be registered in the presence of two witnesses and the officiating civil partnership registrar (**s.2(1) CPA 2004**). This emphasises that marriage and civil partnerships are relationships of public importance. In both cases, a formal legal record is required because marriage and

[4] Fifteen days' notice was changed to 28 days' notice by **Part 4** of **the Immigration Act 2014,** which was implemented on 2 March 2015.

[5] In exceptional situations marriages and civil partnerships can take place in prison, hospital or a person's home, if housebound.

civil partnerships have automatic consequences. However, civil partnerships differ from marriage because the former comes into existence when the parties sign the civil partnership document: there is no obligation on the parties to exchange oral vows (**s.2(1) CPA 2004**). In addition, **s.2(5)** of **the Civil Partnership Act 2004**, provides that no religious service is to be used while the civil partnership registrar is officiating at the signing of the civil partnership document, even if this takes place in a religious building. This does not mean that a religious blessing cannot take place before or after the official signing of the civil partnership document. It can therefore be argued that the distinction is inconsequential.[6]

[6] This is an example of evaluating the differences between marriage and civil partnerships, rather than merely explaining them.

The Rights of Spouses and Civil Partners

In *Secretary of State for Work and Pensions v M* **[2006] 1 FCR 497** Baroness Hale declared that civil partnerships 'have virtually the same legal consequences to marriage' (para. 499). Civil partners, same-sex spouses and opposite-sex spouses have the same rights[7] in relation to financial relief, inheritance, taxation, protection from domestic violence, the adoption of children and the acquisition of parenthood and parental responsibility in cases of assisted reproduction. In relation to occupational pensions, civil partners have survivor pension rights, just as opposite-sex spouses do, but they are only based on contributions made after 5 December 2005, when **the Civil Partnership Act** came into force. **The Marriage (Same Sex Couples) Act 2013** provides that same-sex spouses should be treated in the same way as civil partners in terms of survivor pension rights. There is thus a distinction between heterosexual marriages on the one hand and civil partnerships and same-sex marriages on the other.

[7] It is not possible to discuss these areas of law in any detail.

Annulment and Dissolution

Certain minor differences exist between same-sex marriage, opposite-sex marriage and civil partnerships in terms of nullity and dissolution.[8]

The marriage of a man and a woman shall be voidable on eight grounds set out in **s.12(1)** of **the Matrimonial Causes Act 1973**. **Section 12(1)(a)** and **(b)**, which concern non-consummation, do not apply to same-sex marriages (**s.12(2)**). Civil partnerships cannot be annulled on the grounds of non-consummation either and, in addition, they are not voidable on the ground that the respondent was suffering from a communicable form of venereal disease (**s.50 Civil Partnership Act 2004**). Excluding these particular grounds for annulment from **the Civil Partnership Act** suggests that civil partnerships were not intended to be sexual relationships, but the same cannot be said for same-sex marriage. The Consultation Paper 'Equal Civil Marriage' stated that all grounds for annulment would apply to same-sex marriages and that the courts would develop appropriate

[8] You may point out the different terminology. The word 'dissolution' is used in relation to civil partnerships, rather than divorce.

definitions through case law. However, this was criticised due to lack of certainty, and rather than defining consummation for the purpose of same-sex marriage, it was decided that non-consummation would not be grounds for annulling a same-sex marriage.

Adultery can be used to prove irretrievable breakdown of marriage for the purpose of divorce (**s.1(2)(a) Matrimonial Causes Act 1973**). This applies to same-sex and opposite-sex marriages, but **s.1(6)** makes it clear that 'only conduct between the respondent and a person of the opposite sex may constitute adultery'.[9] As a consequence, the adultery fact will rarely be utilised by same-sex spouses. If the party to a same-sex marriage has a homosexual affair, his or her spouse would have to use the behaviour fact as proof of irretrievable breakdown. The same can be said for civil partners, because adultery is not a fact that can be used to establish breakdown for the purpose of dissolving a civil partnership (**s.44(5) Civil Partnership Act 2004**).

[9]The point made at the end of the last paragraph in relation to the definition of consummation also applies to adultery.

Conclusion

The discussion above has demonstrated that there are a number of differences between opposite-sex marriage, same-sex marriage and civil partnerships in terms of formation and termination of the relationships, most of which are of conceptual, but not practical significance. The rights granted to same-sex spouses, opposite-sex spouses and civil partners are generally identical.

LOOKING FOR EXTRA MARKS?

▪ Show your knowledge of recent developments by discussing the Consultation Paper on Civil Partnerships 2014.

▪ If this question was set as an in-course assignment, you could research the position in other jurisdictions that have introduced same-sex marriage, for example the Netherlands, which permits same-sex and opposite-sex couples to marry or form a registered partnership.

QUESTION | 4

Angela and Ben met at university and have been in a relationship since they were 20. They graduated five years ago and are both building successful careers in accounting and finance. They have lived together in a rented flat for two years and are now considering their future together. Angela wants to get married, but Ben does not think that this is necessary as he believes that cohabiting couples have the same rights as spouses after living together for a few years. He thinks that they should buy a house together but not marry.

Advise Angela and Ben as to the main differences between the rights of spouses and the rights of cohabitants.

CAUTION!

- You should avoid explaining the differences between the formation and termination of marriage and cohabiting relationships, as the question requires students to focus on the parties' rights.

- Given the wide range of subjects that this question covers, it is not possible to discuss any of them in great depth.

DIAGRAM ANSWER PLAN

Identify the issues	- Identify the legal issues - Is Ben correct when he says that cohabitants have the same rights as spouses after living together for a few years?
Relevant law	- Rights of spouses to claim financial relief—MCA 1973 - Claiming an equitable interest in the home—*Lloyds Bank v Rosset* [1991] - Child Support—CSA 1991 and Children Act 1989 - Inheritance—Administration of Estates Act 1925 and Inheritance (Provision for Family and Dependants) Act 1975 - Parental Responsibility—Children Act 1989 - Domestic Violence—Family Law Act 1996
Apply the law	- Compare the rights of cohabitants with the rights of spouses in relation to separation, child support, inheritance, parental responsibility, domestic violence, etc.
Conclude	- Conclusion—advise Angela and Ben

SUGGESTED ANSWER

Since reaching a peak of 480,285 in 1972, the number of marriages taking place in England and Wales declined steadily for almost 40 years. But in 2012 numbers increased to 262,240 from 249,133 the previous year (ONS 2014). In contrast, the number of couples

[1] In a coursework question you might explore the various reasons why couples cohabit rather than marry.

living together[1] outside of marriage has almost doubled from 1.5 million in 1996 to 2.9 million in 2013 (ONS, 2013). People (such as Ben) often believe that cohabiting couples have the same rights as spouses after living together for a certain period of time. This is known as the common law marriage myth because it is not true that cohabiting couples are treated as common law spouses and have the same rights as married couples (see Probert, 2011).

Rights on Separation

[2] This answer will only refer to the rights of spouses because Angela and Ben cannot form a civil partnership. Throughout, you can assume that the rights of spouses are also applicable to civil partners.

Spouses[2] have the right to apply for financial relief under **Part II** of **the Matrimonial Causes Act 1973** when the relationship comes to an end. The court can make pension sharing orders, lump sum orders, property adjustment orders or periodical payment orders in favour of the spouse or a child. If a cohabiting couple separate, the parties are not in a position to apply for financial relief. In such cases, each cohabitant takes away their own property, which is determined in accordance with general principles of contract, conveyancing, equity and trusts. This distinction is illustrated by *McFarlane v McFarlane* [2006] **UKHL 24**, which concerned spouses and *Burns v Burns* [1984] **Ch 317**, which concerned a cohabiting couple. Mrs McFarlane had given up a successful career to care for the children and look after the home and was consequently awarded half of the couple's three million capital and periodical payments of £250,000 per year when her

[3] The rights of spouses and cohabitants will be compared in each section of the answer.

marriage of 16 years came to an end. In marked contrast, the female cohabitant in *Burns*, who had taken her partner's name, looked after his home, redecorated it twice and raised their two children, was left with nothing when their relationship of 19 years ended. A similar decision was reached in *Curran v Collins* [2015] EWCA Civ 404.[3]

Claiming an Equitable Interest

It is possible to claim an equitable interest in property registered in the other cohabitant's name if a constructive trust can be established (*Lloyds Bank Plc v Rosset* [1991] **AC 107**). This requires the claimant to prove a common intention to share the property and prove that he or she relied on this to his or her detriment. Common intent could take the form of an express agreement or be inferred from behaviour, for example a direct contribution to the purchase price. As Mrs Burns had no evidence of an express agreement to share the property and had not contributed to the purchase price or paid mortgage instalments, she was not entitled to a share of the property. In *Stack v Dowden* [2007] **1 FLR 1858**, Baroness Hale and Lord Walker both indicated that, in relation to matrimonial or quasi-matrimonial property, the narrow approach adopted in *Rosset* was outdated. Despite this, it remains difficult for a cohabitant to claim a beneficial interest in property that is registered in the sole name of her partner, as *James v Thomas* [2007] EWCA Civ 1212 and *Curran v Collins* demonstrate.

Proposals for Reform

Because of the hardship that a cohabitant may suffer when the relationship comes to an end, there have been several calls for reform in this area.[4] For example, in 2007 the Law Commission recommended the introduction of a statutory scheme of financial relief based on the contributions made to the relationship by the parties but the recommendations were not implemented (Cohabitation: The financial consequences of relationship breakdown, Law Com. No. 307). Similar proposals were incorporated into **the Cohabitation Rights Bill 2014–15**, but it did not proceed through Parliament.

[4] Here you may include reference to the law in Scotland.

Rights of Cohabitants on Separation

Although a cohabitant cannot claim personal maintenance, a property transfer or share of a pension, and may find it difficult to establish a constructive trust, he or she can request the transfer of certain tenancies under **Schedule 7** to **the Family Law Act 1996** and can claim child support under **the Child Support Act 1991** or **the Children Act 1989**, just as a spouse can. Child support is strictly speaking, a right of the child, rather than the parent, but inevitably benefits the resident parent as well as the child in question. It should also be noted that cohabiting couples can enter into binding cohabitation contracts which determine what will happen to their property on separation (*Sutton v Mischon de Reya* [2004] 3 FCR 142), whereas pre-nuptial contracts are not automatically binding (*Radmacher v Granatino* [2010] UKSC 42). This could be regarded as an advantage or a disadvantage of each relationship, depending upon one's situation.

Inheritance and Financial Provision on Death

The law relating to inheritance and financial provision on death makes a significant distinction between married and cohabiting couples. If a person dies intestate, **the Administration of Estates Act 1925** provides that the surviving spouse or civil partner inherits most, if not all of the estate, whereas a surviving cohabitant has no entitlement at all. In addition, a surviving cohabitant cannot apply for a grant of representation and is not automatically entitled to register the death of his or her partner. Furthermore, a surviving cohabitant's rights differ from those of a surviving spouse under **the Inheritance (Provision for Family and Dependants) Act 1975** as the former can only qualify as of right if he or she had been living with the deceased at the time of death and for at least two years beforehand.[5] This duration requirement also applies if a cohabitant makes a claim under **the Fatal**

[5] It is clear that cohabitants must prove their commitment by meeting a longevity requirement, whereas a spouse has proven their commitment by entering into the marri

Accidents Act 1976, whereas a spouse has an automatic entitlement to claim. In relation to claims under **the Inheritance (Provision for Family and Dependants) Act 1975** a spouse will be awarded such financial 'provision' as it would be reasonable in all the circumstances for a spouse to receive 'whether or not it is required for his or her maintenance' (**s.1(2)(a)**). For other applicants, including cohabitants, the question is one of reasonable maintenance, which indicates that spouses are in a privileged position. The Law Commission has recommended: that a surviving cohabitant should, in certain circumstances share the deceased partner's estate without having to go to court; that no duration requirement should exist under **the Inheritance (Provision for Family and Dependants) Act 1975** if the couple have a child; and that the **s.1(2)(a)** referred to above, should also apply to claims by surviving cohabitants (2009). The recommendations have not been implemented.

Children

In relation to children,[6] the distinction between those born to married couples and those born to parents who are not married to one another was effectively abolished by **the Family Law Reform Act 1987**. However, there remains an important difference between a father who is married to the mother at the time of the birth and a father who is not. The former has parental responsibility for the child (**s.2(1)** of **the Children Act 1989**), whereas the latter does not automatically have this (**s.2(2)**). An unmarried father can, however, acquire parental responsibility under **s.4** of the Act by jointly registering the child's birth,[7] making a parental responsibility agreement with the mother or by obtaining a court order. But unlike a father who is married to the mother, his parental responsibility can be terminated by an order of the court (**s.4(2A)**).

Other Areas of Law

There are a number of other areas where married couples are treated differently from cohabiting couples. For example, a person can apply for maintenance from his or her spouse while the marriage subsists, but cohabitants cannot. Such claims are, however, rare. Spouses are also better protected in the event of bankruptcy than cohabitants. In addition, spouses can benefit from tax exemptions that are not made available to cohabiting couples and are in a better position in terms of pensions. In relation to domestic violence, cohabitants are treated differently from spouses if they are seeking an occupation order and have no right to occupy the relevant property. For example, the court will consider the 'level of commitment' involved in the relationship under **s.36(6)(e)** of **the Family Law Act 1996** when considering an

[6] In 2013, 47.4 per cent of babies were born outside marriage/civil partnerships—ONS 2013.

[7] If the parents are cohabiting, they usually jointly register the birth.

[8] This is a disadvantage rather than an advantage—one partner is expected to financially support the other, just as spouses are, even though they are not married.

[9] The conclusion sums up the application of the law contained in each section of the answer and concludes by advising Angela and Ben.

application by a cohabitant or former cohabitant with no interest. The only area where cohabiting couples are truly equated with married couples is in relation to means-tested benefits in order to ensure that spouses are not in a less favourable position.[8]

Conclusion[9]

The discussion above has demonstrated that spouses and cohabiting couples are treated differently in relation to financial relief on separation, intestate succession, financial provision on death, parental responsibility and occupation orders. Ben is therefore incorrect when he states that cohabiting couples acquire the same rights as married couples after living together for a few years. Certain rights *are* acquired after living together for two years, for example the right to claim under **the Fatal Accidents Act 1976** and **the Inheritance (Provision for Family and Dependants) Act 1975**, but these are limited. Whether Ben and Angela are advised to marry or to cohabit depends upon whether they wish to acquire the rights and responsibilities of marriage or avoid them. In addition, they should be advised that many of the 'disadvantages' of cohabitation can be avoided by registering the family home in joint names, drafting a cohabitation agreement and writing wills to provide for the other party.

LOOKING FOR EXTRA MARKS?

- Include statistics (available from the Office for National Statistics, ONS) relating to marriage and cohabitation—the high number of cohabiting couples demonstrates why this issue is important.

- You might compare the position in England and Wales to the position in Scotland under **the Family Law (Scotland) Act 2006**, particularly if completing this question as an in-course assignment.

TAKING THINGS FURTHER

- Gaffney-Rhys, R. 'Same-sex marriage but not mixed-sex partnerships: Should the Civil Partnership Act 2004 be extended to opposite-sex couples?' (2014a) Child and Family Law Quarterly 26(2) 173.
  Considers whether refusing to allow opposite-sex couples the right to form a civil partnership contravenes the European Convention on Human Rights.

- Gaffney-Rhys, R. 'The future of civil partnerships in England and Wales' (2014) Fam Law 1694.
  Considers the future of civil partnerships following the Civil Partnership Review 2014.

■ Gilbert, A. 'From pretended family relationships to ultimate affirmation: British conservatism and the legal recognition of same-sex relationships' (2014) Child and Family Law Quarterly 26(4) 463.

Examines the approach of the Conservative Party to the development of the law relating to same-sex couples.

■ Gill, K. and Van Engelend, A. 'Criminalisation or multiculturalism without culture—Comparing British and French approaches to tackling forced marriage' (2014) Journal of Social Welfare and Family Law 36(3) 241.

Argues that the politics of France and GB concerning religious and cultural difference have driven their approaches towards tackling forced marriage.

■ Home Office, Forced Marriage Consultation (2011).

Contains the arguments for and against criminalising forced marriage.

■ Probert, P. 'The evolution of the common law marriage myth' (2011) Fam Law 283.

Explains the origins of the common law marriage myth, which many believe continues to exist.

■ Van der Sloot, B. 'Between fact and fiction: An analysis of the case-law on Article 12 of the European Convention on Human Rights' (2014) Child and Family Law Quarterly 26(4) 397.

Reviews the case law of the European Court of Human Rights on article 12.

Online Resource Centre   www.oxfordtextbooks.co.uk/orc/qanda/

Go online for extra essay and problem questions, a glossary of key terms, online versions of all the answer plans and audio commentary on how selected ones were put together, and a range of podcasts which include advice on exam and coursework technique and advice for other assessment methods.

3 Void, Voidable and Non-existent Marriages

ARE YOU READY?

In order to tackle the questions in this chapter you will need to have covered the following:

- the distinction between a void marriage, a voidable marriage and a non-existent marriage and the consequences of each form of marriage;
- the grounds for a void marriage under **the Matrimonial Causes Act 1973**;
- the grounds on which a marriage is voidable under **the Matrimonial Causes Act 1973**;
- the bars and time limits that apply to voidable marriage under **the Matrimonial Causes Act 1973**;
- the circumstances when a marriage ceremony has no legal significance and is labelled a non-marriage or non-existent marriage.

KEY DEBATES

Debate: Should voidable marriage be abolished?

The concept of voidable marriage was abolished in Australia in 1961 (**Marriage Act 1961**). What would the positive and negative consequences of abolishing voidable marriage in England and Wales be? Is the (small) number of nullity decrees granted each year a good reason to abolish voidable marriage?

Debate: The formalities required to create a valid marriage

Failure to adhere to the formal requirements for marriage can result in a marriage being declared non-existent. It can be argued that the law disadvantages people from ethnic minority communities. Should the formalities for marriage be simplified and should individuals have a greater degree of choice as to where and when they marry in order to prevent this from happening? The latter issue is currently being considered by the Law Commission.

Debate: The legal status of sham marriages or marriages of convenience

Sham marriages—those entered into for immigration purposes alone—are valid, i.e. they only come to an end on death or dissolution. Do you think that this is right? Should they be classed as void, voidable or non-existent, given that they are not recognised for immigration purposes?

(Q) **QUESTION** | **1**

Analyse the differences between void and voidable marriages.

(!) **CAUTION!**

- In order to answer this question you need to be able to explain how void and voidable marriages are treated differently *and* discuss the similarities between them.

- It is not necessary to consider void and voidable civil partnerships as the question does not require this.

 DIAGRAM ANSWER PLAN

Explain the concept of a void marriage and voidable marriage

▼

Discuss the grounds on which a marriage is void—s.11 Matrimonial Causes Act 1973

▼

Discuss the grounds on which a marriage is voidable—s.12 Matrimonial Causes Act 1973

▼

Discuss the differences between void and voidable marriages

▼

Discuss the similarities between void and voidable marriages

▼

Conclusion

SUGGESTED ANSWER

In order to create a valid marriage, the parties must have the capacity to marry and the correct formalities must be complied with. If these requirements are not satisfied or if the union is defective in some other way, it may be categorised as a void, voidable or non-existent marriage.[1] This answer focuses on the first two categories.

[1] It is worth mentioning non-existent marriage or non-marriage because it demonstrates that you are aware that certain flawed marriages are not considered void or voidable.

Definitions

A void marriage is one with a fundamental flaw, which means that a lawful marriage never came into existence: the marriage is void *ab initio*.[2] It will never be considered valid in the eyes of the law, regardless of the parties' intentions or wishes, because there are public policy objections to the marriage. It is not necessary to obtain an annulment from the court, although as Gilmore and Glennon explain, 'the advantage of obtaining a decree of nullity is that it removes any uncertainty as to the status of the parties' (2014, p. 6). A voidable marriage is also defective, but not to the same extent as a void one. There are no public policy objections to the marriage, but there is a problem that one or both parties might consider serious enough to justify annulling the union. Voidable marriages are therefore valid unless and until they are annulled by the court (**s.16 Matrimonial Causes Act 1973**).

[2] This Latin term means 'void from the start'.

Grounds on which a Marriage is Void *ab initio*

Section 11 of **the Matrimonial Causes Act 1973** lists the grounds on which a marriage is void.[3] First, a marriage is void if it infringes the provisions of **the Marriage Acts 1949** to **1986**; that is to say, the parties are within the prohibited degrees of relationship, either party is under the age of 16 or the parties have intermarried in disregard of certain requirements as to the formation of marriage (**s.11(a)**). In relation to the latter, the marriage is only considered void if the parties knowingly and wilfully breached the formal requirements (**s.49 Marriage Act 1949**). Secondly, a marriage is void under **s.11(b) Matrimonial Causes Act 1973** if either party was already lawfully married or in a civil partnership at the time of the marriage and in the case of polygamous marriages entered into outside the jurisdiction, the marriage is void if either party was domiciled in England and Wales (**s.11(d)**). **Section 11(c)**, which provided that a marriage was void if the parties were not respectively male and female, was repealed by **the Marriage (Same Sex Couples) Act 2013**.[4] The flaws referred to above are considered so grave that no marriage should come into existence on the ground of public policy. As a result of the public policy

[3] The purpose of this paragraph is to explain the grounds on which a marriage is void. The evidence is provided by **s.11 MCA**. The paragraph ends by analysing the grounds on which a marriage is void.

[4] Note that the equivalent provision of **the Civil Partnership Act 2004** was not repealed.

objections to the marriage, any interested party (for example, a relative or the trustee of a pension scheme) can seek a declaration that the marriage is void.

Grounds on which a Marriage is Voidable

As explained above, a voidable marriage contains a defect that one or both parties may consider serious enough to justify annulling the union. Because there are no public policy objections to the marriage, only the parties can petition for annulment.[5] Section 12(1) of the Matrimonial Causes Act 1973[6] provides that marriage is voidable if: it has not been consummated due to the incapacity of either party or due to the wilful refusal of the respondent; either party did not validly consent due to duress, mistake, unsoundness of mind or otherwise; at the time of the marriage either party was suffering from a mental disorder so as to be unfitted for marriage; at the time of the marriage the respondent was suffering from a communicable form of venereal disease; at the time of the marriage the respondent was pregnant by some person other than the petitioner; an interim gender recognition certificate has been issued to either party after the time of the marriage; and finally on the ground that the respondent is a person whose gender at the time of the marriage had become an acquired gender under the **Gender Recognition Act 2004**. It should be noted that **s.12(1)(a)** and **(b),** which concern non-consummation, do not apply to same-sex marriages as a result of **s.12(2)**.

Differences between Void and Voidable Marriages

As explained above, anyone can petition to the court in relation to a void marriage, but only the parties can petition on the grounds that the marriage is voidable.[7] In addition to this distinction, there are bars and time limits that apply to the annulment of voidable marriages, but not to void marriages. **Section 13(1)** of **the Matrimonial Causes Act 1973** indicates that the court will not grant a decree if the petitioner knew that he or she could have the marriage annulled but behaved in such a way as to lead the respondent to believe that he or she would not do so and the court is satisfied that it would be unjust to grant the decree. In *D v D (Nullity)* **[1979] 3 ALL ER 337** the husband petitioned for annulment ten years after the marriage on the ground of his wife's wilful refusal to consummate. The couple had adopted two children during this period, which constituted conduct that 'lead the respondent to believe' that her husband would not petition for nullity. However, the wife did not object to the decree and as a consequence, it was granted because it was not unjust to do so. Such a restriction is not relevant to the annulment of a void marriage, as the latter is void *ab initio*.

[5] The parties may decide not to petition for an annulment.

[6] The Matrimonial Causes Act 1973 re-enacted the Nullity of Marriage Act 1971.

[7] It is not necessary to repeat the same point in great detail, but it is useful to make links with previous sections, particularly when completing coursework.

A petition in relation to a void marriage can be lodged at any point after the marriage ceremony took place, even after one or both parties have died, but a time limit applies to the annulment of a voidable marriage. **Section 13(2)** of **the Matrimonial Causes Act 1973** provides that, with the exception of annulments on the basis of non-consummation or gender reassignment that took place after the couple were lawfully married, the petitioner must institute proceedings for the annulment of a voidable marriage within three years. The purpose of this three-year bar is to ensure that the status of the marriage is not left in doubt for a long period of time. However, the court can grant leave for the institution of proceedings after three years have elapsed if the petitioner has, during that period, suffered from a mental disorder (**s.13(4)**). Given that a void marriage never came into existence, there is no reason to impose an equivalent time limit on the annulment of void marriages.[8]

[8]It is important to explain why distinctions between void and voidable marriages exist.

The court can also refuse to grant a decree of nullity on the grounds that the respondent was suffering from VD, was pregnant by another or is a person whose gender had become acquired under **the Gender Recognition Act 2004** if the petitioner was aware of the facts (**s.13(3) Matrimonial Causes Act 1973**). This is because such circumstances cannot be considered flaws if the petitioner was aware of them. In contrast, a marriage is void on the basis that the parties were closely related, under the age of 16 etc., even if the parties are aware of such facts, because, as explained earlier, it is public policy objections, rather than the objections of the parties, that make the marriage void.

A further distinction exists between void and voidable marriages in terms of the status of children born to the couple. In the case of a voidable marriage, a child born before the annulment is legitimate because the marriage was valid up until that point. The child of a void marriage is only legitimate if at the time of conception either parent reasonably believed that the marriage was valid (**s.1(1) Legitimacy Act 1976**). However, it should be noted that the marital status of a child's parents is now rarely relevant (see **Re Moynihan** [2000] **1 FLR 113** for an example[9]).

[9]In a coursework question you would have time to explain the facts of this case.

Similarities

As explained above, the parties to a void or voidable marriage can petition for an annulment and the children of such unions may be legitimate. In addition, the parties to a void or voidable marriage can *both* apply for financial orders under **Part II** of **the Matrimonial Causes Act 1973**, in the same way that spouses seeking a divorce or judicial separation can.[10] It is thus clear that a void marriage has certain legal consequences, even though it never existed in the eyes of the law.

[10] It should be noted that the court may refuse to grant financial relief: *J v S-T (formerly J)(Transsexual: Ancillary Relief)* [1997] 1 FLR 402.

This fact separates a void marriage from one that is non-existent (see *Hudson v Leigh (Status of Non-Marriage)* [2009] 3 FCR 401).

Conclusion

This essay has demonstrated that there are several conceptual and practical differences between the status of, and the annulment of void and voidable marriages. But despite this, there are also some similarities between them, the most important being the fact that the parties to a void or voidable marriage can apply for financial relief.

 LOOKING FOR EXTRA MARKS?

- Demonstrate the currency of your knowledge by highlighting the changes made by **the Marriage (Same Sex Couples) Act 2013**.

- Gain extra marks by mentioning non-existent marriages: some marriage ceremonies are so flawed that they have no legal consequences at all (see question 2).

- If this question was set as an in-course assignment, it would be useful to summarise the history of void and voidable marriages and to refer to the Law Commission Report No 33.

 QUESTION 2

'Holding a union to be a non-marriage is not a decision that should be taken lightly. In recent years, however, the courts have been more willing to resort to this option.'

Rebecca Probert, 'The evolving concept of "non-marriage"' (2013) CFLQ 25(3) 314 at p. 314

In the light of this quote, analyse the concept of a non-marriage.

 CAUTION!

- You can answer this question in an examination even if you have not read the article, provided that you have sound knowledge and understanding of the concept of non-marriage.

- Non-marriages are also referred to as non-existent marriages—do not let this confuse you.

DIAGRAM ANSWER PLAN

> Explain the meaning of non-marriage and contrast with a void marriage

▼

> Discuss *Hudson v Leigh*—the criteria for determining whether a marriage is non-existent

▼

> Explain the cases relating to forced marriage

▼

> Explain the cases relating to non-compliant marriage ceremonies

▼

> Discuss the role of intention

▼

> Conclusion

SUGGESTED ANSWER

If two parties take part in a ceremony that purports to be a marriage, but it bears little or no resemblance to an ordinary marriage, it is classified as a non-existent or non-marriage. A non-marriage never existed in the eyes of the law and has no legal consequences. This means that it is not possible to apply for a decree of nullity or for financial orders under **the Matrimonial Causes Act 1973**.[1] In addition, any children born to the couple are technically illegitimate[2] because **s.1(1)** of **the Legitimacy Act 1976**, which provides that a child is legitimate if, at the time of conception either parent reasonably believed that the marriage was valid, only applies to void marriages. A non-marriage can also be distinguished from a void marriage because the parties to the latter can apply for a decree of nullity and for financial orders.[3] The reason for the distinction is that although a void marriage is fundamentally flawed, there is some semblance of marriage. For example, a stranger who observed the ceremony would not be able to tell that the parties were closely related. In contrast, non-marriages have little or no semblance of marriage and should therefore have no legal consequences. A declaration that a marriage is non-existent can be made under **s.55** of **the Family Law Act 1986**.

[1] It is important to explain the implications of declaring a union to be a non-marriage in order to understand the case law that follows.

[2] Illegitimacy is rarely relevant, but see *Re Moynihan* **[2000] 1 FLR 113** for a case where it was significant.

[3] The fact that the parties to a void marriage can apply for financial relief explains why an individual will argue that his or her marriage is void.

Hudson v Leigh

The concept of a non-existent marriage has been considered in several cases during the past two decades, for example in *Ghandi v Patel* [2001] 1 FLR 603 a Hindu marriage ceremony that took place in a restaurant bore very little resemblance to an English marriage and as a result was held to be non-existent. But none of the cases set criteria for determining whether a marriage is void or non-existent. This finally occurred in *Hudson v Leigh (Status of Non-Marriage)* [2009] 3 FCR 401, where Bodey J indicated that the following factors should be considered:[4]

a) 'whether the ceremony or event set out or purported to be a lawful marriage,

b) whether it bore all or enough of the hallmarks of marriage,

c) whether the key participants (most especially the officiating official) believed, intended and understood the ceremony as giving rise to the status of lawful marriage, and

d) the reasonable perceptions, understandings and beliefs of those in attendance' (para. 78).

In this case, a religious ceremony, which was to be followed by a civil ceremony in a register office, constituted a non-marriage, because the event did not purport to be a lawful marriage, the parties and the officiating minister did not intend the ceremony to constitute a marriage and the traditional order of service was altered to reflect the fact that the event was a blessing rather than a marriage ceremony. The High Court made a declaration under **s.55** of **the Family Law Act 1986** that there never was a marriage and the applicant was denied financial relief. The decision of the High Court, which was confirmed by the Court of Appeal, was welcomed as there was previously uncertainty as to whether the law recognised the concept of non-marriage (see Gaffney-Rhys, 2010).

Forced Marriages

The first two cases heard after *Hudson v Leigh* concerned forced marriage, i.e. one that is entered into without the free and full consent of one or both parties. In *SH v NB (Marriage: Consent)* [2009] **EWHC 3274**, a 16-year-old girl of Pakistani descent (NB) had been forced to participate in a marriage ceremony in Pakistan in 2001. She returned to the UK in 2003, and later married another man. SH petitioned for divorce, and in response NB stated that her marriage had been forced. NB was unable to obtain a decree of nullity under **the Matrimonial Causes Act 1973** because more than three years had expired since the ceremony had taken place,[5] but the court declared that NB could apply for a declaration that the marriage was

[4] The decision of the High Court was confirmed by the Court of Appeal.

[5] **Section 13(2) of the Matrimonial Causes Act 1973** requires most petitions for annulment of a voidable marriage to be instituted within three years.

non-existent. In *B v I (Forced Marriage)* [2010] 1 FLR 1721, a young English woman of Bangladeshi origin (B) was forced to take part in a marriage ceremony in Bangladesh. B was unable to petition for an annulment because she was timed out and therefore applied for a declaration that no marriage existed. The court accepted that B had been forced into marriage and made the requested declaration.[6] In these two cases, there were no negative implications of declaring the marriage to be non-existent as the parties did not wish to apply for financial relief (unlike the applicant in *Hudson v Leigh*). In addition, the fact that NB's marriage was non-existent meant that her subsequent marriage was valid and her child legitimate.

[6] A similar approach was adopted in *City of Westminster v IC* [2008] EWCA Civ 198.

Marriage Ceremonies that do not Comply with the Marriage Acts[7]

[7] It is worth pointing out that the Law Commission is currently reviewing how and where people can marry, which may result in a change to the law relating to formalities.

Most cases concerning non-marriage involve ceremonies that do not comply with the formal requirements of **the Marriage Acts**, as *Ghandi v Patel* did. In *Al-Saedy v Musawa (Presumption of Marriage)* [2010] EWHC 3293 (Fam), an event that took place in a flat in London during which the parties entered into an agreement that enabled them to live together and have children constituted a non-marriage as it did not purport to be a marriage, did not bear the hallmarks of marriage and the participants did not believe it to create a lawful marriage. In *El Gamal v Al Makatoum* [2011] EWHC 3763 (Fam), the applicant alleged that an Islamic marriage ceremony had taken place in a London flat between herself and the respondent: the latter denied this assertion. According to Bodey J, there was 'wholesale failure to comply with the formal requirements of English law' (para. 23) because the marriage had not been authorised by the superintendent registrar, had not taken place in a registered building and the marriage had not been registered. The applicant claimed that she believed that the ceremony would create a marriage recognised under English law, but Bodey J indicated that the belief or intent of one party is not sufficient to convert a non-marriage into a void one (para. 86). The applicant was denied a decree of nullity and could not obtain financial relief, as the marriage was non-existent. The same conclusion was reached in *Dukali v Lamrani (Attorney General Intervening)* [2012] EWHC 1748, which concerned a marriage ceremony that took place at the Moroccan consulate in London, but in this case, both parties intended and believed the ceremony to give rise to a marriage recognised under English law, as did the relatives in attendance. When the relationship broke down the wife petitioned for divorce, and after consulting solicitors, the husband discovered that the consulate was not registered for the purpose of marriage,[8] which meant that the marriage had not been authorised or properly registered. Following

[8] The wife made a claim under **the Matrimonial and Family Proceedings Act 1984** following a foreign divorce—in a coursework question you should explain this.

VOID, VOIDABLE AND NON-EXISTENT MARRIAGES 37

the decision in *El Gamal v Al Makatoum*, Holman J declared that the wholesale failure to comply with the requirements of **the Marriage Acts** resulted in a non-marriage. As Probert explains, 'form has been prioritised over intention' (p. 319).[9] The decision in *Dukali v Lamrani* was later upheld by the Court of Appeal in *Sharbatly v Shagroon* [2012] EWCA Civ 1507.

[9] This is an example of utilising the opinion of the author of the quote, which would be expected in an in-course assignment.

MA v JA and the Attorney General [2012] EWHC 2219 (Fam) differed from the cases above as it concerned an application for a declaration that the marriage was valid under **s.55** of **the Family Law Act 1986**. The relationship between the parties had not broken down and the parties wished to remain married. In this case, the Islamic marriage ceremony had taken place in a mosque that was registered for the purpose of marriages, in the presence of the chairman, who was authorised to conduct marriage ceremonies. The parties intended to form a marriage recognised under English law and believed that they had done so, but the imam who performed the ceremony was not, at that time, authorised under **the Marriage Acts**, due notice had not been given to the superintendent registrar and the marriage was not registered. Despite this, Moylan J stated that the marriage was 'of the kind' permitted by English law and in the form capable of producing a valid marriage (para. 101). It satisfied the hallmarks test, the parties to the marriage intended to effect a marriage recognised under English law and those in attendance believed this to be the case. As a result, the marriage could not be declared non-existent and because the breach of formal requirements was not deliberate, the marriage could not be void. The declaration that the marriage was valid was therefore granted.[10]

[10] You may also discuss *Asaad v Kurter* [2013] EWHC 38, where the breach of formal requirements was not sufficient to render the union a non-marriage.

Lack of Intention

The parties in *Galloway v Goldstein* [2012] EWHC 1748 (Fam) were married in Connecticut and then arranged a wedding in England for family and friends to attend. The ceremony in England wholly complied with the formal requirements under **the Marriage Acts**. The couple later divorced in the USA, following which the husband applied for a declaration that the ceremony that took place in England did not effect a valid marriage and did not require dissolution. The High Court declared that the English ceremony was a non-marriage because the parties had not intended it to create a lawful marriage. It is therefore clear that lack of intention can render a compliant ceremony a non-marriage.

Conclusion

The cases discussed in this answer demonstrate that, as Probert asserts, the courts have been more willing to declare a union to be a non-marriage. In some cases, for example *Galloway v Goldstein*, there were no adverse implications for the parties, but in others, for example *Dukali v Lamrani*, the 'wife' was disadvantaged as she was denied a fair financial settlement. This emphasises that 'holding a union to be a non-marriage is not a decision that should be taken lightly'.

LOOKING FOR EXTRA MARKS?

■ Consider the implications of the law relating to non-marriage for members of ethnic minority communities.

■ If this question is set as an in-course assignment, ensure that you read the article and utilise it.

QUESTION | 3

In 2008, Colin married Denise. Denise was born male, but underwent gender reassignment surgery two years before she met Colin. Colin was aware of this fact when he married Denise. Colin and Denise were unable to have sexual intercourse and after a few months they gave up trying. The relationship deteriorated and just before their first anniversary Colin and Denise separated. Colin told Denise that it was not necessary to obtain a divorce, as their marriage was not valid. A year later, Colin met Elaine. They married soon after because Elaine fell pregnant. After the baby was born, Elaine admitted that Colin was not the child's father, which put considerable strain on the relationship. Elaine recently left when she found out that Colin had lied about how rich his parents are. Colin has since met Fiona, whom he wishes to marry. It transpires that Fiona is Denise's daughter from the brief relationship that he had with Gina, several years before the gender reassignment surgery. Fiona lived with Gina throughout her childhood and Gina refused to allow Denise contact with Fiona after the sex change operation. Because of this, Denise never told Colin about Fiona.

Discuss the validity of the marriages to Denise and Elaine and advise Colin in relation to his proposed marriage to Fiona.

CAUTION!

■ Read the question carefully—it contains a lot of information.

■ The question does not tell you whether Denise obtained a gender recognition certificate. You need to explain the legal position if she did and if she did not obtain a certificate.

■ It is not necessary to consider ancillary matters, as the question only asks you to discuss the validity of the marriages.

DIAGRAM ANSWER PLAN

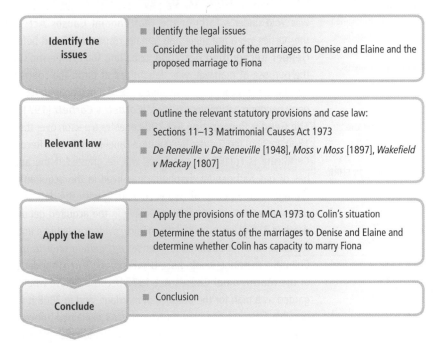

Identify the issues	■ Identify the legal issues ■ Consider the validity of the marriages to Denise and Elaine and the proposed marriage to Fiona
Relevant law	■ Outline the relevant statutory provisions and case law: ■ Sections 11–13 Matrimonial Causes Act 1973 ■ *De Reneville v De Reneville* [1948], *Moss v Moss* [1897], *Wakefield v Mackay* [1807]
Apply the law	■ Apply the provisions of the MCA 1973 to Colin's situation ■ Determine the status of the marriages to Denise and Elaine and determine whether Colin has capacity to marry Fiona
Conclude	■ Conclusion

SUGGESTED ANSWER

This question concerns the validity of two marriages entered into by Colin and as a result it is necessary to discuss the law of nullity, which is contained in **ss.11–16** of **the Matrimonial Causes Act 1973**. A petition can be made to the court utilising the nullity procedure on the basis that a marriage is void under **s.11** of **the Matrimonial Causes Act 1973** or voidable under **s.12**. The difference between these two types of marriage was explained by Lord Greene MR in ***De Reneville v De Reneville* [1948] p. 100**:

A void marriage is one that will be regarded as never having taken place and can be so treated by the parties to it without the necessity of any decree annulling it. A voidable marriage is one that will be regarded as valid until a decree annulling it has been pronounced.

Status of the Marriage to Denise if Full Gender Recognition was not Obtained

[1] The Act came into force in March 2014. If Colin and Denise married after March 2014, whether Denise obtained a gender recognition certificate would be immaterial.

Prior to the Marriage (Same Sex Couples) Act 2013, a marriage was void under s.11(c) of the Matrimonial Causes Act 1973 if the parties were not male and female, respectively[1] and before the Gender Recognition Act 2004 came into force, a person's sex for the purpose of marriage was determined at birth. The courts would not therefore recognise the acquired sex of a person who had undergone gender reassignment surgery (*Corbett v Corbett* [1971] P 83).

[2] You could point out that the Gender Recognition Act 2004 was introduced following *Goodwin v UK* [2002] 35 EHRR 18 and *Bellinger v Bellinger* [2003] UKHL 21.

The Gender Recognition Act 2004 enables a person over the age of 18 to apply to the Gender Recognition Panel for a Gender Recognition Certificate (s.1(1)).[2]. A certificate will be granted if the applicant has or has had gender dysphoria, has lived in the acquired gender throughout the period of two years ending with the date on which the application is made, intends to live in the acquired gender until death (s.2) and has provided the medical evidence required under s.3. If Denise had not obtained full gender recognition prior to marrying

[3] The marriage would be void from the outset and so it is not necessary to discuss voidable marriage.

Colin, the marriage would have been void *ab initio*[3] under s.11(c) of the Matrimonial Causes Act 1973 because Denise would be regarded as a man for the purpose of marriage, and in 2008 it was not possible for same-sex couples to marry. As explained above, a void marriage is one that 'is regarded as never having taken place and can be so treated by the parties to it without the necessity of any decree annulling it' (*De Reneville v De Reneville*). Colin would therefore be free to marry Elaine.

Status of the Marriage to Denise if Full Gender Recognition was Obtained

If Denise did acquire a full gender recognition certificate prior to marrying Colin, the marriage would not be void, but a marriage involving

[4] This is the case even after the Marriage (Same Sex Couples) Act 2013.

a person whose gender is acquired under the Gender Recognition Act can be voidable under s.12(1)(h)[4] of the Matrimonial Causes Act 1973 if the petitioner was ignorant of the fact that the respondent's gender was acquired (s.13(3) MCA 1973)[5]. As Colin was aware

[5] Section 13(3) also applies to annulments based on s.12(1)(e) venereal disease and s.12(1)(f) pregnancy.

that Denise was born male, he could not petition for an annulment on the basis of s.12(1)(h). However, he could petition on the basis that the marriage was not consummated, as the question indicates that the couple was unable to have sexual intercourse. Section 12(1)(a) of the Matrimonial Causes Act 1973 provides that a marriage is voidable on the ground that 'the marriage has not been consummated owing to the incapacity of either party to consummate it', while s.12(1)(b) states that a marriage is voidable 'owing to the wilful refusal of the respondent to consummate it'. Consummation requires sexual intercourse to be 'ordinary and complete, not partial and imperfect' (*D-E v*

A-G (1845) 1 Rob Eccl 279). The question suggests that **s.12(1)(a)** would apply, which means that Colin or Denise could have petitioned for an annulment, but it seems that they have not done so. The three-year bar contained in **s.13(2)** of the Act does not apply to petitions on the ground of non-consummation.

Status of the Marriage to Elaine if the Marriage to Denise is Void

If the marriage to Denise is void, because Denise had not obtained a full gender recognition certificate, the marriage to Elaine is not void, but could be voidable. **Section 12(1)(f)** of **the Matrimonial Causes Act 1973** provides that a marriage is voidable on the ground 'that at the time of the marriage, the respondent was pregnant by some person other than the petitioner' (see *Moss v Moss* [1897] P 263). Colin would therefore have the right to petition for an annulment because Elaine was pregnant by some other person at the time of the marriage, but Elaine cannot do so on this basis. **Section 13(3)** of the Act, which bars a decree if the petitioner is aware of the alleged fact, would not be applicable in this case, as Colin discovered that he was not the baby's father after the marriage. But **s.13(2)**, which requires proceedings to be instituted within three years from the date of the marriage, would bar a petition as the question suggests that Colin and Elaine married in 2010. The court can grant leave to initiate proceedings after three years have elapsed if the petitioner suffered from a mental disorder at some point during that three-year period (**s.13(4)**), but there is no evidence that this would apply to Colin. Colin will therefore have to utilise the divorce procedure, as he is barred from initiating nullity proceedings under **s.13(2) MCA**.[6]

Elaine may wish to end the marriage because Colin lied about his parents' wealth. **Section 12(1)(c)** of **the Matrimonial Causes Act 1973** provides that a marriage is voidable on the ground that either party 'did not validly consent to it, whether in consequence of duress, mistake, unsoundness of mind or otherwise'. A mistake as to the identity of the other party or a mistake as to the nature of the ceremony justifies an annulment, but a mistake as to the attributes of the other party does not (*Wakefield v Mackay* [1807] 1 Hag Con 394). Elaine would not therefore be granted an annulment, but in any event, would be timed out, under **s.13(2)**. If Elaine wants to end the marriage she will therefore have to petition for divorce.

Status of the Marriage to Elaine if the Marriage to Denise is Valid

If the marriage to Denise is valid and has not been annulled due to non-consummation, then the marriage to Elaine is void under **s.11(b)** of **the Matrimonial Causes Act 1973** on the basis 'that at the time of the marriage either party was already lawfully married or a civil partner'.[7]

---

[6] It is not necessary to discuss the ground and facts for divorce, as the question asks you about the validity of the marriages.

[7] A polygamous marriage contracted overseas will not be void if the parties were not domiciled in England and Wales (**s.11(d)**). This does not assist Colin.

Bigamy is also a criminal offence under **s.57** of **the Offences Against the Person Act 1861** and is punishable by up to seven years in prison.

[8] You could discuss *Dredge v Dredge* [1947] 1 ALL ER 29.

A bigamous marriage remains void even if the first spouse dies or the first marriage is later dissolved.[8] It would not therefore be possible to legalise the marriage to Elaine by applying to the court for an annulment of the marriage to Denise on the basis of **s.12(1)(a)**.

Proposed Marriage to Fiona

If the marriage to Elaine is void due to bigamy, it is not necessary to obtain a decree to annul it, but of course Colin would have to dissolve or annul the marriage to Denise in order to have the capacity to remarry. If he does not do so, the marriage to Fiona would be bigamous and therefore void under **s.11(b) MCA 1973**. Similarly, if the marriage to Elaine is valid, Colin would need to obtain a divorce, otherwise the marriage to Fiona would be bigamous and therefore void.

Assuming that action is taken to end the relevant marriage, Colin

[9] You could state that this is known as 'consanguinity'.

is free to remarry, but is he able to marry Fiona? **Section 1** of **the Marriage Act 1949** prohibits marriages between persons closely related through blood[9] and through marriage.[10] **Part 2** of **Schedule 1** to **the Marriage Act** indicates that a man may not marry, inter alia,

[10] You could state that this is known as 'affinity'.

the child of a former spouse. **Section 1(3)** of the Act proceeds to qualify this by providing that the marriage between such persons will not be void 'if both parties have attained the age of twenty one at the time of the marriage and the younger party has not at any time before attaining the age of eighteen been a child of the family in relation to the other party'. **The Marriage Act 1949** thus prohibits the marriage between step-parent and step-child, unless both parties are over 21 and the older party did not act as a parent to the younger party. In this case, Fiona may be the child of a former spouse, but Colin did not treat her as a child of the family while she was under the age of 18. Colin will therefore be able to marry Fiona if/when she is 21, provided of course, the marriage to Elaine has come to an end.

Conclusion

As the status of the marriage between Colin and Denise is unclear, so too is the status of the marriage to Elaine, and because of this we do not know if Colin is free to remarry.

✚ LOOKING FOR EXTRA MARKS?

- Gain extra marks by discussing the bars to a decree contained in **s.13(1)(2)** and **(3)** of **the Matrimonial Causes Act 1973**.

- Mention the changes made by **the Marriage (Same Sex Couples) Act 2013** and the parts of the law that were not altered by this legislation.

QUESTION | 4

Should the concept of voidable marriage be abolished?

CAUTION!

- The question does not ask you to discuss the abolition of void marriages.
- You need a sound understanding of the grounds on which a marriage is voidable to answer this question. You should consider whether each ground should be retained.
- Ensure that you discuss the consequences of abolishing voidable marriage.

DIAGRAM ANSWER PLAN

Explain the meaning of voidable marriage

Discuss the grounds on which a marriage is voidable under s.12(1) Matrimonial Causes Act 1973: Non-consummation—s.12(1)(a) and (b)

Lack of consent—s.12(1)(c)

Non-disclosure—s.12(1)(d)(e) and (f)

Gender reassignment—s.12(1)(g) and (h)

Discuss the implications of abolishing voidable marriage

Conclusion

A voidable marriage is one that is flawed in some way, but the defect is not as fundamental as those that render a marriage void. A voidable marriage is valid unless and until it is annulled by the court (**s.16 Matrimonial Causes Act 1973**) and only the parties to the marriage can lodge a petition. Over 99 per cent of petitions filed for matrimonial proceedings are for divorce, which means that less than 1 per cent are for judicial separation, annulment of a void marriage and annulment of a voidable marriage combined (Ministry of Justice Statistics 2014). The number of decrees granted to annul voidable marriages each year is therefore very small indeed. As a result, it is often suggested that voidable marriage should be abolished.

Non-consummation

The Matrimonial Causes Act 1973 provides that a marriage is voidable on the ground that the marriage has not been consummated due to the incapacity of either party (**s.12(1)(a)**) or the wilful refusal of the respondent (**s.12(1)(b)**). It can be argued that inability to consummate the marriage should not be ground for annulment: because it is a relic of the Canon law and is not therefore relevant to most people; because most couples will have entered into a sexual relationship prior to marriage; and because it may involve a medical examination and will normally involve a full court hearing. But **s.12(1)(a)** may still be relevant to those whose beliefs forbid sexual activity prior to marriage, particularly as divorce is less acceptable amongst such groups. Wilful refusal to consummate was not part of the Canon law, but was added by statute in 1937. According to Lowe and Douglas, this ground is particularly hard to justify as it 'arises purely from a post-marital decision' and should thus be 'regarded as a reason for divorce' (2015, p. 86).[1] Finally, it should be noted that inability and wilful refusal to consummate do not apply to same-sex marriages (**s.12(2)**): abolishing both grounds for annulment would therefore ensure equality between same-sex and opposite-sex couples.

[1] This is an example of academic opinion that can be inserted into your answer. All major textbooks will contain a section that considers whether voidable marriage should be abolished.

Lack of Consent

Section 12(1)(c) provides that a marriage is voidable if either party did not validly consent to it due to duress, mistake, unsoundness of mind or otherwise. The ability to annul, rather than dissolve a marriage due to lack of consent is crucial as consent should be essential to the creation of a valid marriage. This ground has become more significant in recent years as awareness of the problem of forced marriages has grown. In *P v R (Forced Marriage: Annulment: Procedure)* [2003]

1 FLR 661, the court heard evidence that a lesser stigma is attached to a woman who obtains a decree of nullity than a woman who obtains a divorce. One way to resolve this issue is to render forced marriages (and those where consent is lacking due to mistake or mental incapacity), void *ab initio*, as in Australia.[2] Indeed, adopting this approach would overcome the problem faced by the victims of forced marriage who do not seek an annulment during the first three years of marriage and find themselves statute-barred under **s.13(2)**.[3]

Non-disclosure

The grounds contained in **s.12(1)(d), (e)** and **(f)** were originally introduced by **the Matrimonial Causes Act 1937** because of the lack of relief for fraud or the deliberate concealment of material facts. Non-disclosure of other material facts does not render a marriage voidable and in such cases, the aggrieved party would have to petition for divorce. There is no reason why spouses who find themselves in the circumstances contained in **s.12(1)(d–f)** could not utilise the divorce procedure. **Section 12(1)(d) MCA 1973** states that a marriage is voidable 'if at the time of the marriage either party, though capable of giving valid consent, was suffering from a mental disorder . . . of such a kind or to such an extent as to be unfitted for marriage'. 'Unfitted for marriage' means that the person is 'incapable of carrying out the ordinary duties and obligations of marriage' (*Bennett v Bennett* [1969] **1 ALL ER 539**). To abolish this ground for annulment would mean that the person suffering from the mental illness would be unable to end the marriage unless the ground for divorce is established. But given that **s.12(1)(d)** was intended to protect the 'innocent' spouse from wilful concealment of a material fact, there is no reason why s/he could not petition for divorce based on the respondent's behaviour.[4]

A marriage is voidable under **s.12(1)(e)** if 'at the time of the marriage the respondent was suffering from a communicable form of venereal disease'[5] and under **s.12(1)(f)** if 'at the time of the marriage the respondent was pregnant by some person other than the petitioner'. **Section 13(3)** provides that a decree cannot be granted on the basis of **s.12(1)(e)** or **(f)** unless the petitioner was ignorant of the facts. It is thus clear that these provisions were designed to provide a remedy for the victim of fraud, but given that a woman cannot obtain an annulment if she discovers that her husband has impregnated another woman, it is asserted that these grounds should be abolished and such victims of fraud should petition for divorce.

Gender Reassignment

Section 12(1)(g) and **(h)** were inserted by **the Gender Recognition Act 2004** and relate to marriages involving a person who has

[2] The Australian Marriage Act 1961 provides that a marriage is void if consent is not real due to duress, mistake or mental incapacity.

[3] You could point out that making a forced marriage void, would emphasise the importance of consent and stress that forced marriage is unacceptable.

[4] You could mention *Thurlow v Thurlow* [1976] **Fam 32**, where the husband was granted a divorce based on his wife's behaviour, caused by her severe epilepsy.

[5] It is worth noting that venereal disease is not a ground for annulling a civil partnership.

acquired a new gender. **Section 12(1)(g)** states that a marriage is voidable if an interim gender recognition certificate has been issued to either party after the time of the marriage. The purpose of this provision was to prevent the formation of same-sex marriages, which were not permissible in 2004.[6] Despite the passage of the **Marriage (Same Sex Couples) Act 2013**, post-marital gender reassignment remains a ground for annulment. It can be argued that it is not appropriate to annul a marriage on the basis that one spouse has acquired a new gender as the marriage was not 'defective' when it was formed. If a spouse has gender reassignment and either party do not wish to remain married, they should divorce.

Section **12(1)(h)** provides that a marriage is voidable if 'the respondent is a person whose gender at the time of the marriage had become an acquired gender under the **Gender Recognition Act 2004**'. This is intended to provide the same protection against fraud as those relating to pregnancy and venereal disease, as **s.13(3)** bars a decree on the basis of gender reassignment if the petitioner was aware of the fact prior to the marriage. The arguments in favour of abolishing venereal disease and pregnancy as grounds for annulment would apply equally to gender reassignment. In addition, **s.12(1)(h)** is at odds with **s.9(1)** of **the Gender Recognition Act 2004**, which states that a person's reassigned gender should be recognised as their gender for all purposes. It can therefore be argued that a person who marries in ignorance of the other party's acquired gender should petition for divorce.

The Consequences of Abolishing Voidable Marriage[7]

The discussion above has demonstrated that most grounds for voidability could be abolished, as those who find themselves in such circumstances could utilise divorce procedure instead. Given that the family courts have the same powers to make financial orders and orders relating to children in nullity proceedings as they do in divorce proceedings, the effect of the two procedures is very similar. However, there are certain differences between nullity and divorce proceedings. First, a petition for divorce cannot be lodged during the first year of marriage, whereas a petition for nullity can (**s.3 MCA 1973**). Although this may seem to justify retaining the concept of a voidable marriage, those that wish to separate and organise their affairs during the first year of marriage could initially apply for judicial separation (**s.17 MCA**), which is available prior to the first anniversary and then petition for divorce after one year of marriage.

The second distinction between nullity and divorce proceedings is that the former tends to involve a full hearing, whereas the latter does not if the special procedure is utilised. The unpleasantness and the

[6] You could point out that the law in England and Wales did not breach the European Convention on Human Rights—see *Parry v UK* [2006] App. No. 42971/05.

[7] You should consider the advantages and disadvantages of abolishing voidable marriage.

cost of nullity proceedings contribute to the argument that voidable marriage should be abolished. However, those who oppose divorce on religious or cultural grounds would not wish to see voidable marriage abolished. Initially, nullity proceedings were typically utilised by Roman Catholics and other Christians who do not believe in dissolving a valid marriage. If voidable marriage was to be abolished, those who find themselves in the circumstances listed in **s.12(1)** could obtain a civil divorce and initiate action in the ecclesiastical courts for a religious decree of nullity. However, the importance of nullity has increased in recent years because it is apparently a more acceptable means of ending a marriage amongst certain ethnic minorities. Rendering forced marriages (and those where consent is lacking due to mistake or mental incapacity) void *ab initio* would mean that certain members of ethnic minority communities would not have to resort to divorce, but this would not assist those whose beliefs forbid sexual activity prior to marriage and subsequently find that they cannot consummate.[8] The number of people who fall within this category is likely to be extremely small indeed.

[8]Remember, many ethnic minority couples are not in a position to apply for annulment and therefore have to resort to divorce if their marriage breaks down.

Conclusion[9]

[9]I have suggested that voidable should be abolished, but there is no correct answer. You could argue that it should be retained, as some people would be adversely affected.

This essay has presented the arguments for and against abolishing voidable marriages, and on balance it seems that the former outweigh the latter. It is therefore suggested that voidable marriage could be abolished with very few negative consequences. But there seems to be no political will to realise this proposal.

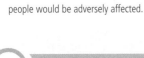

LOOKING FOR EXTRA MARKS?

- To gain extra marks cite statistics on divorce and nullity and use them as part of your argument.
- It is useful to able to discuss the position in other jurisdictions, such as Australia, where voidable marriage has been abolished, particularly in a coursework question.
- Group the grounds for annulment in sections, for example non-consummation, lack of consent, non-disclosure and gender reassignment—this avoids repeating arguments that are applicable to several grounds for nullity.

TAKING THINGS FURTHER

■ Bevan, C. 'The role of intention in non-marriage cases post Hudson v Leigh' (2013) CFLQ 80.
Considers the extent to which the parties' intention determines the court's decision as to whether a marriage is non-existent.

■ Gaffney-Rhys, R. 'Hudson v Leigh [2009]: The concept of non-marriage' (2010) Child and Family Law Quarterly 22(3) 35.1.
Examines the criteria established in Hudson v Leigh, considers whether this better protects ethnic minorities and considers whether English law recognises the concept of a non-existent partnership.

■ Law Commission, Report on Nullity of Marriage (1970) LC33.
Explains the reasons for the grounds for annulment (with the exception of those relating to gender recognition, which were added in 2004).

■ Marriage Act 1961 (Australia).
It is useful to compare the law in England and Wales with the law in another jurisdiction. The Marriage Act 1961 abolished voidable marriage.

■ Probert, R. 'The evolving concept of non-marriage' (2013) Child and Family Law Quarterly 25(3) 314.
Considers the consequences of failing to comply with the formalities required for the celebration of a marriage, i.e. the circumstances in which a marriage will be valid, void or non-existent.

Online Resource Centre   www.oxfordtextbooks.co.uk/orc/qanda/

Go online for extra essay and problem questions, a glossary of key terms, online versions of all the answer plans and audio commentary on how selected ones were put together, and a range of podcasts which include advice on exam and coursework technique and advice for other assessment methods.

Divorce, Dissolution and (Judicial) Separation

4

ARE YOU READY?

In order to attempt the four questions in this chapter you will need to have covered the following topics:

● the ground for divorce and the facts upon which a divorce will be based under **the Matrimonial Causes Act 1973**;

● the grounds for judicial separation under **the Matrimonial Causes Act 1973**;

● the equivalent provisions of **the Civil Partnership Act 2004**;

● proposals to reform the law of divorce;

● the use of mediation in divorce proceedings.

 ## KEY DEBATES

Debate: The reform of the substantive law of divorce

It is often suggested that the ground and facts for divorce are in need of reform. Would the introduction of 'no-fault' divorce be an improvement? If no-fault divorce is introduced, would the approach taken to conduct in financial relief cases need to change?

Debate: Should the process of divorce be judicial or administrative?

The Family Justice Review 2011 recommended that the process of obtaining a divorce should be administrative, rather than judicial in non-defended cases. The process of achieving this goal has already begun. Is it appropriate to treat divorce as an administrative process? What message does it send about marriage and divorce?

Debate: The abolition of judicial separation and separation orders

Do we need to retain judicial separation (marriage) and separation orders (civil partnerships)? What would be the positive and negative consequences of abolishing judicial separation and separation orders? Is the (small) number of decrees granted each year a good reason to abolish judicial separation and separation orders?

QUESTION | 1

Harry, currently aged 30 and Isobel, currently aged 28 met at university. They lived together for three years before marrying six months ago. For the past month, Isobel has felt that Harry has been behaving strangely. She confronted Harry about it, and he confessed that he is bisexual and has had a brief affair with John, a colleague at work. Isobel was distraught and immediately moved out of their house and is currently living with her parents. Harry says that he is sorry, that the relationship with John has ended and that he wants Isobel back. Isobel has refused to return to the matrimonial home: she says that she never wants to see Harry again, and that their marriage is over. Isobel wants everything sorted out as quickly as possible so that she can move on.

a)   **Advise Isobel as to whether she can divorce Harry. [40 marks]**

b)   **What would the legal position be if Harry, was female (short for Harriet) and Harry and Isobel had registered a civil partnership six months ago? [10 marks]**

N.B. You do not have to consider financial issues.

CAUTION!

■ Look at the marks awarded for each section. It is clear that the answer to the second part of the question will be far shorter than the answer to the first part.

■ Do not mix up grounds and facts—there is one ground for divorce, which is established by proving one of five facts. The facts for divorce are grounds for judicial separation.

DIAGRAM ANSWER PLAN

Identify the issues	▪ Identify the legal issues
	▪ Can Isobel divorce Harry (and how would the position differ if they were civil partners)?

Relevant law	▪ Outline tbe relevant law:
	▪ S.3(1) MCA 1973 (one year rule)—s.17 judicial separation
	▪ S.1(1) Ground for divorce—irretrievable breakdown of marriage
	▪ S.1(2) Facts to prove breakdown a) and b)—*Dennis v Dennis* [1995] *Coffer v Coffer* [1964]
	▪ Ss.44 and 56 Civil Partnership Act 2004

Apply the law	▪ Isobel cannot divorce Harry in the first year of marriage but may apply for judicial separation
	▪ Divorce and judicial separation would be based on behaviour
	▪ Briefly explain the procedure that would apply
	▪ Dissolution and separation orders under the Civil Partnership Act cannot be based on adultery

Conclude	▪ Advise Isobel to wait for six months and then petition for divorce based on fact b)
	▪ Conclusion

SUGGESTED ANSWER

[1] The system of divorce contained in **the Matrimonial Causes Act 1973** was introduced by **the Divorce Reform Act 1969**.

[2] The bar was three years until **the Matrimonial and Family Proceedings Act 1984**.

Section 3 (1) of the Matrimonial Causes Act 1973[1] provides that 'no petition for divorce shall be presented to the court before the expiration of the period of one year from the date of the marriage'.[2] Isobel will therefore have to wait until the first anniversary of her marriage before she can file a petition for divorce. But this does not mean that she cannot rely on events that took place during the first year of marriage, as **s.3(2)** indicates that 'nothing in this section shall prohibit the presentation of a petition based on matters which occurred before the expiration of that period'. The case study reveals that Isobel wants everything sorted out as quickly as possible and as a result, it is necessary to advise her that she could obtain a decree of judicial separation during the first year of marriage, which would then enable her to obtain financial orders from the court. A decree of judicial separation can be granted under **s.17** of **the Matrimonial Causes Act 1973** if any of the facts listed in **s.1(2)** are established (see later). The effect of the decree is that 'it shall no longer be obligatory for the petitioner to cohabit with the respondent' (**s.18(1) MCA 1973**). However, a decree of judicial separation does not dissolve the marriage and, as a consequence, Isobel would later have to petition for divorce (**s.4 MCA 1973**). Given that Isobel feels that the marriage has ended, it is advisable to wait six months and then petition for dissolution (assuming that she can establish the ground for divorce).

The Ground for Divorce

Section 1(1) of **the Matrimonial Causes Act 1973** provides that a petition for divorce can be presented 'on the ground that the marriage has broken down irretrievably'. Irretrievable breakdown of marriage can only be proved by establishing one of the five facts listed in **s.1(2)**, namely; adultery, behaviour, desertion, two years' separation with consent and five years' separation.[3] In ***Buffery v Buffery* [1988] 2 FLR 365**, the spouses had been married for over 20 years and had drifted apart. Although they lived in the same property, they did not communicate with one another and had nothing in common. The court accepted that the marriage had broken down irretrievably, but refused to grant a decree because none of the five facts were made out. If the court is satisfied that one of the facts has been established, it is assumed that the marriage has broken down irretrievably (**s.1(4)**) and although the court is required to enquire into facts alleged by the petitioner (**s.1(3)**), in reality the 'special procedure', which applies to undefended divorce involves no actual testing of the evidence.

[3] Do not refer to the facts for divorce as grounds.

Fact (a) Adultery

As the case study indicates that Harry has had an affair, it is necessary to discuss adultery.[4] **Section 1(2)(a) MCA 1973** provides that a marriage has broken down irretrievably if 'the respondent has committed adultery and the petitioner finds it intolerable to live with the respondent'. Adultery was defined in ***Dennis v Dennis* [1995] 2 ALL ER 51** as a voluntary act of sexual intercourse between a spouse and a third party of the opposite sex and this has not changed following **the Marriage (Same Sex Couples) Act 2013**. Indeed, **s.1(6) MCA** now explicitly states that 'only conduct between the respondent and a person of the opposite sex may constitute adultery'. Isobel cannot, therefore, petition for divorce based on Harry's adultery.[5]

[4] You should know that Isobel will not be able to base the petition on adultery, but this does not mean that you should not discuss fact (a)—you need to explain why this is not a case of adultery.

[5] If Harry was female and formed a same-sex marriage with Isobel, Isobel could base the divorce petition on adultery as she has had a heterosexual affair.

⁶Do not make the mistake of referring to fact (b) as unreasonable behaviour.

⁷This paragraph explains the general test for fact (b) and then refers to specific cases that are relevant to Isobel's petition.

Fact (b) Behaviour⁶

Homosexual infidelity may constitute behaviour for the purpose of fact (b).⁷ Under **s.1(2)(b)MCA 1973**, irretrievable breakdown of marriage occurs if 'the respondent behaved in such a way that the petitioner cannot reasonably be expected to live with the respondent'. The behaviour in question may be an act, an omission or course of conduct, which has some reference to the marriage and has an effect on the petitioner (***Katz v Katz* [1972] 3 ALL ER 219**). In ***Livingstone-Stallard v Livingstone-Stallard* [1974] Fam 47** Dunn J indicated that the test is: 'would any right-thinking person come to the conclusion that this husband has behaved in such a way that this wife cannot reasonably be expected to live with him, taking into account the whole of the circumstances and the characters and personalities of the parties' (p. 54). The test is therefore partly objective and partly subjective. In ***Coffer v Coffer* [1964] 108 S.J. 465**, it was held that a homosexual relationship could constitute cruelty (which was one of the grounds for divorce prior to 1969), whilst in ***Wachtel v Wachtel (No. 1) Times* 1 August 1972**, a wife's relationship with another man which did not technically constitute adultery, amounted to behaviour that the husband could not be expected to tolerate. This suggests that Harry's homosexual relationship with John would be considered behaviour that Isobel cannot be expected to tolerate. **Section 2(3)** of the Act provides that if the parties lived with each other for a period not exceeding six months after the incident relied upon by the petitioner, this period is to be disregarded when determining whether the petitioner can reasonably be expected to live with the respondent. This means that if Isobel returned to the matrimonial home for less than six months it would not adversely affect her assertion that she cannot be expected to live with Harry. But if she returned and remained with Harry for more than six months, the court will take it into account when determining whether Isobel can be expected to live with her husband. As Isobel has left the matrimonial home and is currently residing with her parents, **s.2(3)** is unlikely to cause her problems.

Fact (c) Desertion

It should be noted that Harry would not be able to petition for divorce because Isobel has left him. **Section 1(2)(c)** indicates that a divorce can be granted if 'the respondent has deserted the petitioner for a continuous period of at least two years immediately preceding the presentation of the petition'. Desertion is the unjustified withdrawal of cohabitation without the consent of the other spouse with the intention that the separation will be permanent. Even if Harry and Isobel had lived apart for two years, Harry could not claim that Isobel had deserted him as she had reasonable cause to leave (***Quoraishi v Quoraishi* [1985] FLR 780 CA**).[8]

Procedure

The vast majority of divorces are undefended, which means that they are heard in the family court using the special procedure. If Harry does not defend the divorce, the case is entered onto the special procedure list, the legal adviser reads through the documentation and if he or she is satisfied that the ground and fact of divorce have been established, the decree nisi will be pronounced. Six weeks later the petitioner can apply for the decree absolute, the effect of which is to finally dissolve the marriage. If Isobel fails to apply for the decree absolute within three months of the decree nisi, Harry can do so.

Civil Partners

If Harry and Isobel were both female and had formed a civil partnership, Isobel would need to apply for a dissolution order under **s.44** of **the Civil Partnership Act 2004**. The one-year rule referred to above in relation to divorce applies equally to the dissolution of a civil partnership as a result of **s.41** of the Act. Isobel would therefore have to wait until the first anniversary of her partnership before she could petition for dissolution. However, she could apply for a separation order prior to this point under **s.56**. A separation order is equivalent to an order for judicial separation under **the Matrimonial Causes Act 1973**. As the order does not dissolve the partnership and Isobel feels that the relationship has come to an end, it would be advisable to wait six months, at which point she would be able to petition for a dissolution order.

   Section 44(1) of **the Civil Partnership Act 2004** provides that a civil partnership can be dissolved on the ground that the partnership has broken down irretrievably. The petitioner must prove one of the four facts listed in **s.44(5)** in order to satisfy the court that the partnership has broken down irretrievably.[9] The four facts are behaviour, desertion, two years' separation with consent and five years' separation. Even though Harry has had a relationship which would satisfy the definition of adultery for the purpose of **the Matrimonial Causes Act 1973**, as she has had an affair with a person of the opposite sex, a petition for dissolution cannot specifically be based on adultery, as this is not one of the facts listed in **s.44(5)**. Isobel would therefore have to petition for dissolution on the basis that Harry has behaved in a way that Isobel cannot be expected to tolerate.

[10]The conclusion sums up the advice given to Isobel throughout the answer.

Conclusion[10]

Isobel should be advised to wait until the first anniversary of her marriage or civil partnership and then petition for divorce or dissolution. In both cases, she would have to base the petition on Harry's behaviour, as the definition of adultery for the purpose of marriage is not made out and there is no adultery fact in **the Civil Partnership Act 2004**.

LOOKING FOR EXTRA MARKS?

- Mention judicial separation because divorce is not available in the first year of marriage and Isobel wants everything sorted out as quickly as possible.
- Gain extra marks by considering whether Isobel has deserted Harry.

QUESTION | 2

Karen, aged 55 and Lionel, aged 59 were married 30 years ago. Karen gave up work when their twin daughters were born two years later. Their two children moved out of the family home eight years ago. Since then Karen and Lionel's relationship has deteriorated. They no longer socialise together and have separate groups of friends. They have also had separate bedrooms for the past seven years. Four years ago, Karen returned to work on a full-time basis. She told Lionel that she no longer had the time to do the cooking and cleaning. Karen hired a cleaner, who also does the washing and ironing. Karen and Lionel cook their own meals and eat at different times of the day. Lionel feels that the marriage is over and has told Karen that he wants a divorce. Although Karen, accepts that the relationship has deteriorated, she is opposed to divorce, as she is concerned that she will be ousted from the local wives' group.

a) **Advise Lionel as to whether he can divorce Karen. [30 marks]**

b) **What would the position be if Lionel and Karen were Jewish? [8 marks]**

c) **What would the position be if Lionel and Karen were strict Roman Catholics who opposed divorce on religious grounds? [12 marks]**

CAUTION!

- Do not attempt this question unless you are aware of the relevance of the couple being Jewish—this is an invitation to discuss **s.10A MCA 1973**.
- You do not need to know anything about Roman Catholicism to answer part (c). You should immediately recognise the need to discuss judicial separation if a couple are opposed to divorce.

DIAGRAM ANSWER PLAN

Identify the issues	■ Identify the legal issues ■ Can Lionel divorce Karen? ■ What would the position be if the couple were Jewish or Roman Catholics who opposed divorce?
Relevant law	■ Outline the relevant law: ■ S.1(1) MCA 1973—ground for divorce ■ S.1(2)(d) and (e) separation facts—*Hollens v Hollens* [1971] ■ S.5 hardship defence ■ S.10A—religious divorce ■ S.17—judicial separation
Apply the law	■ S.1(2)(d) can only be used if Karen consents ■ S.1(2)(e) may be successful and the hardship defence will probably fail ■ S.10A is unlikely to be required ■ Judicial separation will be available; two years' separation can be utilised as Karen is more likely to consent
Conclude	■ Conclusion—Advise Lionel in relation to divorce, religious divorce and judicial separation

A SUGGESTED ANSWER

As Karen and Lionel were married 30 years ago, **s.3(1)** of **the Matrimonial Causes Act 1973,** which prohibits divorce in the first year of marriage, will not prevent Lionel from filing a petition immediately. However, the petition will only be successful if Lionel can establish the ground for divorce. **Section 1(1)** states that a petition can be presented 'on the ground that the marriage has broken down irretrievably'. Irretrievable breakdown of marriage can only be proved by establishing one of the five facts listed in **s.1(2)**, namely; adultery, behaviour, desertion, two years' separation with consent and five years' separation.[1] In *Buffery v Buffery* [1988] 2 FLR 365, the court

[1] There is nothing to suggest that adultery is relevant and it is unlikely that Karen's refusal to do the housework would constitute 'behaviour'.

accepted that the marriage had broken down irretrievably, but refused to grant a decree because none of the five facts were made out. It is thus essential to base the petition on one of the five facts. If the court is satisfied that one of the facts has been established, it is assumed that the marriage has broken down irretrievably (**s.1(4)**). The facts that are most relevant to Lionel's situation are two years' separation with consent and five years' separation; however, desertion also needs to be mentioned.

[2] It should be noted that divorces based on desertion are very rare.

Fact (c) Desertion[2]

Section 1(2)(c) states that a marriage has broken down irretrievably if 'the respondent has deserted the petitioner for a continuous period of at least two years immediately preceding the presentation of the petition'. Desertion is the unjustified withdrawal of cohabitation without the consent of the other spouse with the intention that the separation will be permanent. A withdrawal of cohabitation can occur even if the parties remain living in the same property, provided that they have separate households (see later in relation to separation). Lionel would only be able to petition for divorce on the basis of desertion if Karen refused to socialise with him, share a bedroom with him and eat with him. As this does not appear to be the case, it is unlikely that Lionel will be in a position to petition for divorce based on desertion.

[3] This is an example of no-fault divorce.

Fact (d) Two Years' Separation[3]

Section 1(2)(d) MCA 1973 provides that a marriage has broken down irretrievably if 'the parties to the marriage have lived apart for a continuous period of at least two years immediately preceding the presentation of the petition and the respondent consents to a decree being granted'. **Section 2(6)** indicates that for the purpose of **s.1(2)(d)** and **(e)** 'a husband and wife shall be treated as living apart unless they are living with each other in the same household'. It is possible for a couple to be treated as living apart even though they live in the same property. For example, in *Hollens v Hollens* **[1971] 115 SJ 327** the parties were living apart because they did not sleep together, eat together or speak to one another. But, in *Mouncer v Mouncer* **[1972] 1 WLR 321** the husband and wife were not treated as living apart, even though they had separate bedrooms, because they usually ate together, spoke to each other and the wife performed domestic chores.[4] The case study indicates that Karen and Lionel have not socialised together for many years and have had separate bedrooms for seven years. This would not be sufficient to constitute separate households, but when the couple stopped eating together and doing chores for one another they could be treated as living apart. As this

[4] The principle established in this case would apply to desertion and five years' separation.

occurred four years ago, the physical element of two years' separation would be made out.

It is also necessary to establish the mental element of separation, which means that one of the parties must recognise that the marriage has ended. In *Santos v Santos* **[1972] Fam 247**, the Court of Appeal stated that 'living apart does not begin to exist until that day on which, if the spouse in question were compellingly asked to define his or her attitude to cohabitation, he (or she) would express an attitude averse to it. Until this state is reached, cohabitation is not . . . broken. When it is reached, living apart begins'. It is not necessary for *both* spouses to recognise that the marriage has ended at the beginning of the two-year period, but the respondent must positively consent to the grant of the decree during the divorce proceedings. This is usually done by answering the appropriate question on the acknowledgement of service form in the affirmative. The case study states that Karen is opposed to divorce, as she is concerned that she will be ousted from the local wives' group. She may therefore refuse to consent, in which case Lionel will have to base the petition on a different fact.

⁵ This is another example of no-fault divorce. You could point out that it was considered controversial as it enabled a blameless spouse to be divorced against his or her will.

Fact (e) Five Years' Separation[5]

Section 1(2)(e) MCA 1973 states that irretrievable breakdown of marriage occurs if 'the parties to the marriage have lived apart for a continuous period of at least five years immediately preceding the presentation of the petition'. The advantage of this fact, compared with two years' separation, is that the respondent's consent to the decree is not required. As explained above, a couple can be treated as living apart even if they live in the same accommodation, provided that they have separate households.[6] The case study suggests that Karen and Lionel ceased living together four years ago: Lionel will therefore have to wait one year before he can present a petition to the court based on five years' separation. If he pursues this course of action, he should be aware that Karen may raise the hardship defence.

⁶ See *Hollens v Hollens* [1971] 115 SJ 327.

⁷ If Karen raises the hardship defence, the divorce cannot proceed as an undefended divorce using the special procedure.

The Hardship Defence[7]

Section 5(1) MCA 1973 provides that the respondent may oppose the grant of a decree 'on the ground that the dissolution will result in grave financial or other hardship to him and that it would in all the circumstances be wrong to dissolve the marriage'. Hardship includes losing 'the chance of acquiring any benefit which the respondent might acquire if the marriage were not dissolved' (**s.5(3)**). In the past, loss of pension rights has constituted grave financial hardship, but the courts were willing to grant the decree if the husband made provision to relieve the wife's hardship (see *Le Marchant v Le Marchant*

[1977] 1 WLR 559). Since December 2000, the courts have been able to make pension-sharing orders under **Part II MCA 1973**, which means that it is more difficult to argue that grave financial hardship will occur.[8]

Karen is likely to assert that the divorce will cause her grave hardship of a non-financial kind, as she is concerned that she will be excluded from the local wives' group if she is divorced. In principle, social ostracism could constitute grave hardship (see ***Banik v Banik* [1973] 3 ALL ER 45**), but there are no reported cases where this has been successfully argued. Even if the court is satisfied that grave financial or non-financial hardship will occur, it must also be convinced that it would be wrong to dissolve the marriage, which will be extremely difficult in this instance. Lionel should therefore be advised that he can petition on the basis of fact (e) provided that he waits one year.[9]

The Legal Position if the Parties are Jewish

If Karen and Lionel were Jewish, **s.10A** of **the Matrimonial Causes Act 1973**, which was inserted by **the Divorce (Religious Marriages) Act 2002**, could come into play. This section allows either party to apply for the divorce not to be made absolute until a declaration is made by both parties that steps have been taken to dissolve the marriage in accordance with their own religious usages. This provision is designed to ensure that a couple divorced in the eyes of the civil law also obtain a religious divorce (in this case a *get*) so that they are no longer regarded as married under Jewish law. It is most relevant where the wife applies for a civil divorce but her husband will not grant her a *get*. As Lionel wishes to divorce Karen, he is unlikely to refuse her a Jewish divorce.

The Legal Position if the Parties are Roman Catholic

If the parties were strict Roman Catholics who opposed divorce on religious grounds, a decree of judicial separation can be granted under **s.17(1) MCA 1973**. It is not necessary to satisfy the court that the marriage has broken down irretrievably because a decree of judicial separation does not dissolve the marriage (**s.17(2)**). The grounds for a judicial separation are the five facts listed in **s.1(2)** of the Act. Lionel could therefore petition for judicial separation on the basis of two years' separation if Karen consents, or five years' separation (provided that he waits one year) if she does not. Although the case study indicates that Karen is opposed to divorce, she may be willing to consent to a decree of judicial separation, as she will technically remain a married woman. The effect of the decree is that 'it shall no longer be obligatory for the petitioner to cohabit with the respondent' (**s.18(1)**) and the parties are able to apply for financial orders

[8] You could point out that **s.10 MCA 1973** enables the court to delay the decree absolute in separation cases until the respondent's financial position has been considered.

[9] This is the conclusion to part a) of the question. As each section covers a different scenario, you can reach a conclusion at the end of each section.

under **Part II MCA 1973** to organise their affairs. Judicial separation is therefore appropriate for a couple that opposes divorce but wishes to separate and to organise their financial affairs. It should be noted that if one of the parties dies intestate while the decree is continuing, the intestate's property devolves as if the other spouse had been dead (**s.18(2)**). Lionel would need to be informed of this and advised accordingly.[10]

[10]You would therefore advise Karen and Lionel to draft appropriate wills if they want to provide for one another on death.

LOOKING FOR EXTRA MARKS?

- Utilise the IRAC method to ensure that you explain and apply the law.
- Be aware that the hardship defence, which applies to petitions based on five years' separation, is rarely successful and gain extra marks by explaining why.

QUESTION | 3

Should the law of divorce be reformed and if so, how?

CAUTION!

- This question requires you to evaluate the law of divorce and to consider whether it needs to be reformed. You should avoid a detailed description of the ground and facts for divorce.
- As the question asks you how the law should be reformed you should discuss some proposals for change.

DIAGRAM ANSWER PLAN

Introduce the current law of divorce

▼

Explain the current ground and facts for divorce

▼

Discuss the criticisms of the MCA 1973 model

▼

Consider the model that was to be introduced by the Family Law Act 1996

▼

Discuss options for reform, e.g. divorce by mutual consent

Conclusion

SUGGESTED ANSWER

The current law of divorce contained in **the Matrimonial Causes Act 1973** was introduced by **the Divorce Reform Act 1969**, which was enacted to implement the recommendations of the Law Commission.[1] In 'Reform of the Grounds of Divorce—the Field of Choice' (1966) the Law Commission concluded that the law should support marriages that have a chance of survival and dissolve those that cannot be saved 'with the minimum of embarrassment, humiliation and bitterness'.

[1] You could mention the Report of the Archbishop of Canterbury's Research Group 'Putting Asunder—A Divorce Law for Contemporary Society' (1966).

The Ground and Facts for Divorce

Section 1(1) of **the Matrimonial Causes Act 1973** states that a petition for divorce can be presented 'on the ground that the marriage has broken down irretrievably'. Irretrievable breakdown of marriage can only be proved by establishing one of the five facts listed in **s.1(2) MCA 1973,** namely; adultery, behaviour, desertion, two years' separation with consent and five years' separation.[2] It is essential to prove one of the five facts in order to obtain a divorce. In *Buffery v Buffery* **[1988] 2 FLR 365**, the court was satisfied that the relationship had broken down irretrievably but would not grant the decree, as none of the five facts had been made out.

[2] It is not necessary to include a detailed explanation of the five facts, but the problems associated with each fact should be considered.

Criticisms of the Current Law[3]

The law initially appears to be non-fault based, as irretrievable breakdown of marriage is the sole ground for divorce, but three of the five facts used to establish breakdown are based on fault and almost two-thirds of divorces are granted on these facts. As a result, the Law Commission criticised the law for being 'confusing and misleading' (The Ground for Divorce, 1990).[4] It further argued that the law increases bitterness, distress and humiliation, because the quickest way to divorce is to base the petition on the respondent's adultery (fact (a)) or behaviour (fact (b)). It may also encourage false claims: if a couple's relationship has broken down, the spouses could fabricate a list of events or pretend that one of them has committed adultery in order to obtain a speedy divorce. As Welstead points out 'occasionally spouses have made totally bogus claims' (2012, p. 24).

[3] The point being made in these two paragraphs is that there are problems with the current law.

[4] In a question on the reform of the law of divorce it is essential to include the Law Commission's criticisms and recommendations.

The Law Commission also criticised the law for being 'discriminatory and unjust' because the separation facts are, in practice, only available to those who are wealthy enough to maintain two properties for the separation period. If the spouses cannot afford to do so, they will have to live in the same property but refuse to speak to one another, eat together, etc. in order to ensure that they are classed as living in 'separate households' (*Hollens v Hollens* [1971] 115 SJ 327). Following **the Marriage (Same Sex Couples) Act 2013**, it can also be argued that the law of divorce is discriminatory because sexual relations between persons of the same sex do not constitute adultery for the purpose of fact (a). Finally, the Law Commission pointed out that the law of divorce does nothing to save marriages that are capable of being saved. The only provision of **the Matrimonial Causes Act 1973** concerned with reconciliation is **s.6**, subsection 1 of which requires a solicitor acting on behalf of the petitioner to certify whether reconciliation has been discussed with the client. He or she is not actually obliged to discuss the possibility of reconciliation, nor is he or she required to encourage it.[5] Furthermore, **s.6** has no impact if the petitioner does not instruct a solicitor. It is clear that the model of divorce contained in **the Matrimonial Causes Act 1973** does not achieve the aims set by the Law Commission in 1966.

[5] Under **s.6(2)**, the court can adjourn proceedings if there is a possibility of reconciliation. You could discuss whether this is likely.

The Family Law Act 1996

It was clear from the Law Commission Report 1990 and the Government Consultation Paper that followed 'Looking to the Future, Mediation and the Ground for Divorce' (1995) that the law of divorce was in need of reform. The Family Law Bill incorporated many of the Law Commission's suggestions and the Act received Royal Assent in 1996. But five years later the Lord Chancellor announced that **Part II**, which contained the reform of divorce law, could not come into force.[6] **The Family Law Act 1996** would have retained irretrievable breakdown of marriage as the sole ground for divorce but would have abolished the five facts as evidence of breakdown. To begin with, a spouse wishing to initiate divorce proceedings would have been obliged to attend an information meeting, during which information relating to mediation would have been disseminated. In addition, legal representatives would have been required to provide their clients with details of qualified mediators and to certify that they have done so (**s.12(2) FLA 1996**). Three months after the information meeting, either party would have been able to file a statement of marital breakdown (**s.6**) and 14 days later, the period of reflection and consideration would have commenced. During this period, which would have lasted nine months or 15 months if the couple had children or applied for an extension, mediation services would have been available and legal aid would

[6] **Part II** of **the Family Law Act 1996** was eventually repealed by **the Children and Families Act 2014**.

have been provided to fund it. There would have been no requirement to separate during this period, and as Lowe and Douglas point
out 'those financially better off would be able to separate and negotiate at a distance; those not able to do so would be forced to live in
what might be an extremely difficult atmosphere for many months'
(2015, p. 239).

After the period of reflection, the parties would have been in a
position to apply for the divorce order if financial issues and arrangements relating to children had been resolved (**s.9**). The provisions of
the Family Law Act 1996 were tested through various pilot studies
conducted throughout the country. The pilot studies revealed dissatisfaction with the information meetings and an unwillingness to utilise
mediation services. As a result of these findings, the implementation
of **Part II** of **the Family Law Act 1996** was abandoned. The system
of divorce contained in **the Matrimonial Causes Act 1973** thus remains current law, but the criticisms of it have not disappeared.

Options for Reform

The Family Law Act 1996 would have introduced a system of no-fault
divorce in England and Wales. Although the information meetings and
mediation services were not popular amongst the participants of the
pilot studies, the removal of fault from divorce proceedings was not
criticised. Indeed, in 2010 a survey conducted by Resolution, the family lawyers' association, indicated that 68 per cent of the public were
in favour of a no-fault model of divorce. Resolution itself has recommended the abolition of fault-based divorce (Resolution Manifesto
for Family Law, 2015). No-fault divorce can take various forms, for
example immediate divorce by mutual consent, and divorce after a
period of separation.[7] The Swedish Marriage Code permits immediate divorce by mutual consent if there are no children under 16 living
with either spouse. If there are children under 16 or if one spouse
does not agree to the divorce, a period of six months' reconsideration
is required (unless the couple have been separated for a period of
two years prior to applying for the divorce). The Law Commission's
criticisms of the law reveal the benefits of a no-fault model—i.e. it
reduces bitterness, distress and humiliation—but it should be noted
that abolishing fault from official proceedings does not necessarily
mean that the divorce will be more congenial. Divorcing spouses
may continue to apportion blame, albeit outside of official divorce
proceedings.[8]

Alternatively, the current law of divorce could be modified to bring
it in line with the law in Scotland. **The Divorce (Scotland) Act 1976**
initially mirrored **the Matrimonial Causes Act 1973**, but following
the Family Law (Scotland) Act 2006: desertion can no longer be
used to prove irretrievable breakdown; two years' separation with

[7] You could point out that **the Family Law Act** model was divorce after a period of separation.

[8] You may therefore argue that it is unrealistic to expect a reform of the law to reduce bitterness between divorcing spouses given the emotional impact of divorce.

consent is reduced to one year's separation with consent; and divorce based on five years' separation (no consent required) is replaced with divorce based on two years' separation (no consent required). Allowing couples to divorce by consent after one year's separation may reduce reliance on the fault-based facts of adultery and behaviour and therefore reduce bitterness, etc.

Finally, the *process* of obtaining a divorce, rather than the ground, could be reformed, for example to implement the recommendations contained in the Family Justice Review Final Report.

The Family Justice Review

The Family Justice Review Final Report (2011) suggested that the process of obtaining a divorce should begin by accessing an online hub, which would provide information and access to the necessary application forms.[9] The application for divorce should be made online and the online form should be sent to a centralised court processing centre and received by a court officer, who would check that it has been completed correctly and serve it on the respondent. If the divorce is uncontested, the court officer should issue the decree nisi, rather than a judge. If the divorce is defended, the court officer would transfer the application to the applicant's local court for consideration by a judge. The process of implementing some of these recommendations has already begun, following **the Crime and Courts Act 2013**. Since November 2014, legal advisers have considered uncontested decrees nisi in certain designated centres. This will save considerable court time and thus expense and will enable judges to hear more family law cases that require the exercise of judicial discretion. But whether it is appropriate for a legal adviser to perform a role that has traditionally been undertaken by a judge is another matter.[10]

[9] This could achieve some of the objectives of the failed **Family Law Act 1996**.

[10] If this question was set as a piece of coursework, you would be expected to find academic opinion on this. See, for example, Jonathan Herring, 2013, *Family Law*, p. 134.

Conclusion

The discussion above has demonstrated that there are problems with the current system of divorce, which was introduced over 45 years ago and is arguably dated. Thus far, attempts to reform the law have been unsuccessful, but the criticisms of the law remain.

LOOKING FOR EXTRA MARKS?

■ Gain extra marks by considering the reforms that have taken place in Scotland as a result of **the Family Law (Scotland) Act 2006**.

■ If this question is set as a coursework task, it is useful to be able to refer to a jurisdiction that has introduced no-fault divorce, for example Sweden.

QUESTION | **4**

Discuss the development of the use of mediation in divorce proceedings.

CAUTION!

- An in-depth evaluation of the advantages and disadvantages of mediation is not possible in a time-constrained examination or an assignment with a restricted word limit.
- Mediation is a form of alternative dispute resolution. If the question had asked about the role of Alternative Dispute Resolution (ADR) in divorce proceedings, you would be expected to discuss collaborative law and arbitration.

DIAGRAM ANSWER PLAN

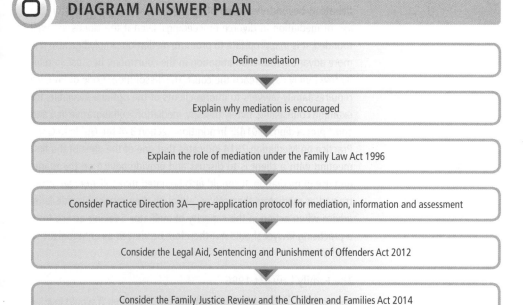

Define mediation

Explain why mediation is encouraged

Explain the role of mediation under the Family Law Act 1996

Consider Practice Direction 3A—pre-application protocol for mediation, information and assessment

Consider the Legal Aid, Sentencing and Punishment of Offenders Act 2012

Consider the Family Justice Review and the Children and Families Act 2014

Conclusion

SUGGESTED ANSWER

The Government White Paper '*Looking to the Future: Mediation and the Ground for Divorce*' defined mediation as 'the process in which an impartial third person, the mediator, assists couples considering separation or divorce to meet together to deal with the arrangements which need to be made for the future' (1995, Para. 5.4). It is a form of 'Alternative Dispute Resolution' (ADR), which according to the Family Justice Review should be rebranded as 'Dispute Resolution Services' (2011, p. 23). This suggests that services such as mediation should be the 'norm', rather than an 'alternative' form of dispute resolution.

Benefits of Mediation

[1] If this question was set as coursework, you would be expected to give examples of supporters and opponents of mediation and cite their work.

Supporters of mediation[1] claim that it is preferable to litigation because: it is a more appropriate forum for resolving family disputes; it enables the parties to communicate more effectively; it enables the parties to reach a solution that is right for them; the agreement is more likely to be effective in the long-term than a court order; and it saves costs. Opponents of mediation are dubious as to its ability to improve communication and save costs and have concerns that it cannot protect the weaker party or the interests of children. This debate is beyond the scope of this answer, which will focus on the *use* of mediation in divorce proceedings. Even if the claims *are* well founded, it is inappropriate to promote mediation simply because it is more advantageous than litigation in the courtroom, because in reality few family cases reach the court. The 'Resolution' Code of Practice requires family lawyers to inform clients of the options available, for example counselling, family therapy, mediation, collaborative law and court proceedings (2014).[2] In addition, section 3 of the Guide to Good Practice on Mediation 2014 indicates that one of the aims of the first meeting with a client is to discuss and provide advice on the merits and use of mediation. It should also be noted that solicitors are often trained as mediators themselves, although they cannot provide legal advice when acting in the capacity of mediator. Seeking advice from a practising lawyer should not therefore be viewed as antagonistic to mediation.

[2] As explained in question 3, Resolution is the family lawyers' association.

The Family Law Act 1996

The benefits of mediation, in particular the hope that it would involve less public expense, were enough to convince the Government that this form of dispute resolution should become central to the divorce process. Part II of **the Family Law Act 1996**, which reformed the law of divorce,[3] but never came into force, sought to achieve this aim by: requiring spouses to attend a meeting where they would receive information relating to mediation; requiring lawyers to provide their clients with details of qualified mediators and funding mediation during the period of reflection, which would have been required to obtain a divorce. The provisions of **the Family Law Act 1996** were tested through pilot studies, which revealed dissatisfaction with the

[3] It is not necessary to provide a detailed account of the model of divorce that would have been introduced by **the Family Law Act 1996**.

information meetings and an unwillingness to utilise mediation services. As a result of these findings, the implementation of **Part II** of **the Family Law Act 1996** was abandoned, but encouraging the use of mediation to resolve family disputes was not. **Section 29** of **the Family Law Act 1996** required publicly funded clients to meet with a mediator, who would assess the case in terms of its suitability for mediation. Although **s.29** was repealed by **the Access to Justice Act 1999**, the Legal Services Commission Funding Code required a person seeking legal aid for representation to first attend a meeting with a mediator to determine whether mediation would be appropriate. The obligation contained in the Code was not limited to divorcing couples who wished to take legal action, but also applied to unmarried parents with disputes relating to children, etc.[4] If the case was deemed suitable for mediation, a refusal to engage could result in the denial of legal aid.

Promoting the Use of Mediation

The use of mediation was further promoted by **the Family Procedure Rules 2010 (SI 2010/2955)** and **Practice Direction 3A—Pre-Application Protocol for Mediation Information and Assessment**, which came into force in April 2011. **Part 3** of **the Family Procedure Rules** enables the court to adjourn proceedings so that the parties can consider and, where appropriate, utilise alternative dispute resolution services whilst **the Practice Direction** extended the duty to consider utilising mediation services to private paying clients. **The Practice Direction** applied to persons considering applying for an order in 'family proceedings'. It applied to divorcing couples that wish to utilise the courts to resolve their disputes, but also to cases relating to children that took place outside of divorce proceedings. The purpose of the practice direction was 'to encourage and facilitate the use of alternative dispute resolution . . . and ensure, as far as possible that all parties have considered mediation as an alternative means of resolving their disputes' (**para. 2.1**). The rationale behind this was the unsuitability of the adversarial court process to resolve family disputes (**para. 3.1**), however **para. 3.5** indicated that 'it is likely to save court time and expense if the parties take steps to resolve their dispute without pursuing court proceedings'.[5]

The court expected all applicants to have complied with the protocol before commencing relevant family proceedings. The protocol required a person making an application to the court (or their legal representative) to contact a family mediator to arrange for the applicant to attend an information meeting about mediation and other forms of alternative dispute resolution (**para. 2**). **Paragraph 3** indicated that the applicant did not have to attend a meeting if any of the circumstances set out in Annex C applied, for example one of the

[4] The question could easily have been: 'Discuss the development of the use of mediation in private law proceedings.' The answer to the question would be the same.

[5] Indicating why **the Practice Direction** was introduced is important, as the question asks you to 'discuss' the development of the use of mediation.

parties has made an allegation of domestic violence which has resulted in a police investigation or civil proceedings or the dispute concerns financial issues and one of the parties is bankrupt.

Reducing Legal Aid[6]

The Legal Aid, Sentencing and Punishment of Offenders Act 2012 restricted the availability of legal aid for representation in the family courts to cases involving domestic violence, child abuse and child abduction.[7] Divorcing couples (and other family members in dispute) who cannot afford to pay their own legal fees will have to utilise mediation (or another dispute resolution service) as public funding for alternatives to litigation will remain. Legal aid will also cover legal assistance to support mediation, for example drafting a legal agreement to incorporate the settlement reached during mediation. The purpose of reducing the availability of legal aid for family proceedings was to save money and to encourage couples to settle disputes out of court, but the impact is likely to be an increase in the number of litigants in person.[8] In September 2014, the Bar Council reported that 90 per cent of those who work with the family courts had seen an increase in the number of self-represented parties. As Lowe and Douglas indicate, there are consequential difficulties for the litigants in person 'in terms of trying to conduct a legal case and examine witnesses and for their family members in the hostility and distress this may engender; and for the courts in having to assist such litigants so that they can receive justice' (2015, p. 13)

The Family Justice Review and the Children and Families Act 2014

The Family Justice Review Final Report (2011) recommended that attendance at a Mediation Information and Assessment Meeting (MIAM) should be compulsory for anyone wishing to make a court application (unless the exemptions listed in the Pre-Application Protocol applied). If the application related to children, the applicant would have to attend a Separating Parents Information Programme (PIP).[9] In both cases, the respondent would be expected, but not required, to attend.[10] If the mediation (or other form of alternative dispute resolution) did not result in an agreement, the mediator would issue a certificate to that effect, which would enable either party to apply to the court. The Review was thus consistent with previous proposals and reforms in promoting the use of mediation and dispute resolution services. The recommendations contained in the review were implemented by **the Children and Families Act 2014. Section 10(1),** provides that before making a relevant family application a person must attend a Mediation Information and

---

[6] The point being made in this paragraph is that reducing legal aid for court proceedings should result in an increase in mediation.

[7] The evidence for this is **the 2012 Act**, which restricts legal aid for court proceedings in family cases, but does not restrict the funding of mediation.

[8] The paragraph ends by analysing the law—it is suggested that the impact of the reform may be an increase in the number of litigants in person.

[9] A Supporting Separated Parents in Dispute Programme (SSPID) is being piloted.

[10] You can discuss whether the process will be effective if the respondent does not have to attend.

Assessment Meeting. **Section 10(2)** of the Act states that Family Procedure Rules can make provision that **s.10(1)** does not apply in certain circumstances. **Rule 3.8 of the Family Procedure Rules** indicates that the MIAM requirement will not apply to cases involving domestic violence or child protection or urgent cases and cases involving financial remedies, where the applicant is bankrupt. There are additional circumstances when the obligation to attend a MIAM will not apply, for example if either party has a disability that would prevent attendance or if there are no authorised mediators within 15 miles. **Practice Direction 3A**—which supplements the Family Procedure Rules has been renamed **Practice Direction 3A Mediation Information and Assessment Meetings.** As Stevenson points out, it is essential that the system of screening is adequate in order to ensure that 'unsuitable cases do not enter the mediation process' (2014, p. 1758).

Conclusion

For the past 20 years successive Governments have sought to encourage the use of mediation to resolve disputes between divorcing couples, culminating in the enactment of **the Children and Families Act 2014**, which makes attendance at a MIAM compulsory in many cases. Whether this will result in a great increase in the use of mediation and fewer family cases reaching the family courts remains to be seen.

LOOKING FOR EXTRA MARKS?

■ The question asks you to discuss the development of the use of mediation: this requires evaluation or critical analysis of the laws and policies that have been introduced to promote mediation.

■ Gain extra marks by referring to reports or research on the likely impact of reducing legal aid, for example the Bar Council Report 2014.

TAKING THINGS FURTHER

■ Dingwall, R. 'Divorce mediation: Should we change our mind ?' (2010) Journal of Social Welfare and Family Law 32(2) 107.
Considers whether the promotion of mediation is appropriate.

■ Herring, J. *Family Law* (2013), Longman Law series.

■ Lowe, N. and Douglas, G. *Bromley's Family Law* (2015) 11th edn, Oxford University Press.

■ Ministry of Justice, The Family Justice Review Final Report (2011).
Contains proposals to make undefended divorce an administrative rather than judicial process.

- Parkinson, L. 'The place of mediation in the Family Justice System' (2013) Child and Family Law Quarterly 25(2) 200.

  Examines concerns about the functions and competence of family mediators.

- Stevenson, M. 'Dispute resolution: Mediation: Screening for suitability' (2014) Family Law 1758.

  Addresses the process of screening cases for suitability for mediation.

- Welstead, M. 'Divorce in England and Wales—Time for reform' (2012) Denning Law Journal 2.

  Argues that defects in the law of divorce are not given sufficient attention.

- Wright, K. 'The evolving role of the family lawyer: The impact of collaborative law on family law practice' (2011) Child and Family Law Quarterly 23(3) 370.

  Considers the use of collaborative law, which is a form of alternative dispute resolution in disputes arising on divorce or separation.

Online Resource Centre   www.oxfordtextbooks.co.uk/orc/qanda/

Go online for extra essay and problem questions, a glossary of key terms, online versions of all the answer plans and audio commentary on how selected ones were put together, and a range of podcasts which include advice on exam and coursework technique and advice for other assessment methods.

Family Property and Domestic Violence

5

ARE YOU READY?

In order to attempt the four questions in this chapter you will need to have covered the following topics:

- the difference between legal and beneficial ownership of real property;
- the acquisition of a beneficial interest in real property through the creation of a trust;
- ownership of personal property and money in joint bank accounts;
- the definition of domestic violence;
- non-molestation orders and occupation orders under **the Family Law Act 1996**;
- **The Protection from Harassment Act 1997**.

Although family property and domestic violence may not appear to be related topics, the right to occupy real property by virtue of a legal or beneficial interest affects the right to apply for an occupation order in domestic violence situations. In addition, occupation orders are used to resolve disputes relating to the right to occupy real property in situations where there is no domestic violence.

KEY DEBATES

Debate: Ownership of matrimonial and quasi-matrimonial property

Unlike many European jurisdictions, there is no matrimonial property regime in England and Wales. Is it appropriate that the general law of property is applied to matrimonial and quasi-matrimonial cases? It can be argued that this causes injustice, particularly to cohabitants or former cohabitants.

Debate: The use of estoppel in disputes between cohabitants regarding ownership of property

The common intention constructive trust has traditionally been used by cohabitants more often than proprietary estoppel. Following the decision of the Court of Appeal in *Southwell v Blackburn* [2014] EWCA Civ 1347, it has been suggested that estoppel could have a greater role to play in disputes between cohabitants.

Debate: The definition of domestic violence

The Cross-Government Definition of Domestic Violence, 2013 defines domestic violence as 'any incident or pattern of incidents of controlling, coercive or threatening behaviour, violence or abuse between those aged 16 or over who are or have been intimate partners or family members regardless of gender or sexuality. The abuse can encompass, but is not limited to: psychological, physical, sexual, financial, emotional abuse …. This definition includes so called 'honour' based violence, female genital mutilation (FGM) and forced marriage …' Do you think it is appropriate that the definition should include financial abuse?

QUESTION | 1

Mary and Nigel met 25 years ago when they worked for the same company. Three years later Mary moved into Nigel's house. Initially Mary paid some of the bills as she felt that it was important that she contributed financially to the household. Nigel continued to pay the mortgage and the property remained registered in his sole name. Two years after Mary had moved in, she gave birth to Olivia. At this point Mary gave up work and was no longer in a position to contribute to the household bills. Nigel was happy for Mary to stay at home to look after Olivia and the home. Mary did all the housework, the cooking and the gardening. She has also done a considerable amount of redecorating. Nigel set up a joint bank account, which he paid money into, so that Mary could purchase things for Olivia, herself and the home. Mary purchased a car, of which she is the registered keeper, using funds from the joint account. Nigel retained the bank account that he had in his sole name and from this, paid the mortgage and the bills. Last year Mary asked Nigel about registering the family home in joint names. Nigel replied that the house was Mary's just as much as his and they did not need a piece of paper to prove it. Last month Nigel informed Mary that he had fallen in love with Penny and wanted to marry her. He has told Mary that she has three months to find somewhere to live. Nigel then intends to move Penny into the property. Olivia no longer lives at home, as she moved to another city for work purposes. The family home is worth £200,000 and the mortgage on the property has been paid off. There is £10,000 in the joint bank account that Nigel set up. The couple has no other significant assets, apart from a painting that Nigel inherited from his aunt Queenie, which is worth £10,000. Mary claims that Nigel gave her the painting for her fortieth birthday, but Nigel denies this.

Advise Mary in relation to this matter.

CAUTION!

- The case study upon which this question is based is lengthy and contains many facts—ensure that you read it carefully and highlight relevant points.
- Although you need to consider several issues, you should spend most time discussing Mary's rights in relation to the family home.

DIAGRAM ANSWER PLAN

Identify the issues	- Identify the legal issues - Does Mary have an interest in the house, bank account and personal property?
Relevant law	- Outline the relevant law: - Acquisition of a beneficial interest by constructive trust—*Lloyds Bank v Rossett* [1991] - Joint bank accounts—*Jones v Maynard* [1951] - Gifts—*Re Cole* [1964]
Apply the law	- Mary cannot establish a constructive trust due to the lack of detrimental reliance - Mary is entitled to a share of the joint bank account and to items purchased for her use - Mary may be able to prove that the painting was gifted to her
Conclude	- Conclusion - Advise Mary in relation to house, bank account, car, personal items and painting

SUGGESTED ANSWER

Mary and Nigel have separated but as they never married, it is not possible for Mary to apply for a periodical payments order or a property adjustment order, which are available to spouses under **the Matrimonial Causes Act 1973.** Nor is it possible to claim child maintenance under **the Child Support Act 1991** or **the Children**

[1] It is useful to begin by explaining that cohabiting couples who have separated do not have the same rights as spouses who separate.

[2] If an individual can establish that s/he has a beneficial interest, s/he will have a right to occupy the property and a right to a share of the proceeds.

[3] See, for example, *Walker v Hall* [1984] FLR 126.

[4] The point of this paragraph is to explain that intention needs to be established to claim a beneficial interest via a constructive trust. It concludes that Mary may be able to establish common intention.

Act 1989, as Olivia is an independent adult. The division of assets in this case is thus based on ownership.[1]

Ownership of the Family Home

The family home is registered in Nigel's sole name. **Section 52(1) of the Law of Property Act 1925** requires a deed to convey the legal estate in land, which means that Mary would only have a legal interest in the family home if Nigel formally conveyed a share to her. Mary would not therefore acquire a legal interest in the property just because Nigel said that the house is just as much hers. The question is whether Mary can claim a beneficial or equitable interest in the property.[2] A beneficial interest will be acquired if the legal owner creates an express trust. **Section 53(1)(b) LPA 1925** requires a signed written document to create an express trust, so again, Nigel's oral declaration would not suffice. However, it is possible to acquire a beneficial interest in property by the creation of a resulting or constructive trust, neither of which requires written documentation (**s.53(2) LPA 1925**). A resulting trust is created if one party provides all or some of the purchase price for a property that is registered in the name of the other party.[3] Mary did not contribute to the purchase price and so could not claim that a resulting trust exists. In any event, the House of Lords in **Stack v Dowden** [2007] **UKHL 17** indicated that the flexible constructive trust is more appropriate for matrimonial or quasi-matrimonial cases. To establish a constructive trust, Mary would need to prove intention to share the property and detrimental reliance (**Lloyds Bank v Rosset** [1991] AC 107).

Common Intention[4]

A common intention will be found if the parties expressly discussed sharing the property. In **Hammond v Mitchell** [1992] 2 ALL ER 109, the comment: 'don't worry about the future because when we are married [the house] will be half yours anyway and I'll always look after you' constituted evidence of common intention to share the property. But in **James v Thomas** [2007] **EWCA Civ 1212**, the Court of Appeal held that the owner's comment: 'this will benefit us both' which was made when the couple carried out extensive renovations, was not intended to be a promise of an interest in the property. When the owner was questioned about putting the property in joint names he was evasive and unwilling. **Curran v Collins** [2015] **EWCA Civ 404** also demonstrates that it can be difficult to prove the existence of an express agreement to share the property. Mary and Nigel have had an explicit conversation about ownership of the family home, which seems to be stronger evidence of intention to share than that provided in **Hammond v Mitchell**, which seemed to promise rights to the property in the future. Provided that Mary *can* convince the court that this conversation took place, she should be able establish common intention.

[5] This paragraph explains that it is difficult to establish common intention by conduct.

Inferring Intention from Conduct[5]

Intention can also be inferred from conduct, but this is more difficult, for as Lord Bridge stated in *Lloyds Bank v Rosset* **[1991] AC 107**, it is extremely doubtful whether anything other than a direct contribution to the purchase price would suffice. Making mortgage payments constitutes a contribution to the purchase price and will thus be evidence of common intention (*Re Gorman (a Bankrupt)* **[1990] 2 FLR 284**), but this will not assist Mary, as she did not contribute to the mortgage payments. In *Le Foe v Le Foe* **[2001] 2 FLR 970 FD**, the wife paid for day-to-day expenses while the husband made the mortgage payments. The wife acquired a beneficial interest because the husband would not have been able to pay the mortgage if the wife did not take responsibility for household expenditure. However, *Le Foe* has not been confirmed by the Court of Appeal or Supreme Court and cases such as *James v Thomas* and *Curran v Collins* suggest that indirect financial contributions will not suffice. It also remains the case that non-financial contributions to the household—i.e. cooking, cleaning, gardening and decorating—will not be enough to generate a beneficial interest (see *Burns v Burns* **[1984] FLR 216**). Mary's short-term contribution to the bills and her non-financial contribution to the household will not convince the court that the couple intended to share the property.

Detrimental Reliance

Assuming that Mary establishes actual intention to share, she then has to demonstrate the further requirement of 'detrimental reliance', which requires conduct that the claimant could not reasonably be expected to have embarked upon 'unless she was to have an interest in the house' (Nourse LJ in *Grant v Edwards* **[1987]**). Carrying out manual work on the property constituted detrimental reliance by the woman in *Eves v Eves* **[1975] 3 ALL ER 768**, whilst assuming joint liability for mortgage payments did so in *Crossley v Crossley* **[2005] EWCA Civ 1581**. Indirect financial contributions may constitute detrimental reliance on an express agreement, but Mary did not pay the bills after the conversation about joint registration took place and seemed to do so to pay her way rather than to acquire an interest in the property. Furthermore, non-financial contributions, such as Mary's cooking, gardening and decorating will not amount to detrimental reliance. It therefore seems doubtful that Mary will be able to establish a constructive trust.[6] The lack of reliance on the conversation will also prevent Mary from making a claim based on proprietary estoppel.[7]

[6] You might comment on the fairness of the situation.

[7] Proprietary estoppel was outlined by Lord Walker in *Thorner v Majors* **[2009] UKHL 18**.

[8] It is also worth pointing out that claims by former cohabitants are possible in Scotland due to the **Family Law (Scotland) Act 2006**, particularly in a coursework question.

The Law Commission Report and Cohabitation Rights Bill[8]

If the recommendations of the Law Commission contained in 'Cohabitation: The Financial Consequences of Relationship Breakdown' (Law Com No. 307) had been enacted, Mary's position would have been far stronger. The Law Commission recommended that an eligible applicant should be able to apply for financial relief if she had made a qualifying contribution to the relationship that gave rise to enduring consequences, provided that they had not agreed to dis-apply the scheme. Mary would be an eligible applicant as she had a child with Nigel and they lived together for 22 years. She made a qualifying contribution by giving up work to look after Olivia and this has had enduring consequences. Similar proposals were incorporated into **the Cohabitation Rights Bill 2014–15**, but it did not proceed through Parliament.

The Joint Bank Account and Personal Items[9]

[9] It is important to discuss Mary's entitlement to the bank account and personal property, particularly as her claim to a share of the family home is likely to fail.

In terms of the joint bank account, Mary and Nigel have a joint interest in the whole fund, and this is the case even though Nigel contributed all the money (*Jones v Maynard* **[1951] Ch 572**). Mary is therefore entitled to a share of the joint account. The case study indicates that Mary was able to withdraw money to purchase items for herself, Olivia and the home. The ownership of such items depends upon the intention of the parties. It is likely that items purchased for common use in the home will be classed as jointly owned by Mary and Nigel, unless there is an agreement to the contrary. Mary can therefore claim a share of the goods purchased from funds from the joint bank account that were for joint use. Items purchased for Mary's personal use would be considered her own, as this is normally the intention of the parties in such circumstances. Mary would thus argue that the car purchased for her own use was intended to be her property, as it is registered in her name. Similarly, goods purchased for Olivia would probably belong to Olivia.

Ownership of the Painting

The case study also indicates that there is a dispute as to ownership of a valuable painting that Nigel inherited from his aunt. Mary argues that Nigel gifted the painting to her for her fortieth birthday. In order to make an effective gift of a chattel, there must be intent on the donor's part and either a deed or delivery of the chattel. If there is evidence that Nigel presented the painting to Mary on her birthday the courts will accept that Nigel intended to make a gift and that delivery is effective.[10] The courts are less likely to infer delivery if it would deprive the donor's creditors (*Re Cole* **[1964] Ch 175**), but that is not an issue in this case.

[10] Family members and friends may have witnessed the presentation of the painting.

Conclusion

It seems that Mary will be able to claim the painting, a share of the joint bank account, goods purchased for her personal use from funds in the joint bank account, including the car and a share of goods purchased for joint use from funds in the joint bank account. However, it is unlikely that she will acquire a beneficial interest in the family home.

LOOKING FOR EXTRA MARKS?

- Gain extra marks by pointing out that Mary's legal position would have improved if the recommendations contained in the Law Commission Report No. 307 had been enacted or if **the Cohabitation Rights Bill 2014–15** had become law.

- It is also worth mentioning that Mary would be in a better position if the couple had lived in Scotland.

QUESTION | 2

'The starting point where there is joint legal ownership is joint beneficial ownership.'

Baroness Hale in *Stack v Dowden* [2007] UKHL 17 at [56]

In the light of the statement above, discuss how the beneficial estate is shared if the legal title to the family home is registered by a couple in joint names.

CAUTION!

- Do not attempt this question in an examination unless you are very familiar with *Stack v Dowden* [2007]. A discussion of *Jones v Kernott* [2011] UKSC 53 is also essential.

- Read the question carefully—you are only required to discuss joint names cases.

DIAGRAM ANSWER PLAN

> Explain the difference between legal and beneficial ownership

> Explain how the beneficial estate can be shared and the position if there is no indication as to beneficial ownership on the property register

> Discuss the facts and decision in *Stack v Dowden*

> Explain when the presumption of equal beneficial ownership applies

> Discuss changing intention—*Jones v Kernott*

> Conclusion

In order to address the question set, it is important to note the difference between legal ownership and beneficial or equitable ownership. The legal owner is registered on the title register: he or she has the power to sell the property and holds the property on trust for the beneficial owner, who is entitled to the proceeds.[1] It is common that the legal owner is also the beneficial owner, but this is not always the case.

[1] The trustee has a duty to look after the property on behalf of the beneficial owner.

The Beneficial Estate[2]

[2] The point of this paragraph is to explain why it is important to establish how the couple shares the beneficial estate.

This question concerns beneficial ownership in cases where the legal estate is conveyed to a couple in joint names. The beneficial estate may be held as joint tenants, tenants in common in equal shares or tenants in common with unequal shares. If a couple are joint tenants, both parties have an equal right to the whole property, rather than distinct shares. They cannot leave their entitlement to the property to another person by will, as the right of survivorship applies. This means that if one joint tenant dies, the survivor automatically acquires the property. Where couples hold the beneficial estate as tenants in common, each party has a distinct share of the property that can be left by will to a beneficiary of their choice. Tenants in common can have equal or unequal shares.

Prior to 1 April 1998, when the new land registration form came into effect, it was not necessary to indicate how the beneficial estate should be shared in cases where a couple were registered as joint owners. Form TR1 now requires the parties to indicate how they hold the equitable estate but there are many couples who bought property prior to the introduction of this obligation. In addition, the Land Registry will not reject a registration form that has not been correctly completed in terms of the beneficial interest. It is not therefore unusual to find that no written declaration of interests exists. As Baroness Hale indicated in *Stack v Dowden* [2007] **UKHL 17**, 'the starting point' in such cases 'is joint beneficial ownership', i.e. equity follows the law.

Stack v Dowden[3]

[3] As the question is based on *Stack v Dowden*, it is essential to be able to cite the facts of the case.

Stack v Dowden concerned a couple that had formed a relationship in 1975 and moved in together in 1983. Initially they lived in a property owned by Ms Dowden, which was sold in 1993 for £66,613. The couple then purchased a property in joint names for £190,000, which was funded by a joint mortgage, a mortgage in Ms Dowden's sole name and funds from Ms Dowden's bank account, which contained the proceeds of sale from her property. The relationship ended in September 2003 and the claimant sought an order that the beneficial estate was held as tenants in common in equal shares and an order for the sale of the property. The judge granted the requested orders but they were overturned by the Court of Appeal, which declared that Mr Stack was entitled to 35 per cent of the beneficial estate. Mr Stack appealed to the House of Lords.

Presumption of Joint Beneficial Ownership

In *Stack v Dowden*, the House of Lords held that when a couple purchases a family home in joint names, the presumption is that they intended to own the property jointly in equity. This presumption can be rebutted by evidence that it was not, or ceased to be the intention of the parties. The House of Lords indicated that a variety of factors should be taken into account when determining the parties' intention, such as: the reason for joint registration; the advice received prior to purchasing the property; the purpose for which the home was acquired; the nature of the parties' relationship; whether the parties had children for whom they had a responsibility to provide a home; the financial contributions made to the property by each party; and how the parties organised their finances. These factors demonstrate that the courts have developed specific principles that apply to family situations, which Hayward refers to as the 'familialisation' of property law (2012).

The majority of the House of Lords was of the view that it would be 'very unusual' (para. 49) to find that the presumption of joint ownership in equity has been rebutted, but *Stack v Dowden* was held to be 'a very unusual case' (para. 91) because their finances were kept rigidly separate and because the parties made unequal financial contributions.[4] The House of Lords thus upheld the decision of the Court of Appeal.

[4] You can question whether the situation in *Stack v Dowden* is 'very unusual'. It is common for couples to keep their finances separate.

Quantifying Shares

If a court determines that the presumption of joint beneficial ownership has been rebutted, it is then required to determine the parties' actual shares, which is based on their intention. In the absence of clear evidence as to how they would share the beneficial estate, the court can infer or impute intention. An inference will be drawn where intention can be objectively deduced from the dealings of the parties, whereas imputed intention is attributed to the parties by the court.[5]

[5] You could consider whether imputed intention is intention at all. Is the court simply imposing its view?

[6] *Graham-York v York* [2015] EWCA Civ 72 states that the starting point of joint beneficial interest does not apply where the applicant has claimed a constructive trust.

When does the Presumption of Joint Beneficial Ownership Apply?[6]

As explained above, the presumption of joint beneficial ownership will only be rebutted in unusual circumstances. In *Fowler v Barron* [2008] EWCA Civ 377, the Court of Appeal emphasised that unequal financial contributions would not be sufficient to rebut the presumption of joint beneficial ownership in cases where the property is registered in joint names.[7] *Stack v Dowden* was distinguished because in

[7] Do you think the situation in *Fowler v Barron* is very different from *Stack v Dowden*?

Fowler v Barron the parties generally pooled their resources for the benefit of the family. The presumption of joint beneficial ownership applied even though Miss Fowler contributed nothing to the acquisition of the property.

Laskar v Laskar **[2008] EWCA Civ 347** demonstrates that the presumption only applies where the property in question is the parties' home. In this case, a mother and daughter jointly purchased a property as an investment and rented it out.[8] The parties' shares were determined on the basis of resulting trust principles, which meant that the mother and daughter shared the beneficial estate on a 67:33 basis to reflect their contributions to the acquisition of the property.

[8]*Adekunle v Ritchie* [2007] **BPIR 117** is also a case involving a parent and child. In this case the presumption of joint beneficial ownership was rebutted.

Changing Intention

Jones (Appellant) v Kernott (Respondent) **[2011] UKSC 53** concerned a couple that purchased a property in 1985 for £30,000 in joint names without making a declaration as to how the beneficial interest in the property was to be held. The £6,000 deposit that was paid came from the proceeds of sale from Ms Jones's previous home but the mortgage and household expenses were shared. On separation in 1993, Mr Kernott moved out of the property, whilst Ms Jones remained there with the couple's two children. Mr Kernott ceased to make any contribution towards the running of the house. In 1995, the parties cashed in an insurance policy, which enabled Mr Kernott to purchase a property in his own name. Ten years later, Mr Kernott indicated that he wished to claim a beneficial share of the jointly owned property. Ms Jones responded by applying to the county court for a declaration under **s.14** of **the Trusts of Land and Appointment of Trustees Act 1996** that she owned the entire beneficial interest in the property, which was valued at £245,000 in 2008.

The court held that when the house was purchased a presumption arose that they intended to jointly share the beneficial interest. Until 1993, there was no evidence to rebut this presumption,[9] but the intention of the parties had clearly changed after Mr Kernott moved out. The county court judge decided that Mr Kernott should have a 10 per cent share of the beneficial estate. Mr Kernott appealed and the case eventually reached the Supreme Court. The Supreme Court held that joint beneficial ownership had ceased to be the couple's intention at some point after Mr Kernott moved out and that his interest in the property crystallised in 1995 when the parties cashed in an insurance policy to enable Mr Kernott to purchase a property in his own name. This date is significant, as much of the property's increase in value occurred after 1995. The Supreme Court proceeded to indicate that if there is no evidence of an actual agreement as to how the beneficial estate should be shared and it is not possible to infer a

[9] This confirms that unequal contributions alone are insufficient to rebut the presumption

common intention, the court will have to impute an intention to them, which the court considers fair having regard to the whole course of dealing between them in relation to the property. The financial contribution made by each party will be a significant factor, but not the only factor. The court will also consider the conduct of the parties, how they organised their finances, etc. when making its decision. The Supreme Court unanimously restored the decision of the county court.

[10] It is useful to return to the quote in your conclusion.

Conclusion[10]

As Baroness Hale indicated in *Stack v Dowden*, the starting point in joint names cases is joint beneficial ownership. Although it is possible to rebut the presumption of joint beneficial ownership, this will be unusual and it is clear from *Fowler v Barron* that unequal financial contributions will not suffice.

LOOKING FOR EXTRA MARKS?

- Gain extra marks by questioning the outcome in *Stack v Dowden*—should the facts of this case have been regarded as unusual?

- If the question was set as a piece of coursework, you could incorporate several of the points made by Andy Hayward (see Taking Things Further) on the 'familialisation' of property law.

QUESTION | 3

Rebecca is 19 years old and lives with her mother, Susan. Last year she formed a relationship with Thomas, who is 25 and lives next door to them. They never lived together, but Rebecca regularly spent the night at Thomas's house. The relationship deteriorated because Thomas became extremely possessive and complained when Rebecca socialised with her college friends. Rebecca finally ended the relationship after they had an argument, during which Thomas slapped Rebecca across the face. Since then Thomas has been pestering Rebecca and has threatened to post semi-naked photographs of her onto the Internet. Because of this, Susan approached Thomas and asked him to leave Rebecca alone. Thomas shouted obscenities at Susan as she left for work and demanded that 'she stay out of his business or else'. The following day Thomas repeated the threat to Susan, indicating that if she interfered again she would be sorry.

Rebecca and Susan are very frightened and require advice in relation to this matter. If possible, they do not want to involve the police.

CAUTION!

- As Rebecca and Susan have indicated that they do not wish to involve the police, it is not necessary to discuss the criminal law.

- Rebecca has not actually cohabited with Thomas and so you should not discuss occupation orders. Your answer should focus on non-molestation orders under **the Family Law Act 1996** and injunctions under **the Protection from Harassment Act 1997**.

DIAGRAM ANSWER PLAN

Identify the issues	<ul><li>Identify the legal issues</li><li>What protection is available to Rebecca and Susan?</li></ul>
Relevant law	<ul><li>Outline the relevant law: non-molestation orders—s.42 Family Law Act 1996</li><li>Definition of an associated person—s.62(3) Family Law Act 1996</li><li>Protection from Harassment Act 1997</li></ul>
Apply the law	<ul><li>Rebecca can apply for a non-molestation order—explain the application process, the court's decision, the contents of the order and the consequences of breach</li><li>Susan and Rebecca can apply for an injunction under the Protection from Harassment Act—explain the other orders available</li></ul>
Conclude	<ul><li>Conclusion</li><li>Advise Rebecca and Susan as to the orders they can apply for</li></ul>

SUGGESTED ANSWER

[1] If the police are called, the officer can issue a Domestic Violence Protection Notice and then apply for a Domestic Violence Protection Order within 48 hours.

Rebecca and Susan require advice regarding the situation that has arisen with their neighbour, Thomas. They have indicated that they do not wish to involve the police[1] and, as a result, this answer will focus on the civil law remedies that are available under **the Family Law Act 1996** and **the Protection from Harassment Act 1997**.

To begin with **the Family Law Act 1996, s.4[?]** the courts[2] to make a non-molestation order, which is [?] order that prohibits 'a person (the respondent) from [?] other person who is associated with the respondent' or a rel[?] child' **(s.42(1))**. A non-molestation order can be made if an application for such an order has been initiated **(s.42(2)(a))** or during any family proceedings, even though no such application has been made **(s.42(2)(b))**. In this instance, Rebecca and Susan would have to apply to the court for an order, as there are no active family proceedings.

The Definition of Molestation[3]

Molestation is not defined in the statute but 'encompasses any form of serious pestering or harassment and applies to any conduct which could properly be regarded as such a degree of harassment as to call for the intervention of the court' (Law Commission, No. 207, 1992 Domestic Violence and Occupation of the Family Home para. 3.1). *George v George* **[1986] 2 FLR 347** demonstrates that shouting obscenities can constitute molestation, whilst *Johnson v Walton* **[1990] 1 FLR 350** indicates that publishing or attempting to publish semi-naked photographs of the applicant also falls within the definition. The conduct directed at Rebecca *and* Susan would constitute molestation.

Associated Persons

In order to apply for a non-molestation order, the applicant must be *associated with the respondent*, which means that the parties: are or have been married to each other; are or have been civil partners; are cohabitants or former cohabitants; live or have lived in the same household (but not as landlord/tenant, etc); are relatives;[4] have agreed to marry one another or form a civil partnership (whether or not that agreement has been terminated); have or have had an intimate personal relationship with each other of significant duration; are parents of the same child or have PR for the same child; or they are parties to the same family proceedings **(s.62(3))**. The only category that is relevant to Rebecca is persons who have had an intimate personal relationship **(s.62(3)(ea))**.[5] It is unclear what constitutes an intimate personal relationship and what amounts to a significant duration, but in *G v F (Non-Molestation Order: Jurisdiction)* **[2000] 2 FCR 638** the court indicated that a purposive approach should be adopted and that jurisdiction should not be declined unless the facts of the case were plainly incapable of being brought within the statute. It is therefore assumed that Rebecca's relationship with Thomas would be considered an intimate personal relationship of a significant duration, enabling her to apply for a non-molestation order. In contrast,

[4] 'Relatives' covers parents, step-parents, children, step-children, grandchildren, step-grandchildren, siblings, aunts/uncles, nieces/nephews and first cousins **(s.63(1))**.

[5] This provision was inserted by **the Domestic Violence, Crime and Victims Act 2004**, which came into effect in 2007. Prior to this, non-cohabiting or engaged couples could not apply for an order.

Susan is not associated with Thomas and consequently would not be in a position to make an application for this particular type of order.

The Application for a Non-molestation Order

Rebecca should be advised that a non-molestation order can be made ex parte, i.e. without notice to the respondent, if the court considers that it is just and convenient to do so (**s.45(1)**). When deciding whether to make an ex parte order, the court shall have regard to all the circumstances, including any risk or significant harm to the applicant or a relevant child, attributable to conduct of the respondent, if the order is not made immediately, whether it is likely that the applicant will be deterred or prevented from pursuing the application if an order is not made immediately and whether there is reason to believe that the respondent is aware of the proceedings but is deliberately evading service (**s.45(2)**). Although Thomas has hit Rebecca in the past, there is nothing to suggest that she is in immediate danger. An ex parte order is therefore unlikely, but if one was made, Thomas would have the right to a full inter partes hearing and would thus have the opportunity to apply to set the order aside.

The Court's Decision

When deciding whether to exercise its powers and if so, in what manner, the court must have regard to all the circumstances, including the need to secure the health (both physical and mental), safety and well-being of the applicant or the person for whose benefit the order would be made or any relevant child (**s.42(5)**). The court would consider the fact that Thomas has hit Rebecca, is currently threatening to post semi-naked photographs of her on the Internet and is also harassing her mother. It is clear that the court needs to take action to ensure Rebecca's safety. Although the court is able to accept an undertaking from the respondent that he or she will not engage in the conduct that the applicant has complained of,[6] **s.46(3A)** provides that the court shall not do so in any case where 'the respondent has used or threatened violence against the applicant or a relevant child and for the protection of the applicant or child it is necessary to make a non-molestation order so that any breach may be punishable under **s.42A**'. This suggests that if Thomas were to offer an undertaking, the court would not accept it, as Thomas has used violence against Rebecca. However, the court may be willing to accept an undertaking if Rebecca can be adequately protected without a non-molestation order.

If a non-molestation order is granted, it can prohibit molestation in general, can refer to specific acts of molestation, or both (**s.42(6)**). The order might therefore contain a generic prohibition restraining

[6] An undertaking is a formal promise to the court which is enforceable in the same way as a court order.

Thomas from assaulting, molesting, annoying or interfering with Rebecca and then expressly forbid the posting of photographs on the Internet. It can be made for a specified period or until further order (**s.42(7)**). If Thomas does anything that he is prohibited from doing by the order, without reasonable excuse, he would be guilty of a criminal offence (**s.42A**).[7] This provision was inserted by **the Domestic Violence, Crime and Victims Act 2004** and means that it is no longer necessary to attach a power of arrest to a non-molestation order. A person found guilty of this offence may face a prison sentence of up to five years on indictment and 12 months following summary conviction.

[7] Breach of a non-molestation order is also contempt of court.

Harassment

As explained earlier, Susan is not able to apply for a non-molestation order as she is not associated with Thomas. She can, however, apply for an injunction under **the Protection from Harassment Act 1997**, as the latter does not require the applicant to have or have had a relationship with the respondent.[8]

[8] The Protection from Harassment Act 1997 was specifically enacted to deal with stalkers.

Section 1(1) indicates that a person must not pursue a course of conduct which amounts to harassment of another and which he knows or ought to know amounts to harassment of the other. **Section 1(2)** states that the person whose conduct is in question ought to know that it amounts to the harassment of another if a reasonable person in possession of the same information would think the course of conduct amounted to harassment of the other. An injunction can be obtained under **s.3A** where there is an actual or apprehended breach of **s.1(1)**.

Although **the Protection from Harassment Act** does not provide a clear definition of harassment, **s.7(2)** indicates that it includes alarming a person or causing distress, while **s.7(4)** provides that conduct includes speech. It is thus clear that physical or psychological harm is not required (see ***Hipgrave v Jones* [2005] 2 FLR 174**). The threats made to Susan and the obscenities used by Thomas would be sufficient to constitute harassment.

As explained above, **s.1(1)** indicates that a course of conduct is required, which means that the harassment must have occurred on at least two occasions (**s.7(3)(a)**). The separate acts must be connected in order to form a course of conduct (***R v Patel* [2004] EWCA Crim 3284**) and the longer the gap between them, the less likely it is that the court will consider them to be a course of conduct.[9] In this particular case, Susan has been harassed on two occasions and the second took place the day after the first. The court would have little difficulty finding that Thomas knew or ought to have known that his behaviour constituted harassment. Although defences can be raised under

[9] See *Lau v DPP* [2000] 1 FLR 799.

[10] Rebecca could also apply as an alternative to obtaining a non-molestation order.

s.1(3) of the Act, none of them are applicable to Thomas. Susan would therefore be in a position to apply to the court for an injunction to prevent Thomas from harassing her.[10] The court hearing the case can award damages under **s.3(2)** for anxiety and financial loss.

It should also be noted that a person who pursues a course of conduct in breach of **s.1(1)** is guilty of a criminal offence, which is punishable on summary conviction to imprisonment of a term not exceeding six months (**s.2**). However, Rebecca and Susan have indicated that they do not wish to involve the police and as a result a criminal prosecution may not be initiated.

Conclusion

In conclusion, Rebecca is in a position to apply for a non-molestation order under **the Family Law Act 1996** or an injunction under **the Protection from Harassment Act 1997**, whereas Susan can only apply for the latter, as she is not associated with Thomas.

LOOKING FOR EXTRA MARKS?

- Discuss the impact of **the Domestic Violence, Crime and Victims Act 2004** on the law in this area.

- Gain extra marks by mentioning the possibility of a Domestic Violence Protection Notice and Order, which were introduced by **the Crime and Security Act 2010** and were rolled out to all police forces in March 2014.

QUESTION | 4

Discuss the approach taken by **the Family Law Act 1996** in relation to occupation orders.

CAUTION!

- There are five categories of applicants for an occupation order—you will need to be able to summarise the law effectively.

- As the question concerns the legislative approach to occupation orders, it is not necessary to consider practical issues such as the possibility of the court accepting an undertaking (**s.46 Family Law Act 1996**).

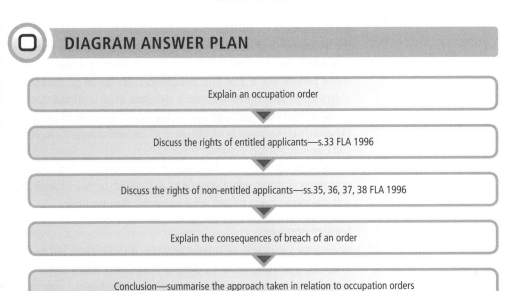

DIAGRAM ANSWER PLAN

Explain an occupation order

▼

Discuss the rights of entitled applicants—s.33 FLA 1996

▼

Discuss the rights of non-entitled applicants—ss.35, 36, 37, 38 FLA 1996

▼

Explain the consequences of breach of an order

▼

Conclusion—summarise the approach taken in relation to occupation orders

A **SUGGESTED ANSWER**

Part IV of **the Family Law Act 1996** empowers the courts to make an occupation order, which 'will often be the only way of supporting a non-molestation order and giving the applicant effective protection' against domestic violence (Law Com No. 207 (1992)). In emergency situations they can be made ex parte, i.e. without notice to the respondent (**s.45(1)**). However, it should be noted that occupation orders can be made in situations that do not involve domestic violence in order to resolve disputes regarding the right to occupy a property (see *S v F (Occupation Order)* **[2000] 1 FLR 255**).[1]

[1] If this question was set as a piece of coursework, you would have time to explain the facts of this case.

The Nature and Scope of an Occupation Order[2]

An occupation order may be declaratory—i.e. it declares, confers or extends occupation rights—or regulatory—i.e. it controls the actual occupation of the property. A regulatory occupation order can enforce the applicant's right to remain in occupation; require the respondent to permit the applicant to enter and remain in the property; regulate the occupation of the property by either or both parties; prohibit or restrict the respondent's right to occupy or exclude the respondent from a defined area (**s.33(3)**). Occupation orders can only be made in relation to a *dwelling-house* that is, was, or was intended to be

[2] The purpose of this paragraph is to explain the nature and scope of occupation orders and to identify the reason for restricting occupation orders.

the family home. In addition, the applicant must be associated with the respondent *and* must have shared or intended to share a home with him or her. As a result of the second requirement, many associated persons will not be in a position to apply for an occupation order. Access to occupation orders is therefore more restricted than access to non-molestation orders, as the former is regarded as 'an extremely serious invasion of the rights of the respondent' (Gilmore and Glennon, 2014, p. 129).

The approach of **the Family Law Act 1996** in relation to occupation orders is to categorise applicants as 'entitled' or 'non-entitled', with the former being treated more favourably than the latter.

Entitled Applicants

Under **s.33** a person is an entitled applicant if he or she 'is entitled to occupy a dwelling-house by virtue of a beneficial estate or interest or contract or by virtue of any enactment giving him the right to remain in occupation', or if he or she 'has home rights in relation to a dwelling-house'. **Section 30** grants 'home rights' to an individual who is not entitled to occupy the home under the general law, but his/her spouse/civil partner is so entitled. An occupation order made in favour of an entitled applicant can be for a fixed term or until further order (**s.33(10)**).

The Balance of Harm Test

[3] The definition of harm is contained in **s.63(1)**. 'Significant' is not defined in the Act, but the approach taken in relation to **the Children Act 1989** would apply.

Section 33(7) provides that if it appears that the applicant or any relevant child is likely to suffer significant harm[3] attributable to the conduct of the respondent if an order is not made, the court *shall* make the order unless it appears that 'the respondent or any relevant child is likely to suffer significant harm if the order is made' and 'the harm likely to be suffered by the respondent or child in that event is as great as or greater than, the harm attributable to conduct of the respondent which is likely to be suffered by the applicant or child if the order is not made'. This is known as the 'balance of harm test' and was considered in *B v B* **[1999] 1 FLR 715**. The case concerned a married couple that lived with their baby and the husband's son from a previous relationship. Because the husband was violent the wife moved into temporary accommodation and applied for an occupation order. The court was satisfied that the wife and baby would suffer significant harm attributable to the husband's conduct if no order was made, but held that the husband and son would suffer a greater degree of harm if required to leave the property, as the local authority would not be obliged to house them and the son's education and welfare would suffer. The balance of harm test was not therefore satisfied.

If the balance of harm test is satisfied, the court has a mandatory duty to make an order. If it is not satisfied, there is no duty to make an order, but the court can use its discretion to make an order. It will consider the factors listed in **s.33(6)**, i.e. the parties' housing needs and resources, their financial resources, the effect of any order or of a decision not to make an order and the conduct of the parties, when deciding whether or not to exercise its discretion and make an occupation order (see *Chalmers v John* [1999] **1 FLR 392**).

Non-entitled Applicants—Former Spouses/Civil Partners

Those who do not have a right to occupy the property are known as non-entitled applicants. A former spouse/civil partner with no right to occupy where the respondent does have a right to occupy must make an application under **s.35**. First s/he must apply for a declaratory order to acquire a right to occupy (**s.35(3) and (4)**).[4] When the court is deciding this issue it will have regard to all the circumstances of the case, including: the parties' housing needs and resources; their financial resources; the effect of any order; the conduct of the parties; the length of time since the parties lived together; the length of time since the marriage was terminated; and the existence of pending proceedings between the parties (**s.35(6)(a)–(g)**). If the court grants a declaratory order, it will then consider making a regulatory order (**s.35(5)**) based on the criteria contained in **s.35(6)(a)–(e)**.[5] The balance of harm test also applies under **s.35(8)**. If the court makes an order, it will only last for six months, but can be extended on one or more occasions for six months (**s.35(10)**). The protection provided to non-entitled applicants is clearly intended to be more temporary than that available to entitled applicants.

Cohabitants and Former Cohabitants

A cohabitant or former cohabitant with no right to occupy where the respondent has a right of occupation applies under **s.36(1)**. Cohabitants are defined as 'two persons who are neither married to each other nor civil partners of each other but are living together as husband and wife or as if they were civil partners' (**s.62(1)(a)**). The court must first make a declaratory order granting the right to occupy (**s.36(3) and (4)**). The court must consider the factors listed in **s.36(6)(a)–(i)**, several of which are the same as the factors contained in **s.35(6)**, but in addition the court must consider the nature of the parties' relationship, the level of commitment involved, the duration of their cohabitation and whether the parties have children. The law is clearly making a judgement about such relationships.[6]

If the court makes a declaratory order, it will then decide whether to make a regulatory order, for example to exclude the respondent

[4] If the applicant is in occupation, the order gives him/her a right not to be evicted. If the applicant is not in occupation, the order gives him/her the right to enter and occupy.

[5] Section 35(7) states that s.35(6)(a)–(e) applies. Section 35(6)(f) length of time since marriage was dissolved and (g) the existence of pending proceedings do not apply.

[6] You should consider whether you think this is appropriate.

(**s.36(5)**). It considers the parties' housing needs and resources, their financial resources, the effect of an order and the conduct of the parties (**s.36(7)**). The balance of harm test applies but it is not determinative (**s.36(8)**), i.e. it does not result in a duty to make an order. An occupation order made under **s.36** cannot exceed six months, but can be extended once for six months (**s.36(10)**), which is in marked contrast to orders made in favour of entitled applicants and former spouses or civil partners.

[7] You could explain when this situation might arise, for example when the couple are living with family or friends or squatting.

[8] This demonstrates how restricted occupation orders are.

Neither Party has a Right to Occupy[7]

Only a non-entitled spouse/civil partner/cohabitant or former spouse/ civil partner/cohabitant can make an application if the respondent is not entitled to occupy the property either.[8] In both cases, the order has no effect on the rights of the third-party owner. Spouses and civil partners (or former spouses/civil partners) apply under **s.37**, and in such cases the court's discretion is governed by the same criteria that apply to entitled applicants (**s.37(4)**). The order can be made for six months and can be extended for further periods of six months (**s.37(5)**). If the applicant is a cohabitant or former cohabitant the application is made under **s.38**. The balance of harm test does not result in a duty to make an order: rather it is a question that the court asks when exercising its discretion (**s.38(4)** and **(5)**). The order can be made for six months but only extended once (**s.38(6)**).

Breach of an Order

Unlike breach of a non-molestation order, breach of an occupation order is not a criminal offence. This reflects the fact that occupation orders can be utilised in situations that do not involve domestic violence. In cases where the respondent has used or threatened violence against the applicant, a power of arrest can be attached to the order, giving the police the automatic power to arrest the applicant if the order is breached (**s.47(2)**). If no such power exists, an application would have to be made to the court for a warrant to arrest the respondent. The respondent can then be prosecuted for contempt of court.[9]

[9] Contempt of court is punishable by a fine or prison sentence not exceeding two years.

Conclusion

The approach of **the Family Law Act 1996** to occupation orders is to limit their availability because they constitute a significant infringement of the rights of the respondent. Entitled applicants are treated more favourably than non-entitled applicants because they have a right to occupy the property. In addition, spouses and civil partners (and former spouses and civil partners) are in a better position than cohabitants and former cohabitants. It is therefore clear that Parliament has made a judgment about such relationships.

LOOKING FOR EXTRA MARKS?

- Gain extra marks by comparing the approach taken in relation to occupation orders with the approach taken in relation to non-molestation orders.

- Utilise the PEA method to ensure that your answer is logically structured and sufficiently analytical.

TAKING THINGS FURTHER

- Burton, M. 'Emergency barring orders in domestic violence cases: What can England and Wales learn from other European countries?' (2015) Child and Family Law Quarterly 27 (1) 25.

  Considers whether the introduction of domestic violence protection notices and orders will improve the policing of domestic violence in England and Wales.

- Edwards, S. 'Domestic violence: Not a term of art but a state of consciousness' (2011) Family Law 1244.

  Discusses the history of the law and implications of the Supreme Court decision in Yemshaw v London Borough of Hounslow *in relation to the housing needs of battered women.*

- Hayward, A. '"Family Property" and the process of "familialisation" of property law' (2012) Child and Family Law Quarterly 24 (3) 284.

  Argues that the 'familialisation' of property law—i.e. the reinterpretation of neutral family law principles to accommodate family situations—is a necessary process and has intensified in recent years.

- Hayward, A. 'Cohabitants, detriment and the potential of proprietary estoppel' (2015) Child and Family Law Quarterly 27 (3) 303.

  Suggests that proprietary estoppel could have a greater role to play in disputes between cohabitants, if it is remodelled in a domestic consumer context.

- Herring, J. 'The meaning of domestic violence: *Yemshaw v London Borough of Hounslow* [2011] UKSC 3' (2011) Journal of Social Welfare and Family Law 33 (3) 297.

  Considers the approach of the Supreme Court to the definition of domestic violence for the purpose of the Housing Act 1996.

- Knight, C.J.S. 'Doing (linguistic) violence to prevent (domestic) violence? *Yemshaw v Hounslow LBC* in the Supreme Court' (2012) Child and Family Law Quarterly 24 (1) 95.

  Discusses the case of Yemshaw v Hounslow LBC, *where the Supreme Court held that psychological, financial and emotional abuse can fall within the definition of domestic violence.*

- Law Commission 'Cohabitation: The Financial Consequences of Relationship Breakdown' 2007 (Law Com No. 307).

  Recommended that cohabitants acquire rights on relationship breakdown in certain circumstances. The Government did not implement the recommendations—See The Law

Commission's Statement on the Government Response to 'Cohabitation: The Financial Consequences of Relationship Breakdown' (2011).

- Sloan, B. 'Keeping up with the Jones case: Establishing constructive trusts in "sole legal owner" scenarios' (2015) Legal Studies 35 (2) 226.

   Considers the influence of the decision of the Supreme Court in Jones v Kernott *on subsequent cases relating to ownership of the family home.*

Online Resource Centre   www.oxfordtextbooks.co.uk/orc/qanda/

Go online for extra essay and problem questions, a glossary of key terms, online versions of all the answer plans and audio commentary on how selected ones were put together, and a range of podcasts which include advice on exam and coursework technique and advice for other assessment methods.

Financial Relief and Child Support

6

ARE YOU READY?

In order to attempt the four questions in this chapter you will need to have covered the following topics:

- the financial orders available under **the Matrimonial Causes Act 1973** and **the Civil Partnership Act 2004**;
- the factors the court must take into account when making a decision as listed in **s.25** of **the Matrimonial Causes Act 1973**;
- appeals against financial orders and variation of financial orders;
- pre-nuptial and post-nuptial agreements;
- child support under **the Child Support Act 1991 (as amended)**;
- financial orders for children under **the Matrimonial Causes Act 1973** and **the Children Act 1989**.

KEY DEBATES

Debate: Time limits on applications for financial relief on divorce

In *Wyatt v Vince* [2015] **UKSC 14**, the Supreme Court held that an ex-wife was not barred from submitting a claim for financial relief 27 years after the marriage had ended. Should a time limit be imposed on applications for financial relief? It can be argued that the decision will encourage spouses to seek a court order, which declares that no award is required in order to prevent future claims.

Debate: The relevance of conduct in financial relief applications

Conduct will only be considered by the court if it would be inequitable to disregard it, i.e. it must be extremely serious. Do you think that this is the correct approach to conduct in financial relief cases? Do you think the law would need to be reformed if no-fault divorce was introduced?

$\circlearrowright$

Debate: The effectiveness of the child support system

The administrative system introduced by **the Child Support Act 1991** has been amended on a number of occasions. Is the current system finally fit for purpose?

QUESTION | 1

Una, who is 32 and Victor, aged 35, met 12 years ago while working as marketing executives for a large advertising company. They married six years later. Una gave up her job when she gave birth to their daughter Wendy, one year after they were married. Wendy was born with a rare blood disease and died at the age of three. Una became very depressed after Wendy's death and has not returned to work. Since then, Victor and Una's marriage has deteriorated and a few months ago Una began an affair with Xavier, Victor's younger brother. Victor found out about the relationship three weeks ago. He changed the locks when Una was out of the house so that she could not return. Una is currently sleeping on the sofa in her sister, Yvonne's one bed-roomed flat. She has submitted a claim for social security benefits as she has no means of supporting herself. Victor has refused to pay Una any money and their joint bank account is empty. Una says that she is sorry and wants to reconcile, but Victor refuses to speak to her and says that he wants a divorce. The matrimonial home, which is registered in joint names, is worth £300,000 and is subject to a mortgage of £100,000. The couple has no savings or other significant assets.

Advise Una as to the applications she can currently make and the financial position if Victor petitions for divorce.

N.B. It is not necessary to discuss the ground for divorce.

CAUTION!

- Read the question carefully—it is not necessary to discuss the ground for divorce.
- Una is in need of immediate financial relief and does not intend to petition for divorce, so it is necessary to discuss financial provision during marriage.
- As Victor has indicated that he wants a divorce, it is necessary to advise Una about financial relief on divorce.

DIAGRAM ANSWER PLAN

Identify the issues
- Identify the legal issues
- What rights does Una have to claim immediate financial support?
- What is the financial position if Victor petitions for divorce?

Relevant law
- Outline the relevant law:
- Financial relief during marriage—s.27 MCA, s.2 Domestic Proceedings and Magistrates Court Act 1978
- Maintenance pending suit—s.22 MCA
- Application for financial relief on divorce—Part II MCA
- S.25—factors for the court to consider
- Key cases: *White v White* [2001], *McFarlane v McFarlane* [2006]

Apply the law
- Identify the orders that a court is likely to make in this case
- Apply the factors contained in s.25(2) MCA 1973 to Una and Victor

Conclude
- Conclusion
- Advise Una in relation to the possible award she may be granted

SUGGESTED ANSWER

Una and Victor have separated and Victor is refusing to provide Una with money: it is therefore necessary to discuss financial relief during marriage.[1] Una can apply under **the Domestic Proceedings and Magistrates' Court Act 1978** or **the Matrimonial Causes Act 1973** for a lump sum or penalty payments on the ground that the respondent has failed to provide reasonable maintenance for the applicant, but it should be noted that such applications are rare. If Victor initiates divorce proceedings, the court could make an order for maintenance pending suit prior to the final order under **s.22** of **the Matrimonial Causes Act** 1973.[2] These awards are also rare, but they remain an option open to the court.

[1] The Common law duty for a husband to maintain a wife was abolished by **the Equality Act 2010** because it was discriminatory.

[2] You could point out that there are few reported cases dealing with maintenance pending suit. See *MET v HAT (No. 2)* [2014] EWHC 717 (Fam) for a recent example.

Financial Relief on Divorce

If Victor petitions for divorce it will be necessary to advise Una regarding financial relief. Although a Mediation Information and Assessment Meeting (MIAM) would be compulsory prior to initiating court action, it seems unlikely that Victor will be willing to negotiate a settlement that adequately provides for Una.[3] If this is the case, Una will need to make an application for financial relief under **Part II** of **the Matrimonial Causes Act 1973. Section 21** empowers the court to make an order for financial provision or property adjustment. Orders for financial provision cover:[4] orders for periodical payments, secured periodical payments and lump sum orders. Orders for the transfer of property, settlements and orders to vary a settlement constitute property adjustment orders. **Section 21A** allows the court to make pension-sharing orders, whilst **s.24A** enables the court to make an order for sale. In this particular case Una is likely to request periodical payments as she is presently unable to support herself. It is unclear whether Victor has a private pension and as a result pension-sharing orders will not be discussed. Although Una might request a property transfer or settlement, the circumstances of the case render such options unlikely. The court might, however, order the sale of the matrimonial home and the division of the proceeds. There appear to be no other funds available to enable a separate lump sum order.

Factors to Consider

When hearing an application for financial relief the court is required to consider various factors listed in **s.25 MCA 1973. Section 25A(1)** requires the court to consider whether to exercise its powers so 'that the financial obligations of each party towards the other will be terminated as soon after the grant of the decree as the court considers just and reasonable'.[5] In other words, the court has a duty to consider whether to make a clean break order. Clean break orders can be advantageous, but they are inappropriate if there is uncertainty over the recipient's financial future. For example, in **Whiting v Whiting [1988] 2 FLR 189** it appeared that the wife would be in a position to become self-supporting at some point in the future but it was not possible to predict when this would occur. In this particular case, Una will require periodical payments as she is currently unemployed: a clean break order is not therefore possible, but a delayed clean break order might be appropriate. This is achieved by limiting the period of time over which payments would be made and including a term that prohibits an application for an extension of the order (**s.28(1A) MCA 1973**). The court will only do this if it is satisfied that the recipient will be financially independent at the end of the term (**C v C (Financial Provision: Short Marriage) [1997] 2 FLR 26**). Although Una has

[3] Even where a couple undertakes mediation, the agreement reached will be influenced by the legal advice that each party receives.

[4] Lump sum orders cannot be varied but an order for periodical payments can. A lump sum order is unaffected by remarriage but an order for periodical payments would end.

[5] This paragraph focuses on **s.25A(1)**. The law relating to clean breaks is explained and applied to Una's situation.

only been out of the workforce for four years, her depression makes it difficult to determine whether a delayed clean break order would be appropriate.

Section 25(1) MCA requires the court to 'have regard to all the circumstances of the case, first consideration being given to the welfare, while a minor of any child of the family who has not attained the age of 18'.[6] **Section 25(2)** places a duty on the court to consider a list of factors discussed below.

Income, Earning Capacity, Property and Resources

Section 25(2)(a) requires the court to consider the income, earning capacity, property and other financial resources, which each of the parties has or is likely to have. In terms of income and earning capacity, Victor has remained in, what is assumed to be, a well-paid job, whereas Una has no current income and her earning capacity has been restricted. These factors suggest that a periodical payments order would be required. The couple jointly own the matrimonial home, which is worth £300,000 with £200,000 equity. This property appears to be the couple's only asset and as a result it may need to be sold in order to ensure that the property is divided on divorce. The precise shares will be discussed below.

Financial Needs and Responsibilities[7]

[7] The Law Commission Report 'Matrimonial Property, Needs and Agreements' (2014) recommends the development of written guidance to explain needs.

Under **s.25(2)(b)**, the court must consider the financial needs and responsibilities of the parties. In this case, both parties need accommodation, whilst Una also requires income. As there are no children to house, both parties could be accommodated in a relatively small property. The court might therefore make an order for sale under **s.24A** and order the division of the proceeds. The equity in the property may not be sufficient to enable both parties to purchase a property outright and Una is not currently in a position to obtain a mortgage, whereas Victor is. The court might therefore award Una a greater share of the proceeds in order to meet her housing needs and to compensate her for the lack of earning capacity, which has resulted from her childcare responsibilities. In *White v White* **[2001] 1 AC 596**, the Court of Appeal held that equality of division of family assets should be seen as a 'yardstick' and that it is appropriate to depart from equality in order to achieve fairness. A departure from equal sharing will be justified if it is required to meet the basic needs of the parties or if it serves to compensate one party for losses suffered as a result of the marriage. In *McFarlane v McFarlane* **[2006] 3 ALL ER 1**, the wife was granted more than 50 per cent of the assets to compensate her for the loss of earning capacity she suffered as a consequence of the marriage. The court may therefore be minded to award Una a greater share of the proceeds of sale than Victor.

Standard of Living, Age, Duration of Marriage and Disability

The third factor that the court is obliged to consider is the standard of living enjoyed by the family before the breakdown of the marriage (**s.25(2)(c)**). This is most relevant to wealthy couples and will have little bearing on a case such as this, where there are insufficient funds to house both spouses in the sort of property that they are used to. **Section 25(2)(d)** then provides that the court must have regard to the age of the parties and the duration of the marriage.[8] Age affects a person's earning capacity, and although Una is young enough to work or even retrain, her depression may impact upon her ability to work. The relatively short duration of the marriage is unlikely to influence the court's decision in this case because Una's need for maintenance, her loss of earning capacity caused by her childcare responsibilities and the fact that she jointly owned the matrimonial home will be more significant (see *C v C (Financial Relief: Short Marriage)* [1997] 2 FLR 26). Under **s.25(2)(e)**, the court has a duty to consider any physical or mental disability of either of the parties. Una's depressive state may constitute a disability and, as explained above, this may affect her capacity to work.

[8] We do not know if the couple cohabited before marriage. Although **s.25(2)** does not refer to cohabitation, it would be considered under **s.25(1)**.

Contributions

The contributions which each of the parties has made or is likely to make to the welfare of the family, including looking after the home or caring for the family, must be considered under **s.25(2)(f)**. In *White v White* [2001] 1 AC 596, the Court of Appeal emphasised that there should be no bias against the homemaker and child-carer and no bias in favour of the breadwinner. This point was reiterated by the House of Lords in *Miller v Miller; McFarlane v McFarlane* [2006] 3 ALL ER 1. Presumably, Una made a financial contribution prior to giving up work and after this point she undertook child and home care responsibilities. Both spouses have therefore made important contributions to the welfare of the family.

Conduct

Finally, **s.25(2)(h)** states that the court must have regard to the conduct of each of the parties if it would be inequitable to disregard it. The conduct must be extreme to have an impact on any award made by the court;[9] for example, in *K v L* [2010] EWCA Civ 125 the husband sexually abused the wife's grandchildren. He was entitled to his share of jointly owned property, but additional financial claims were rejected due to his conduct. Una's adultery would not be considered sufficiently serious to influence the court's decision in this matter.

[9] Do not assume that adultery will be taken into account.

Conclusion

Una is in a position to apply for maintenance during marriage as Victor is refusing to support her. If the couple divorce, the court may order the sale of the matrimonial home and the division of proceeds. Una may also be awarded periodical payments for a fixed period of time, but due to the uncertainty surrounding her condition, the court might refuse to bar an application for an extension. Hopefully, Victor will agree to such an arrangement, thus obviating the need for the court to adjudicate.

LOOKING FOR EXTRA MARKS?

- If Una makes an application, a MIAM will be compulsory, but this does not mean that clients will not seek legal advice. You could point out that if mediation is successful, the agreement should be incorporated into a consent order.

- You could mention the Financial Dispute Resolution Appointment, which will be required if an application is made to the court.

QUESTION | 2

Zoe and Anthony, who are both aged 45, met at university. When Anthony qualified as a solicitor and Zoe qualified as an accountant, they married. The couple purchased a three-bedroomed house in joint names, which is now worth £400,000 and mortgage free. The couple have two children: Belinda, aged ten and Conor, aged six. Zoe and Anthony both work full time and have high salaries and their own private pensions. They have no savings. Zoe's mother looks after the children while Zoe and Anthony work.

Zoe has just discovered that Anthony has been having an affair with his secretary, Debbie, for the past five years. Anthony claims that the relationship is over, but Zoe is furious and wants a divorce after almost 16 years of marriage. Belinda and Conor will live with Zoe.

a) **Advise Zoe as to the financial position in this case. [35 marks]**

b) **Discuss the circumstances in which the orders made by the court can be changed or overturned. [15 marks]**

N.B. It is not necessary to discuss the ground for divorce.

CAUTION!

- Read the question carefully—it is not necessary to discuss the ground for divorce. You only need to consider financial provision.

- You should notice that part a) is worth far more than part b). Your answer to part a) should be longer than your answer to part b).

DIAGRAM ANSWER PLAN

Identify the issues	▪ Identify the legal issues ▪ What sort of financial settlement is Zoe likely to receive? ▪ Identify the circumstances when a court order can be changed, overturned or set aside
Relevant law	▪ Outline the relevant law: ▪ Application for financial relief on divorce—Part II MCA 1973 ▪ S.25—factors for the court to consider ▪ Application to vary a periodical payments order—s.31 MCA ▪ Appeals and set aside applications—*Barder v Barder* [1987]
Apply the law	▪ Identify the orders that a court is likely to make ▪ Apply the factors contained in s.25(2) MCA to Zoe's case ▪ Identify the circumstances when a court order can be changed, overturned or set aside
Conclude	▪ Conclusion ▪ Advise Zoe in relation to the possible award she may be granted and appeals

SUGGESTED ANSWER

[1] You should explain what a consent order is.

Zoe wishes to divorce her husband Anthony. If they can reach an agreement regarding their finances, either of their own volition or during mediation, the agreement can be incorporated into a consent order.[1] If they cannot do so, Zoe will have to make an application for financial relief under **Part II** of **the Matrimonial Causes Act 1973**. Orders can be made for the benefit of the applicant or a child. **Section 21** of the Act empowers the court to make an order for financial provision (which includes periodical payments and lump sum orders) or property adjustment (which includes transfers and settlements). **Section 21A** allows the court to make pension-sharing orders, whilst **s.24A** enables the court to make an order for sale. In this case, Zoe will require maintenance for the children and the matrimonial home may be subject to a transfer order or a settlement.

Factors

When hearing an application for financial relief the court is required to consider various factors listed in **s.25 MCA 1973**. **Section 25A(1)** requires the court to consider whether a clean break can be ordered. In this case, a complete clean break is inappropriate as there are young children. **Section 25(1)** requires the court to 'have regard to all the circumstances of the case, first consideration being given to the welfare, while a minor of any child of the family who has not attained the age of 18'. The welfare of Belinda and Conor will therefore be the court's first consideration, but it is not the overriding consideration. **Section 25(3)** lists the factors that the court must take into account, when hearing an application from a spouse with a child, for example the financial needs of the child and the manner in which he was being and is expected to be educated. Nothing in the case study suggests that the children have any special needs, etc. but the children may be expected to attend university.[2]

[2] Explain why this is relevant—if the court orders a settlement, the property may be sold once the children complete higher education.

Section 25(2)

The court must consider the factors contained in **s.25(2) MCA 1973**.

In terms of income, earning capacity and assets, which must be considered under **s.25(2)(a)**, both spouses have well-paid jobs and can therefore support themselves. The couple jointly own the matrimonial home, which is worth £400,000 and is free of mortgage. In *White v White* [2001] 1 AC 596, the Court of Appeal held that equality of division of family assets should be seen as a 'yardstick'. It is therefore likely that the property would be shared equally. However, the housing needs of the children and their primary carer, Zoe, mean that the home may not be sold immediately.

Under **s.25(2)(b)**, the court must examine the financial needs and responsibilities of the spouses. The primary need for both spouses is housing and priority is given to the children and their carer. Zoe will need a three-bedroomed property for herself and the children and it is preferable for them to remain in the current family home. Zoe may be able to obtain a mortgage to purchase Anthony's share of the property. The court could then order a transfer of Anthony's share to Zoe and a lump sum order in favour of Anthony. Alternatively, Zoe and the children could live in the family home under a settlement, such as a Mesher order (*Mesher v Mesher* [1980] 1 ALL ER 126).[3] Zoe and Anthony would continue to jointly own the property, which would be sold and the proceeds divided, when the children complete full-time education. In *Sawden v Sawden* [2004] 1 FCR 776, the order provided that the home would be sold when the children had left home, rather than when they finished their studies, which reflects the fact that many children remain in the family home after completing their education. Anthony's salary would mean that he could afford

[3] The court could transfer the home to Zoe with a charge in favour of Anthony, which would entitle him to a share of the proceeds when the property is sold.

to obtain a mortgage to purchase a small property or live in rented accommodation.

Zoe will also need maintenance for the children. Zoe may apply for maintenance under **the Child Support Act 1991**, which requires Anthony to pay 16 per cent of his gross weekly income up to £800 and 12 per cent of his gross weekly income that is between £800 and £3,000.[4] If Zoe requires more than the maximum available, she will have to apply to the courts. It is also possible that child maintenance is agreed by the parties and incorporated into a consent order. Even if the parties cannot agree the amount of maintenance, the court can make a nominal periodical payments order by consent, which can later be varied.

Section 25(2)(c) directs the court to take into account the standard of living enjoyed by the family. In this case, the family should be able to enjoy a comparable standard of living as both parties have high salaries. **Section 25(2)(d)** then provides that the court must have regard to the age of each spouse and the duration of the marriage. Zoe and Anthony are both 45 years of age and may therefore have the capacity to work for a further 20 years. The marriage appears to have lasted a significant duration, but this factor is of greater relevance to wives who have stayed at home and have lesser earning capacity than their husbands. Neither Zoe nor Anthony have a disability (**s.25(2)(e)**).

The contributions which each party has made or is likely to make to the welfare of the family must be considered under **s.25(2)(f)**. It is assumed that Zoe and Anthony made equal financial and parenting contributions, but the fact that the children will live with Zoe, means that her contribution to the upbringing of the children will increase. Zoe's role as primary carer will influence the court's decision in relation to the order made in respect of the family home. However, Anthony's affair is not conduct that the court has regard to under **s.25(2)(h)**.

[5]This short conclusion sums up the orders that are likely to be made. It is not possible to ascertain how much the periodical payments will be.

In conclusion,[5] Zoe will receive child maintenance (which may be ordered by the court or the Child Maintenance Service) and the family home may be subject to a transfer order or settlement.

[6]This section considers variation of court orders. Child maintenance obtained through the CSA can be changed periodically.

Variations[6]

[7]You could refer to **Wright v Wright** [2015] EWCA Civ 201, which is a recent example of the husband successfully applying to vary the order—the wife's appeal failed.

It is possible to make an application to vary or discharge an order for periodical payments (**s.31 MCA 1973**).[7] The recipient of periodical payments might apply to extend the order, unless a bar has been included under **s.28(1A)**. An application for an extension must be submitted before the original order has expired. If the parties agreed nominal periodical payments for the children, an application to vary may follow soon after the consent order. At a later date either party

[8]Capitalisation is appropriate if the payer has acquired capital, since the making of the periodical payments order and a clean break is desirable.

may apply to increase or decrease the periodical payments. In addition, either party can apply for capitalisation under **s.31(7A)**,[8] but this may be inappropriate where the payments are for the benefit of a child. In *Omielan v Omielan* **[1996] 2 FLR 306**, the Court of Appeal stated that Mesher-type orders are final orders and cannot be varied, but if the order contains a 'liberty to apply' provision, one party can apply for an early order for sale.

Appeals

It is not possible to vary a lump sum order or transfer, but one of the parties could appeal against these or any other type of court order. An appeal must be lodged within 14 days. Once 14 days have expired, the applicant will have to apply for leave to appeal or to set aside the original order. This may be due to a flaw in the trial process—for

[9]Another example is mistake of fact—you could refer to *Richardson v Richardson* [2011] EWCA Civ 79.

example non-disclosure[9]—or due to an unforeseen change of circumstances. In *Hutchings-Whelan v Hutchings-Whelan* **[2011] EWCA Civ 1048**, a consent order required the husband to pay a lump sum of £176,000 to the wife. The wife later discovered that her former husband had sold property for £1.3 million and thus applied to have the order set aside due to non-disclosure. The application was successful and the husband was ordered to pay £384,000.

An order can also be set aside if a fundamental unforeseen change of circumstances occurs after the order has been made. This is referred to as a 'Barder Event', after *Barder v Barder (Calouri Intervening)* **[1987] 2 FLR 480**. In this case, a consent order required the husband to transfer the home to the wife. Soon after, the wife killed herself and the two children. The wife had drafted a will leaving her property to her mother. The husband successfully applied to set aside the consent order and recovered the matrimonial home. The court hearing the application will only set aside an order if the subsequent unforeseen event destroys the basis of the order. In *Williams v Lindley* **[2005] 1 FCR 813**, the wife was granted a lump sum to meet her housing needs. Within weeks, she became engaged

[10]If the purpose of the lump sum is to compensate the wife for loss of earning capacity, her subsequent marriage would not be a Barder event.

to a wealthy man and later married him. The husband's application to set aside the order was successful because the purpose of the lump sum was to provide housing, which the wife no longer needed.[10] It should be noted that a fluctuation in the value of property does not constitute an unforeseen change of circumstances (see *Myerson v Myerson* **[2009] ALL ER (D) 05**). Similarly, the husband's redundancy did not constitute a Barder event in *Maskell v Maskell* **[2001] 3 FCR 296**.

At this stage, it is impossible to advise whether a variation or appeal would be appropriate in Zoe and Anthony's case.

LOOKING FOR EXTRA MARKS?

- Utilise the IRAC method to ensure that you answer this problem question properly.
- Refer to the Law Commission Report 'Matrimonial Property, Needs and Agreements: The Future of Financial Orders on Divorce and Dissolution' (2014).
- Gain extra marks by including the most up-to-date cases relating to variations—for example *N v N* [2014] **EWCA 314 Civ**—and out-of-time appeals/applications to set aside, for example *Sharland v Sharland* [2015] **UKSC 60**.

QUESTION | 3

Evaluate the development of the law relating to pre-nuptial and post-nuptial contracts.

CAUTION!

- You should focus on pre-nuptial and post-nuptial contracts—the question does not require a discussion of post-separation agreements, which are commonly reached by divorcing couples and are often encapsulated into a consent order.
- Do not attempt this question unless you are aware of the leading case: *Radmacher v Radmacher (formerly Granatino)* [2010] **UKSC 42**.

DIAGRAM ANSWER PLAN

Explain the powers of the court to make financial orders on divorce and dissolution

⬇

Explain the approach of the courts to pre- and post-nuptial contracts prior to *Radmacher*

⬇

Discuss the facts and decision in *Radmacher v Granatino* [2010]

⬇

Discuss subsequent case law, e.g. *Kremen v Agrest* [2012]

⬇

Consider proposals for change—the Law Commission Report and Draft Nuptial Agreements Bill

⬇

Conclusion

The courts have wide-ranging powers to make financial orders on divorce under the **Matrimonial Causes Act 1973**[1] and because it is not possible to deprive the courts of such powers, pre- and post-nuptial contracts are not strictly binding. Initially, pre-nuptial agreements were void under the common law because they envisage divorce before the marriage has even begun, but the Supreme Court in *Radmacher v Radmacher (formerly Granatino)* **[2010] UKSC 42** stated that 'the rule was obsolete and should be swept away' (para. 52). As Parker points out, there is uncertainty as to whether the rule still exists (2015, p. 63).

[1] Equivalent provisions are contained in **the Civil Partnership Act 2004**.

Pre-nuptial Agreements Pre-*Radmacher*

Although a court hearing an application for financial relief is not obliged to enforce a pre-nuptial agreement, it must not disregard it completely, as **s.25(1) MCA 1973** directs the court to take into account *all* circumstances when deciding whether to exercise its powers. This includes the existence of a pre-nuptial agreement (*N v N (Jurisdiction: Pre-Nuptial Agreement)* **[1999] 2 FLR 745**). Initially, the judiciary was hostile towards ante-nuptial agreements (see *F v F (Ancillary Relief: Substantial Assets)* **[1995] 2 FLR 45**), but since then, support for such contracts has grown (see *K v K (Ancillary Relief: Prenuptial Agreements)* **[2003] 1 FLR 120**). Whether the parties received legal advice and whether one party failed to make full disclosure have affected the court's perception of pre-nuptial agreements (*J v V (Disclosure: Offshore Corporations)* **[2003] EWHC 3110 (Fam)**). The courts have been most willing to enforce them if the marriage was short, childless and both parties were wealthy, as in *Crossley v Crossley* **[2007] EWCA Civ 1491**.

Post-nuptial Contracts[2]

[2] This paragraph explains the different approach to post-nuptial contracts that was taken before *Radmacher*, as evidenced by *Macleod v Macleod*.

[3] In a coursework question with an extended word limit, you would be expected to provide more detail regarding the facts of the case.

In the past, the courts treated post-nuptial contracts, which are agreed after the marriage, differently from pre-nuptial contracts. As Baroness Hale pointed out in *Macleod v Macleod* **[2008] UKPC 68**,[3] a pre-nuptial contract may be the price that one party extracts from the other in return for his or her willingness to marry, but in the case of post-nuptial contracts the couple have already undertaken responsibilities towards one another and so this risk does not exist. In this case, the Privy Council overturned the lump sum awarded to the wife because the post-nuptial agreement that the parties had signed should have been enforced. The Privy Council held that post-nuptial agreements are capable of being enforced, provided that no vitiating factors are present, such as undue influence as in *NA v MA* [2006] **EWHC 2900 (Fam)**. The court also pointed out that they are capable of being varied in the same way that a post-separation agreement can be varied under **s.35 MCA**. In *MacLeod*, the Privy Council indicated that the same approach should apply to post-nuptial contracts. Post-nuptial contracts were thus treated in the same way as post-separation contracts, but differently from pre-nuptial contracts.

[4] As *Radmacher* is the leading case on pre-nuptial agreements, you would be expected to provide a considerable amount of detail on it.

Radmacher[4]

In 2010, the Supreme Court was given the opportunity to clarify the status of pre-nuptial (and post-nuptial agreements). *Radmacher v Radmacher (formerly Granatino)* **[2010] UKSC 42** concerned a German heiress who had married a French man in England. Prior to the marriage they signed an agreement that restricted the parties' rights to make financial claims against one another in the event of divorce. When the couple separated, the husband petitioned for financial relief and was awarded over £5.5 million. However, the Court of Appeal reduced this to approximately £1 million because due weight had not been given to the pre-nuptial contract. The husband appealed to the Supreme Court, which indicated that three issues arose for consideration.

First, were there circumstances surrounding the formation of the contract which should detract from the weight which should be accorded to it, for example undue pressure, lack of awareness of the implications, non-disclosure? Secondly, are there circumstances that enhance the weight that should be accorded to the agreement? Finally, did the circumstances prevailing at the time of the court order make it fair or just to depart from the agreement, for example the agreement prejudices the children or the applicant's needs have changed substantially? In this particular case there were no circumstances surrounding the formation of the contract that should detract from the weight accorded to it. The fact that the agreement was binding under German law demonstrated that the parties intended to be bound and there were no circumstances prevailing at the time of the court order that would make it just to depart from the agreement (apart from the fact that the husband required provision as father of the two children). The Supreme Court thus agreed with the Court of Appeal, that the husband should be granted provision for his role as father of the two children, but not for his own long-term needs. In relation to the latter, the pre-nuptial agreement was decisive.

In relation to post-nuptial contracts, the Supreme Court indicated (obiter dicta) that the factors that a court must consider when determining the weight to be accorded to a pre-nuptial agreement should

[5] Lady Hale thus maintained the viewpoint she expressed in *Macleod v Macleod*.

apply to post-nuptial contracts. Lady Hale opined that there remain 'important policy considerations justifying a different approach for agreements made before and after a marriage' (para. 162), but the majority disagreed.[5] It thus appears that pre-nuptial and post-nuptial contacts should no longer be distinguished.

[6] There are many post-*Radmacher* cases that you could consider, for example *BN v MA* [2013] EWHC 4250 (Fam), *M v W* [2014] EWHC 925 (Fam).

Post-*Radmacher* Cases[6]

Z v Z [2011] EWHC 2878 was the first case involving a pre-nuptial contract decided after *Radmacher*. It concerned a French couple who had signed a pre-nuptial agreement opting out of the French 'community of property' regime[7] and later moved to London. On separation,

[7] The community of property regime is a default regime, which provides that marital property is jointly owned. Couples can opt out of it.

the wife petitioned for financial relief, claiming an equal share of the assets worth £15 million, and child maintenance. The court accepted that the husband would not have married the wife unless she had signed a pre-nuptial agreement. It held that the contract had been entered into freely and that there were no circumstances prevailing at the time of the order that would make the agreement unfair. It was thus appropriate to depart from equal sharing, which would have

[8] The agreement dealt with property on divorce but not maintenance after divorce.

been ordered in the absence of the contract. As the agreement did not exclude maintenance, the court was able to make an award to meet the needs of the wife and children.[8] The court thus applied the principles established in *Radmacher*.

In *Kremen v Agrest* [2012] EWHC 45 (Fam), the principles established in *Radmacher* were applied to a post-nuptial contract entered into by a Russian couple. The agreement, which was highly disadvantageous to the wife, was accorded no weight as the wife had not received independent legal advice, she did not appreciate the implications of the agreement and the husband had failed to disclose the extent of his wealth. Consequently, an award was made to the wife

[9] Contrast the case of *Hopkins v Hopkins* [2015] EWHC 812 (Fam).

on a needs basis. Similarly, in *Gray v Work* [2015] EWHC 834 (Fam) no weight was attached to the post-nuptial agreement as the wife did not appreciate its implications.[9]

In *Luckwell v Limata* [2014] EWHC 502 (Fam), the court considered a pre-nuptial agreement (which was supplemented by post-nuptial agreements) restricting the husband's right to apply for financial relief. The wife's assets, namely £6.74 million equity in property registered in her sole name, had been provided by her wealthy father. The husband had freely entered into the agreements and had received legal advice. The High Court stated that great weight should be attached to the agreement and as a result, the husband received nothing based on contribution, compensation or sharing, but the terms of the contract were not strictly enforced because the husband was in real need of housing. The wife was thus ordered to provide £900,000 for the purchase of a property for the husband's use. When the youngest child reached the age of 22, the property would be sold and 45 per cent of the net proceeds would return to the wife. The High Court thus applied the principles established in ***Radmacher*** as it was fair and just to depart from the agreement.

The Law Commission Recommendations

[10] You could summarise the provisional recommendations made by the Law Commission in relation to marital agreements in 2011.

In January 2011, the Law Commission Consultation on Marital Property Agreements was launched (No. 198).[10] It was later extended to review the extent to which one spouse should be obliged to meet the other's needs after divorce and how the courts should treat non-marital property. The Law Commission Report 'Matrimonial Property, Needs and Agreements: The Future of Financial Orders on Divorce and Dissolution' 2014 (No. 343) recommends that 'qualifying nuptial agreements' are enforceable and not subject to the courts' assessment of fairness. In order to be 'qualifying' the agreement must: be contractually valid; be made by deed; contain a statement signed by both parties that they understand the binding nature of the agreement; not be made within the 28 days preceding the wedding. In addition, the parties must have made full disclosure and received legal advice before the contract was formed. The agreement cannot remove a spouse's right to apply for a financial order to meet their needs or those of any children. These recommendations were incorporated into the Law Commission's Draft Nuptial Agreements Bill, but it has not yet been presented to Parliament. As Parker indicates, Parliament will need to consider whether to recognise the autonomy of adults to determine their own future (2015, p. 80), but also 'whether allowing couples to contemplate a future separation would encourage divorce' is appropriate (2015, p. 79).

Conclusion

This essay has demonstrated that the law relating to pre- and post-nuptial agreements has developed considerably over the past 30 years. Originally, pre-nuptial contracts were void on the ground of public policy, but today pre- and post-nuptial contracts must be considered and are often of great significance. If the Draft Nuptial Agreements Bill becomes law, qualifying nuptial contracts will be binding.

LOOKING FOR EXTRA MARKS?

- Utilise the PEA method to ensure that you answer this essay question properly.

- Demonstrate the currency of your knowledge by referring to recent cases on pre-nuptial contracts, for example ***Luckwell v Limata*** **[2014] EWHC 502.**

QUESTION 4

Child support is primarily regulated by **the Child Support Act 1991** (as amended) but the courts continue to have a role to play in relation to financial support for children.
Evaluate this statement.

CAUTION!

- Do not attempt this question unless you have knowledge of **the Child Support Act 1991** *and* the role of the courts in terms of financial provision for children.

- It is not necessary to provide a detailed explanation of the old CSA schemes.

- You should be aware that there is very little case law on **the Child Support Act 1991** because cases rarely reach the courts.

DIAGRAM ANSWER PLAN

Explain the Child Support Act 1991 system of child maintenance

▼

Explain the amount payable under the CSA

▼

Discuss the enforcement of child support awards

▼

Discuss the jurisdiction of the courts under the Matrimonial Causes Act 1973

▼

Discuss the jurisdiction of the courts under Schedule 1 to the Children Act 1989

▼

Conclusion

SUGGESTED ANSWER

The Child Support Act 1991 introduced a statutory maintenance scheme based on a formula to (largely) replace the discretionary jurisdiction of the courts to order child support. Since the introduction of this scheme, the role of the courts has diminished considerably.

The CSA Scheme

The Child Support Act 1991 (as amended) enables a claim to be made to the Child Maintenance Service (CMS)[1] for a maintenance calculation.[2] In addition, the recipient can ask the CMS to collect the maintenance.[3] A claim can be made if the child is under the age of 16 or under 20 and in full-time, non-advanced education (**s.55 CSA 1991**). In addition, the child must be 'qualifying', which means that one (or both) of his parents is in relation to him, a non-resident parent (**s.3(1)(a)**). A non-resident parent is one who is not living in the same household as the child and the child has his home with a person who is in relation to him a person with care (**s.3(2)(a)**). The latter is defined as a person with whom the child has his home and who usually provides day-to-day care for the child (whether exclusively or in conjunction with any other person (**s.3(3)**). **Section 54** states that a parent is 'any person who is in law the mother or father of the child'. The Act thus imposes responsibilities on legal parents, but not on step-parents.

Parents are not obliged to use the CMS to calculate and collect maintenance: they are free to reach a maintenance agreement (**s.9(2) CSA 1991**). Indeed, the fees that have recently been introduced encourage parents to do so. Nevertheless, in December 2014 the CMS was handling approximately 1.3 million cases (DWP, 2014).

The Amount Payable

The initial scheme introduced by **the Child Support Act 1991** was extremely complex and was consequently replaced by the simpler 'net-income scheme' in March 2003. Although the net-income scheme continues to apply to some old cases, new applications are based on the non-resident parent's gross salary (introduced by **the Child Maintenance and Other Payments Act 2008**), so that the CMS can easily obtain information from HMRC. The basic rate[4] is 12 per cent, 16 per cent or 19 per cent of the non-resident parent's gross weekly income, for one child, two children and three or more children, respectively (**Schedule 1 Para. 2(1) CSA 1991**). These percentages apply to income up to £800 per week. If the non-resident parent earns more than £800, 9 per cent, 12 per cent and 15 per cent of the gross weekly income above £800 is payable in addition to the basic rate

[1] The Child Support Agency was established in 1991 and deals with old cases. The Child Maintenance Service administers the 2012 scheme.

[2] A £20 application fee applies.

[3] If maintenance is collected by the CMS, the non-resident parent must pay a 20 per cent collection fee for every payment. The recipient has 4 per cent deducted from the payments.

[4] A nil rate, flat rate or reduced rate will be payable in certain circumstances.

(**Schedule 1 Para. 2(2)**). This is subject to a maximum income of £3,000 (**Schedule 1 Para. 10(3)**), which means that the maximum payable using **the CSA** is £482 per week (plus fees).

The amount payable will be reduced by 11 per cent, 14 per cent or 16 per cent if the non-resident parent has another child or children living with him or her. Lowe and Douglas explain that this is 'an attempt to encourage non-resident parents to pay at least something by way of child support in the knowledge that at least their current family's needs are not being squeezed' (2015, p. 811). The amount payable will also be reduced if the parents share the care of the child/children, for example by 1/7 if the child stays with the non-resident parent 52–103 nights per year (**Schedule 1 Para. 7**). In addition, the amount payable may be altered by applying for a variation (**s.28A**).

Enforcement of CMS Awards

The CMS can take action to collect maintenance arrears if the recipient has requested collection, using a variety of enforcement mechanisms, for example deduction from earnings, regular deductions from bank accounts, lump sum deductions from bank accounts, liability orders, etc. In such cases, the recipient cannot take court action to enforce the award (**R v Secretary of State for Work and Pensions ex parte Kehoe [2005] UKHL 48**).

The Courts' Powers under the Matrimonial Causes Act

Section 8(1) and (**3**) of **the Child Support Act 1991** provide that where the CMS has jurisdiction to make a maintenance calculation, the courts do not have the power to make an award. The courts cannot therefore order maintenance for children during contested financial relief proceedings on divorce, nullity or judicial separation, but they can order periodical payments for children by consent under **the Matrimonial Causes Act 1973**.[5] Once a consent order is made, the court has the power to vary it. The courts can also make periodical payment orders for children if the CMS lacks jurisdiction, for example if the child is over the age of 16 and not in full-time education, if the non-resident parent, the person with care or the child are resident outside the UK or if the applicant's spouse is not the child's legal parent. In addition, the CMS only has the power to make a maintenance calculation. The courts can make lump sum orders, transfers and settlements for the benefit of a child under **the MCA 1973** during divorce proceedings, even if contested. When considering making an order under **the MCA 1973** the court will consider the factors contained in **s.25**. In 2011, the courts made approximately 14,000 orders in respect of children under **the MCA 1973** (Judicial and Court Statistics, 2012).

[5] Or **the Civil Partnership Act 2004**.

Schedule 1 to the Children Act 1989

Applications for financial orders for children can be made under **Schedule 1 to the Children Act 1989**. A parent, guardian, special guardian or person with residence[6] can apply for an order for periodical payments, a lump sum order, a settlement of property or a transfer of property order (**Schedule 1 Para. 1(1)**). An adult child can submit a claim him/herself under **Para. 2 Schedule 1**, which is not possible under **the Child Support Act 1991** or **the Matrimonial Causes Act 1973**. However, restrictions are imposed on this; for example, an order cannot be made if the parents are living together and the court cannot order a settlement of property.

[6] I.e. a person who has been granted a child arrangements order that states that the child should live with him/her—this was previously called a residence order.

Claims will be made under **the Children Act 1989**.[7] if the CMS does not have jurisdiction to make a calculation. In *B v B (Adult Student: Liability to Support)* [1998] 1 FLR 373, a claim was made by an adult child for maintenance from his father to support his further education,[8] whilst in *CF v KM* [2010] EWHC 1754 (Fam) an award was made to the mother to enable her to travel to see her child who had been abducted to Sudan. This was regarded as a financial order 'for the benefit of the child'. **The Children Act** can also be utilised to obtain lump sum orders, transfers or settlements, which the CMS cannot make. In *J v C (Child: Financial Provision)* [1999] 1 FLR 152, FD, the mother, who was living in a housing association property with the child and her half-sisters, made a claim against the father, who had won £1.4 million. The court ordered the father to provide £70,000 to purchase a house for the mother and children to live in. The capital would revert to the father when the child reached the age of 21 or six months after she finished full-time education. The father was also ordered to pay £12,000 to furnish the house and £9,000 to buy the mother a car. As Mehta points out, such claims are not restricted to situations where the non-resident parent is wealthy: they are also made where assets are modest but a lump sum or other order is required to meet the child's needs (2015). The difference between proceedings under **the Children Act 1989** and claims under **the Matrimonial Causes Act 1973** is that the latter are ancillary to divorce, nullity or judicial separation, whereas the parties to a **Children Act** claim may not have been married.[9]

[7] The purpose of this paragraph is to explain when an application can be made under the **Schedule 1 to the Children Act 1989**.

[8] The evidence is provided by the cases discussed in the paragraph, which show when **the Children Act** can be utilized.

[9] The paragraph concludes by comparing **Schedule 1 to the Children Act** and **the Matrimonial Causes Act 1973**.

When the courts are determining applications under **the Children Act 1989**, they are required by **Schedule 1 Para. 4(1)** to have regard to all the circumstances of the case,[10] including: the income, financial resources, financial needs and responsibilities of each parent; the financial needs of the child; the income, earning capacity, property and other financial resources of the child; any disability of the child; and the manner in which the child was being or was expected to be educated or trained. In addition, the courts have held that the parents'

[10] It is worth pointing out the similarities between this and **s.25 MCA 1973**.

standard of living (*F v G (Child: Financial Provision)* **[2004] EWHC 1848 (Fam)**) and the length of their relationship (*N v D* **[2008] 1 FLR 1629, FD**) are factors that can be considered. In 2011, the courts made 614 financial orders under **the Children Act** (Judicial and Court Statistics, 2012).

Top-up Maintenance

Under **s.8(6)** of **the Child Support Act 1991** a claim can be made to the courts for child maintenance if the CMS has made a maximum calculation (see *Dickson v Rennie* **[2014] EWHC 4306**). If the non-resident parent is wealthy, the person with care of the child may therefore obtain a maximum award from the CMS and top-up maintenance from the courts. Similar powers exist under **s.8(7)** and **(8)** to obtain a periodical payments order for the child's education or if the child has a disability.

Conclusion

The discussion above has demonstrated that the majority of child support cases are handled by the CMS. But the residual role of the courts is significant as it enables the making of orders that are not available under **the Child Support Act 1991** and in circumstances when the CMS lacks jurisdiction. This ensures that children's needs may be effectively met.

LOOKING FOR EXTRA MARKS?

- Utilise the PEA method to ensure that you answer this essay question well.
- Include data relating to the number of orders made by the courts and the number of cases dealt with by the Child Maintenance Service. This will help you to evaluate the role each plays in child support matters.

TAKING THINGS FURTHER

- Bendall, C. 'Some are more "equal" than others: Heteronormativity in the post-White era of financial remedies' (2014) Journal of Social Welfare and Family Law 36 (3) 260.

  Suggests that civil partnership dissolution presented an opportunity to challenge heteronormativity, but the first case dealing with financial remedies on the dissolution of a civil partnership (Lawrence v Gallagher) indicates that aspects of the normative framework are being applied to same-sex relationships.

- Gheera, M. 'Child support: When the non-resident parent lives abroad' (2014) House of Commons Standard Note SN/SP/3405.

Considers when the Child Support Agency has jurisdiction to make a child maintenance calculation and when it does not due to the fact that the potential payer is not resident in England and Wales.

- Ferguson, L. '*Wyatt v Vince*: The reality of individualised justice—Financial orders, forensic delay and access to justice' (2015) Child and Family Law Quarterly 195.

  Discusses the decision of the Supreme Court in Wyatt v Vince, *which held that the ex-wife was not barred from making a claim for financial relief 27 years after the marriage had ended.*

- Law Commission 'Matrimonial property, needs and agreements: The future of financial orders on divorce and dissolution' 2014 (Law Com No. 343).

  Recommended that the law relating to financial needs should be clarified through the provision of guidance by the Family Justice Council and recommended the introduction of qualifying nuptial agreements.

- Mehta, A. 'Schedule 1 to the Children Act 1989: Not just for WAGS' (2015) Family Law Week. http://www.familylawweek.co.uk.

  Argues that Schedule 1 to the Children Act 1989 is a powerful tool for meeting children's needs in a variety of circumstances.

- Parker, M. 'The draft Nuptial Agreements Bill and the abolition of the common law rule: 'Swept away or swept under the carpet?' (2015) Child and Family Law Quarterly 27 (1) 63.

  Examines the draft Nuptial Agreements Bill, considers whether it proposes to abolish the common law rule that invalidates agreements contemplating separation in the future and whether this should be the case.

- Skinner, C. 'Child maintenance reforms: Understanding fathers' expressive agency and the power of reciprocity' (2013) International Journal of Law, Policy and the Family 27 (2) 242.

  Argues that child maintenance policy is difficult because it involves the management of the competing interests of the state, the child and the parents.

- Thompson, S. 'Behind the veil: Company or family property' (2014) Journal of Social Welfare and Family Law 36 (2) 217.

  Considers the case of Prest v Petrodel Resources Ltd *[2013] UKSC 34, which determined whether Mr Prest's company resources could be transferred to the wife on divorce.*

- Woolridge, B. 'Nuptial agreements: The search for intention' (2015) Family Law week. http://www.familylawweek.co.uk.

  Reviews the approach of the courts to nuptial agreements since the decision of the Supreme Court in Radmacher v Granatino *[2010] UKSC 42.*

Online Resource Centre   www.oxfordtextbooks.co.uk/orc/qanda/

Go online for extra essay and problem questions, a glossary of key terms, online versions of all the answer plans and audio commentary on how selected ones were put together, and a range of podcasts which include advice on exam and coursework technique and advice for other assessment methods.

Parenthood and Parental Responsibility

7

ARE YOU READY?

In order to attempt the four questions in this chapter you will need to have covered the following topics:

- the difference between legal parenthood, genetic parentage and parental responsibility;
- common law presumptions relating to paternity and common law rules relating to parenthood;
- the acquisition of parenthood under **the Human Fertilisation and Embryology Act 2008**;
- the law relating to surrogacy;
- the attribution of parental responsibility under **the Children Act 1989**.

KEY DEBATES

Debate: Restrictions on legal parenthood

The law in England and Wales does not allow a child to have more than two legal parents. Do you agree with this approach? When lesbian couples have a child using artificial insemination, **the Human Fertilisation and Embryology Act 2008** states that the woman who carries the child is the legal mother and her partner or wife can be the 'other legal parent'. Should *both* women be designated as the child's mothers?

Debate: Unmarried fathers and parental responsibility

A father who is not married to the mother of his child does not automatically have parental responsibility for the child, although he can acquire it. Does this constitute an infringement of the father's human rights? Should the law be changed? Would it benefit the child?

Ellen is married to Frank and they have two children, Grace, aged six and Henry, aged three. Last year Ellen had an affair with Ian, a work colleague. Ellen ended the relationship when she found out that she was pregnant. She did not tell Ian that she was expecting a child, as she believed Frank to be the father. Shortly after the affair had ended, Ian left the company to work for another employer. Ellen did not tell Frank about her relationship with Ian and eight months ago, Jeremy was born. Last month Ellen, Frank and the children were out shopping when they passed Ian on the street. Ian noticed the baby and the following day sent a text message to Ellen asking her if he was the baby's father: he had realised that the baby would have been conceived at the time they were having an affair. Ellen replied that Frank was the father, but Ian did not believe her. He keeps sending her messages demanding to meet the baby, but Ellen has ignored them. Last week Ellen received a letter from Ian's solicitor asking Ellen to consent to a paternity test. The letter indicated that if Ian was found to be the father of the child, he would provide child support and apply to the court to be able to see the child on a regular basis. That day, Ellen confessed all to Frank. Frank stated that he is willing to forgive Ellen and to accept that Jeremy is his son, but if Jeremy is DNA tested and it transpires that Ian is his father, he will apply for divorce and will not have anything to do with Jeremy.

Advise Ellen as to who is considered to be Jeremy's father and whether the courts will order paternity tests.

N.B. You do not need to consider the applications that Ian might make under **the Children Act 1989**, child support or the law relating to divorce.

CAUTION!

- The case study upon which this question is based is lengthy and contains many facts—ensure that you read it carefully.

- As Ian is seeking a paternity test, it is not necessary to include case law relating to the refusal of putative fathers to supply samples, for example *Re A (A Minor) (Paternity: Refusal of Blood Test)* [1994] 2 FLR 463.

DIAGRAM ANSWER PLAN

Identify the issues	▪ Identify the legal issues ▪ Who is assumed to be Jeremy's father? ▪ Will tests be conducted to determine who is Jeremy's biological father?
Relevant law	▪ Outline the relevant law: ▪ Common law presumptions of paternity ▪ Applications for declarations of paternity—s.55A Family Law Act 1986 ▪ Scientific tests—s.20(1) Family Law Reform Act 1969 ▪ *Re H (A Minor) (Blood Tests: Parental Rights)* [1996], *Re H and A (Children)* [2002]
Apply the law	▪ Apply the law above to the scenario ▪ Determine who is the legal father of Jeremy ▪ Decide whether the courts would order scientific tests ▪ Consider the human rights implications
Conclude	▪ Conclusion ▪ Sum up the consequences of parenthood

SUGGESTED ANSWER

This question concerns paternity, which is important from a legal perspective, because under the common law, the genetic father of a child is treated as the legal father of that child. In this particular case, the paternity of Jeremy is in doubt and in order to ensure that he has a legal father, certain presumptions will apply until paternity is ascertained or in the event that paternity is never determined.[1]

[1] These presumptions were developed at a time when a finding of illegitimacy had severe consequences.

Presumptions

If a woman married to a man gives birth, it is presumed that her husband is the father of the child (***Banbury Peerage Case* (1811) 1 Sim & St 153**). This is known as '*pater est quem nuptiae demonstrant*' and applies even if conception took place prior to marriage, provided that the birth took place after the couple was married. As Ellen was married to Frank when Jeremy was conceived and when he was born, Frank is presumed to be his father (**Brierly v Brierly [1918] P257**). There is also a presumption that the man named on the birth certificate is the child's father. As Ellen and Frank were married when Jeremy was born, Frank would have been registered as his father (**s.2 Births and Deaths Registration Act 1953**). There is no conflict between this presumption and the *pater est* presumption in this particular case.[2]

[2] There may be conflict in other cases.

Rebutting the Presumptions

Ian can apply for a declaration of parentage under **s.55A of the Family Law Act 1986**, but will have to provide evidence to prove that he is the father. **Section 26 of the Family Law Reform Act 1969** states that the presumptions of paternity can be rebutted on the balance of probabilities.[3] According to Lord Reid, little evidence is required to rebut the presumptions because they are so weak (**S v S, W v Official Solicitor (or W) [1972] AC 24**). In this case, there is no immediate evidence to rebut the presumptions that Frank is Jeremy's father. It is therefore necessary to conduct scientific tests in order to rebut the presumption. As Ellen is unlikely to cooperate in this matter, Ian will have to bring the matter before the court.

[3] Prior to **the Family Law Reform Act 1969** it was necessary to establish beyond a reasonable doubt that the woman's husband was not the child's father.

Scientific Tests

The court is able to direct the use of scientific tests to ascertain parentage under **s.20(1) of the Family Law Reform Act 1969**. The court can make the direction of its own motion or upon application during civil proceedings. For example, if Ian applies to have contact with the child under **s.8 of the Children Act 1989**, the court could direct scientific tests (**Re E (Parental Responsibility: Blood Test) [1995] 1 FLR 392**).[4] The tests can only be carried out by a body which has been accredited for those purposes by the Lord Chancellor or a body appointed by him (**s.20(1A)**).

[4] Contact and residence orders have been replaced by Child Arrangement Orders, which deal with where the child will live and with whom he will have contact.

Ellen could consent to a sample being taken from Jeremy as she has 'care and control' of him (**s.21(3)(a)**), but as Ellen is unlikely to do so, the court would have to consent (**s.21(3)(b)**). It should be noted that **s.1 of the Children Act 1989**, which provides that the child's welfare is paramount, does not apply to decisions regarding DNA tests,[5] because the application does not concern the child's upbringing. This does not mean that the court does not consider the child's welfare, as **s.21(3)(b)**, provides that the court will consent to a sample being taken from a minor if it considers that it would be in his best interests. As the House of Lords explained in **S v S, W v Official Solicitor (or W) [1972] AC 24**, the court ought to permit the testing of a young child unless it would be against the child's interests. The court will

[5] See chapter 8.

often have to balance the child's right to know his or her genetic parents against the possibility that the family unit within which the child resides may be disrupted if it is found that the mother's current husband or partner is not the child's father.

In *Re H (A Minor) (Blood Tests: Parental Rights)* [1996] 2 FLR 65, the importance of knowing the truth was crucial. In this case, it was alleged that the woman's husband was not the father of her youngest child. Ward LJ indicated that a child has the right to know the truth and that concealing the truth is only permissible if it is in the child's interests. In support of this contention, Ward LJ referred to **art. 7** of **the UN Convention on the Rights of the Child**, which contains a right to know and be cared for by one's parents. The tests were consequently ordered, but it should be stressed that the child's relationship with his mother's husband was not likely to be affected by the tests.[6]

In certain cases, the courts have refused to order tests because of the impact that such tests would have on the family unit. For example, in *Re F (A Minor) (Blood Test: Parental Rights)* [1993] Fam 314 the Court of Appeal did not order tests because there was evidence that the mother's marriage would be harmed and the child's security would be impacted if the mother's husband was not the child's father. The court concluded that the advantages of a secure family unit outweighed the benefits of knowing the truth. The same conclusion was not reached in *Re H and A (Children)* [2002] EWCA Civ 383,[7] where the Court of Appeal directed tests due to the importance of ascertaining the truth, despite the fact that the woman's husband indicated that if the tests established that he was not the father of his wife's twins, he would leave his wife and the children.

In more recent cases, special circumstances existed that do not apply in Ellen and Ian's case. For example, in *J v C* [2006] **EWHC 2837 (Fam)** the person who alleged to be the child's father had disappeared since making the application and the mother's health would have been adversely affected by ordering the tests due to her vulnerability. The court refused to direct tests. In *L v P (Paternity Tests: Child's Objection)* [2011] **EWHC 3399 (Fam)**, the court refused to direct scientific tests as the child in question was a 15-year-old mature boy and he objected.[8]

The Approach of the ECHR

The European Court of Human Rights has also emphasised the importance of determining the truth. For example, in *Mikulic v Croatia* [2002] 1 FCR 720, the Court held that the right to respect for private and family life contained in **art. 8** of **the European Convention on Human Rights** encompasses the right of a child to know his or her

[6]In addition, the child was likely to become aware that there were doubts over his paternity because his two older brothers were cognisant of the fact.

[7]Why do you think these cases were decided differently?

[8]See also *Re D (Paternity)* [2006] EWHC 3545.

genetic parentage. However, the court has also pointed out that a balance has to be struck between the right to challenge presumptions of paternity and protecting legal certainty of family relations (***Shofman v Russia* [2005] 3 FCR 581**).

[9]See also **Ahrens v Germany (App No 45071/09)**, which was joined with ***Kautzor v Germany***.

In ***Kautzor v Germany* [2012] (App No 23338/09)**, the applicant believed himself to be the father of his former wife's daughter.[9] The child's mother, Ms D, lived with Mr E, who acknowledged paternity of the child. They later had two more children and married. Mr Kautzor was not permitted to challenge Mr E's status and the court refused to allow scientific tests to establish biological paternity, because both could harm the family unit. The European Court of Human Rights held that Mr Kautzor's relationship with the children did not fall within the scope of family life, contained in **art. 8** of the Convention, because there was no personal relationship between them. However, the decision not to allow them to challenge paternity fell within the scope of private life, also protected by **art. 8**. The Court proceeded to point out that a significant minority of nine member states do not permit a man to challenge another's paternity and as a result, there was no consensus amongst contracting states. The decision as to whether to permit paternity challenges thus fell within the state's margin of appreciation and as a consequence, the application was unsuccessful.

Application

The case law above seems to suggest that a court hearing an application from Ian would direct paternity tests to take place, despite the fact that Frank has threatened to divorce Ellen. This approach is consistent with **art. 8** of **the European Convention** as the European Court has clearly indicated that contracting states have a wide margin of appreciation in relation to such matters.

Conclusion

[10]The legal father of a child has an automatic right to apply for an order under **s.8** of **the Children Act 1989** (see chapter 8).

If Ian is found to be Jeremy's father, the court will then have to decide whether contact should be ordered.[10] The judge will also have to consider whether the child should be told who his biological father is and if so, when. For as the Court of Appeal indicated in ***Re F (Paternity: Jurisdiction)* [2007] EWCA Civ 873**, determining the disclosure of paternity results falls within the court's jurisdiction. It should therefore be emphasised that if DNA tests establish that Ian is Jeremy's father, it does not necessarily follow that Ian will have contact and that Jeremy will be told the truth. However, Ian will be liable to pay child support under **the Child Support Act 1991** regardless of the decision the court makes in relation to contact and the revelation of paternity.

LOOKING FOR EXTRA MARKS?

- Gain extra marks by including the jurisprudence of the European Court of Human Rights on this matter, for example *Ahrens v Germany* (App No 45071/09) March 2012.
- Utilise the IRAC method to ensure that you answer this problem question properly.

QUESTION | 2

How does the law assign parenthood when couples use sperm, egg or embryo donations to procreate?

CAUTION!

- The question asks how the law assigns parenthood in cases involving donations—in most cases **the Human Fertilisation and Embryology Act 2008** applies, but sometimes the old common law rules apply.
- The question refers to *couples* that use sperm, egg or embryo donations—it is important to discuss heterosexual and same-sex couples.

DIAGRAM ANSWER PLAN

Introduction

▼

Consider who is the legal mother when egg donations are used

▼

Consider who is the legal father when sperm donations are used

▼

Discuss the position in relation to DIY insemination

▼

Discuss IVF mix-ups

▼

Explain legal parenthood when same-sex couples utilise sperm donations

▼

Conclusion

When couples receive assisted reproduction services and utilise sperm, egg or embryo donations, the provisions of **the Human Fertilisation and Embryology Act 2008,** which replaced **the HFEA 1990,** will be applicable. The question is, who are the legal mother and father if sperm and egg donations are used?

The Legal Mother

Section 33(1) HFEA 2008 states that 'the woman who is carrying or has carried the child as a result of the placing in her of an embryo or of sperm and eggs, and no other woman, is to be treated as the mother of a child'. The egg donor is not therefore considered the legal mother even in surrogacy situations where the genetic mother is intended to act as the social parent. In such cases, legal parenthood can be transferred by the making of a parental order under **s.54** of the Act (or an adoption order under **the Adoption and Children Act 2002**). But until this happens, the woman who carried the child is the legal mother. **Section 33(1)** applies in relation to children carried as a result of insemination/implantation that took place after 5 April 2009, even if the woman was not in the UK (**s.33(3)**).[1] The identical provision of the 1990 Act applies where a woman was inseminated/implanted between 1 August 1991 and 5 April 2009. In relation to children born as a result of insemination/implantation that took place prior to 1 August 1991, the common law rule applies. This provides that the woman who gave birth to the child is the legal mother (*The Ampthill Peerage Case* [1977] AC 547). The law clearly gives priority to the woman who carries the child over the genetic mother.[2] As Baroness Hale explained in *Re G (Children) (Residence: Same-Sex Partner)* [2006] 1 FCR 436, 'while this may be partly for reasons for certainty and convenience, it also recognises a deeper truth: that the process of carrying a child and giving him birth brings with it, in the vast majority of cases, a very special relationship between mother and child' (para. 34).

The Legal Father

If a couple receive treatment at a licensed clinic, using a sperm donor, **s.41(1) HFEA 2008** provides that the sperm donor is not treated as the child's legal father. This does not mean that children born as a result of sperm donor insemination will always be fatherless, as the Act enables the mother's husband or partner to be treated as the child's legal father.

Section 35(1) states that if at the time of insemination/implantation, a woman is married to a man,[3] the woman's husband 'is to be treated

[1] It is not therefore necessary for the woman to receive treatment in a clinic licensed under the HFEA.

[2] In a coursework question, you would have time to consider whether this approach is appropriate.

[3] **Section 35** does not apply to same-sex marriages as it specifically deals with the assignment of legal fatherhood.

as the father of the child unless it is shown that he did not consent to the placing in her of the embryo or the sperm and eggs or to her artificial insemination'. This provision applies whether or not the woman was in the UK when the insemination took place. It replaced **s.28(2)** of the 1990 Act, which was almost identical. If the husband did not consent, the child will have no legal father.

If the woman is in a relationship with a man, but not married to him, **s.36** enables the male partner to be treated as the child's legal father if the requirements set out in **s.37** (the agreed fatherhood conditions) are satisfied. Under **s.37(1)(a)**, the man in question must give the person responsible at the clinic licensed under the Act a notice stating that he consents to being treated as the father of any child resulting from treatment provided to his partner, and the woman in question must give notice that she consents to her partner being treated as her child's father (**s.37(1)(b)**). In both cases, the notice must be in writing and signed by the parties (**s.37(2)**) and must not have been withdrawn (**s.37(1)(c)**). The woman must not have given a further notice indicating that she consents to another man being treated as the father of any resulting child or that she consents to a woman being treated as the other parent of any resulting child[4] (**s.37(1)(d)**) and the parties must not be within the prohibited degrees of relationship (**s.37(1)(e)**). This amended the position under **the 1990 Act, s.28(3)** of which provided that a male partner would be treated as the child's father if the woman was implanted or inseminated in the course of treatment services provided for her and the man together.[5] Proof of cohabitation was not required, as it does not follow that a couple were receiving treatment together simply because they cohabited (*Re Q (Parental Order)* **[1996] 1 FLR 369**). An example of receiving treatment together was attending the clinic together in the knowledge that donor sperm was to be utilised that day (*Re B (Parentage)* **[1996] 2 FLR 15**). The requirement to give written notice that was introduced by the 2008 Act avoids the need to determine whether a couple was receiving treatment together.

DIY Insemination

Section 35 applies whether or not treatment was received in a licensed clinic. If a married couple asks a male friend to provide sperm for self-insemination, the woman's husband will be treated as the legal father under **s.35** unless he did not consent. If he did not consent, the common law rule would apply, which provides that the genetic father is the legal father. The donor does not have the protection of **s.41 HFEA 2008**. However, **s.36**, which enables a woman's male partner to be treated as the father of a child created using donated sperm, only applies if the woman receives treatment at a licensed

[4] It is thus clear that the child can only have two legal parents.

[5] Consider the problems defining 'receiving treatment together'.

clinic (**s.36(b)**). If an unmarried woman self-inseminates using sperm donated by a male friend, her partner will not be treated as the legal father, even if he consented to the arrangement. The common law rule that the genetic father is the legal father will apply.

IVF Mix-ups

[6] This case did not involve 'sperm donors' as the couples were supposed to receive treatment utilising the husband's sperm. However, it demonstrates the limits of **s.35**.

Sections 35–37 HFEA 2008 do not apply to IVF mix-ups. In *Leeds Teaching Hospital NHS Trust v A* [2003] EWHC 259, two couples, one black and one white, were receiving treatment at the same time.[6] When Mrs A gave birth to mixed-race twins, it was evident that her eggs had been mixed with Mr B's sperm. The court held that Mr A could not be considered the father of his wife's children as he did not consent to the use of another man's sperm. Mr B could not claim the exemption contained in **s.28(6)(a)** of **the 1990 Act** (now **s.41(1)** of **the 2008 Act**) as he had not consented to his sperm being used to treat others. As none of the provisions of **the HFEA** were applicable, the common law rule, which provides that the genetic father is the legal father, was applied. Mr B was thus considered the legal father of Mrs A's twins.

Same-sex Couples[7]

[7] This paragraph considers legal parenthood in cases involving same-sex couples, which is primarily governed by **HFEA 2008**, as amended by **the Marriage (Same Sex Couples) Act 2013**.

Under **the 1990 Act** a woman could not be treated as the legal parent of a child born to her female partner even after **the Civil Partnership Act 2004** was passed. A lesbian couple could, however, be granted a joint residence order to reflect the social role that the mother's partner played. In 2006, the Department of Health concluded that reform was required 'to better recognize the wider range of people who seek and receive assisted reproduction' (*Review of the Human Fertilisation and Embryology Act* (2006) para. 2.67).

[8] See for example, *Re A (Joint Residence: Parental Responsibility)* [2008] EWCA Civ 867.

Section 42 of the 2008 Act as amended by **the Marriage (Same Sex Couples) Act 2013** provides that a woman's civil partner or wife will be treated as a legal parent unless it is shown that she did not consent to the treatment.[8] The mother's civil partner or wife is not technically the child's mother: she is a second legal parent. This is the case even if the wife or civil partner provided the egg used to create the embryo. However, this difference is a matter of terminology rather than a matter of substance.[9] Under **s.43** a woman's unregistered/unmarried partner can be treated as the other legal parent if the 'agreed female parenthood conditions' set out in **s.44** are satisfied. These provisions mirror the agreed fatherhood conditions set out in **s.37**.

[9] Discuss whether you think this approach is right.

Sections 42–44 HFEA indicate that when lesbian couples procreate utilising assisted reproduction services there will be a legal mother, a second legal parent but no legal father. **Section 42** applies whether or not treatment was received in a licensed clinic, just as **s.35** does. However, **ss.43–44** only apply if the woman received treatment at a licensed clinic. If a lesbian couple asks a friend to provide sperm for self-insemination, the legal mother's partner will not be treated as the second legal parent, even if she consented to the arrangement. As explained earlier in relation to unmarried heterosexual couples, the common law dictates that the sperm donor is the legal father. As Smith indicates, there 'is a lack of an appropriate framework to facilitate and regulate the use of known donors' (2013, p. 356).

Conclusion

The discussion above has demonstrated that the assignment of legal parenthood in situations where couples utilise sperm or egg donations is a complex matter and will depend upon a number of factors, such as whether the couple was married and whether treatment was received in a licensed clinic.

LOOKING FOR EXTRA MARKS?

- Gain extra marks by considering the limits of **s.35 HFEA**, for example IVF mix-ups.
- Give your opinion on the law; for example, do you agree that a woman's wife is not regarded in law as a *mother*?

QUESTION | 3

Analyse how the law assigns legal parenthood in cases involving surrogacy.

CAUTION!

- It is essential that you understand the status of a surrogacy agreement.
- An explanation of the law relating to parental orders contained in **s.54 Human Fertilisation and Embryology Act 2008** is also crucial. In addition, you should be aware of the alternatives to a parental order.

DIAGRAM ANSWER PLAN

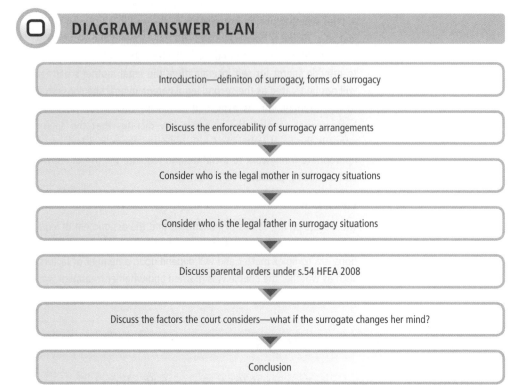

Introduction—definiton of surrogacy, forms of surrogacy

Discuss the enforceability of surrogacy arrangements

Consider who is the legal mother in surrogacy situations

Consider who is the legal father in surrogacy situations

Discuss parental orders under s.54 HFEA 2008

Discuss the factors the court considers—what if the surrogate changes her mind?

Conclusion

A **SUGGESTED ANSWER**

Section 1(2) of the Surrogacy Arrangements Act 1985 defines a surrogacy arrangement as one made by a woman (known as the surrogate or gestational mother) 'before she began to carry the child and made with a view to any child carried in pursuance of it being handed over to, and parental responsibility being met (so far as practicable) by another person or persons'. Surrogacy will be 'partial' if the surrogate mother is also the genetic mother, because her egg has been used to create the embryo. 'Full' or 'host' surrogacy occurs if the surrogate is implanted with an embryo created using the egg and sperm of the 'commissioning couple' (or donors or a combination of the two). In the latter case, assisted reproduction will be utilised, but in the former instance the pregnancy could come about due to assisted reproduction, self-insemination or sexual intercourse between the intended father and surrogate mother.

Enforcement of Surrogacy Agreements

Although surrogacy arrangements are permissible in England and Wales,[1] s.1A of the Surrogacy Arrangements Act 1985 states that

[1] N.B. it is a criminal offence for a third party to negotiate such arrangements on a commercial basis (s.2 Surrogacy Arrangements Act 1985).

a surrogacy agreement is unenforceable 'by or against any of the persons making it'. This means that if any of the parties change their mind, they cannot be compelled to go through with the arrangement. It also means that the parties cannot determine by prior agreement, the legal parenthood of any child born as a result of the arrangement.

The Legal Mother

A surrogate mother is treated as the legal mother of a child born as a result of a surrogacy arrangement under the common law and under **the Human Fertilisation and Embryology Act 2008. Section 33(1) HFEA** makes it clear that the woman who is carrying or has carried a child, and no other woman, is to be treated as the mother of the child and this is the case in full or partial surrogacy situations. The genetic link between the intended mother and a child is, therefore, irrelevant in terms of establishing legal motherhood.

The Legal Father

If the pregnancy results from sexual intercourse between the intended father and surrogate mother or self-insemination using the intended father's sperm, the common law provides that the genetic father is the legal father. Similarly, if the mother becomes pregnant having received treatment at a clinic, utilising the sperm of the intended father, the latter is the genetic and legal father. However, **s.35(1) HFEA 2008** states that if the woman is married to a man and the embryo was not brought about with the sperm of her husband, then the husband is treated as the father unless it is shown that he did not consent.[2] **Section 35** does not require the sperm to be donated by an anonymous party, nor does it require treatment to take place in a licensed clinic. It is assumed that **s.35** will rarely apply in surrogacy situations, as the surrogate mother will often be unmarried or her husband will not consent. The surrogate's male partner could also be treated as the child's legal father under **s.36**, but the agreed fatherhood conditions contained in **s.37** will rarely be satisfied.[3] In addition, treatment must be received in a licensed clinic, and as a result, **s.36** will not apply to cases of self-insemination.

If the genetic father is an anonymous sperm donor, the latter is not to be treated as the father of the child (**s.41(1) HFEA 2008**). This means that the child will have no legal father when it is born unless the surrogate's husband or partner is treated as the child's father under **ss.35** and **36**. If these provisions are not applicable, the child will only have one legal parent, i.e. the gestational mother.[4] This situation is unavoidable, for the law does not wish to assign parenthood to a sperm donor and cannot assign parenthood to the intended father at the point of birth, as the effect of this would be partial enforcement of the surrogacy agreement, possibly against the will of the mother.

[2] The surrogate's wife or civil partner could also be a legal parent under **s.42 HFEA**.

[3] A female partner could become a legal parent under **ss.43–44**, but the agreed female parenthood conditions will rarely apply.

[4] Unless the surrogate's civil partner/wife/female partner is considered the other legal parent as a result of **ss.42** or **43–44**.

Parental Orders

Although the common law and **HFEA** determine the legal parents at the point of birth, it is possible for legal parenthood to be transferred to the intended parents, by the court making a parental order. **Section 54(1) of the Human Fertilisation and Embryology Act 2008** indicates that an application must be made by two people who are a married couple, civil partners or 'two persons living as partners in an enduring family relationship'[5] who 'are not within prohibited degrees of relationship in relation to each other' (**s.54(2)**). In addition, both applicants must be over 18 when the order is made (**s.54(5)**).

[5]What do you think is meant by an 'enduring' relationship?

The court can only grant a parental order if the child carried by the surrogate resulted from artificial insemination (**s.54(1)(a)**). It is not therefore possible to make a parental order if the surrogate mother became pregnant as a result of sexual intercourse with the intended father. In such cases, the couple would have to pursue adoption or apply for parental responsibility and residence under **the Children Act 1989**, but the latter will not give the intended mother the status of legal parent. A parental order can only be made if 'the gametes of at least one of the applicants' were used to create the embryo (**s.54(1)(b)**). An order cannot therefore be made if an embryo is created using the surrogate's egg and an anonymous sperm donation, or sperm and egg donations. The requirement contained in **s.54(1)(b)** indicates that the law will only permit the transfer of parenthood if there is a genetic link between the child and the commissioning couple.[6]

[6]This emphasises the importance the law places on biological ties.

The application for a parental order must be made within six months of the child's birth (**s.54(3)**).[7] In addition, 'the child's home must be with the applicants' at the time of the application and the making of the order (**s.54(4)(a)**) and one or both parties must be domiciled in the UK (**s.54(4)(b)**). It is therefore clear, that a parental order will only be made if the child has actually been handed over to the commissioning couple and has continued to reside with them. A parental order cannot be used to compel the surrogate mother to transfer the child, which is confirmed by **s.54(6)**, which states that 'the woman who carried the child' must have freely and with full understanding of what is involved, agreed unconditionally to the making of the order. The consent of the mother is not effective if it is provided within the first six weeks (**s.54(7)**). **Section 54(6)** also requires the consent of 'any other person who is a parent of the child but is not one of the applicants', for example the surrogate's husband. The final requirement, contained in **s.54(8)** is that the court must be satisfied that no money (other than for reasonable expenses) has changed hands. In *Re S (Parental Order)* [2010] 1 FLR 1156, expenses totalling over £23,000 were considered legitimate because they were not greatly disproportionate to the expenses incurred and were not 'tainted with

[7]In **JP v LP and others (Surrogacy Arrangement: Wardship) [2014] EWHC 595 (Fam)**, the time limit was not complied with but wardship was utilised to resolve the issue.

bad faith'. The court was not therefore prevented from making a parental order under **s.54(8)**. Fenton-Glynn argues that the courts have adopted a liberal approach to reasonable expenses because they have focused on the best interests of the child (2015).

The Court's Decision

The court is not obliged to make a parental order simply because the requirements set out in **s.54** are satisfied. When making its decision the child's welfare is of paramount consideration and the court considers a checklist of factors listed in **s.1** of **the Adoption and Children Act 2002**.[8] The court can make alternative orders, for example under **s.8** of **the Children Act 1989**.[9] If the court does make a parental order, the effect of it is to vest parental responsibility exclusively with the applicants. It extinguishes the parenthood and parental responsibility of the gestational mother (and any other parent).

Although the court will not make a parental order if the surrogate mother does not consent, the court can order that the child lives with the commissioning parents if the surrogate mother changes her mind. In *Re P (Surrogacy: Residence)* **[2008] Fam Law 18**, the surrogate had told the intended father that she had miscarried and there was evidence that she had done the same to other men. When the father discovered that a child had been born, he and his wife applied for residence.[10] Their application was successful because the mother's psychological state was such that she would not be able to parent in the long term. In contrast, the commissioning couple in *CW v NT and another* **[2011] EWHC 33** were not granted residence of a child born as a result of a surrogacy arrangement. This was because the surrogate mother did not set out to deceive the couple: she genuinely changed her mind after the child was born. In addition, the child had formed an attachment to the surrogate mother and the mother was more likely to promote contact with the father than vice versa. Residence was therefore granted to the mother with contact to the father. The same decision was reached by the court in *Re TT (Surrogacy)* **[2011] EWHC 33 (Fam)**. Case law thus indicates that the courts will rarely grant residence to the commissioning couple if the surrogate mother changes her mind.

Conclusion

The provisions of **the Human Fertilisation and Embryology Act 2008** and the common law rules determine the legal parents of a child born as a result of a surrogacy arrangement, rather than the terms of the surrogacy agreement. However, **s.54** of the Act makes it possible to transfer parenthood to the commissioning couple, but only if the surrogate agrees.

[8] These factors apply as a result of **the Human Fertilisation and Embryology (Parental Orders) Regulations SI 2010/985**.

[9] The court might direct the local authority to conduct an investigation under **s.37** of **the Children Act**, which may result in an application for a care order.

[10] Today the application would be for a child arrangements order granting residence.

LOOKING FOR EXTRA MARKS?

- Utilise the PEA method to ensure that you answer this essay question well.
- Do not simply describe the rules regarding parenthood, but consider why they are in place and whether they are appropriate.
- Gain extra marks by referring to recent cases.

QUESTION | 4

Karl and Lauren started going out together when they were at school. Their relationship became more serious whilst they were in sixth form. In May 2007, Lauren became pregnant. In October of that year Karl went away to university and the couple split up soon after. Lauren gave birth to Melissa in February 2008. As Karl was away at university, he did not see his daughter until he returned home for the Easter holidays in April. Lauren refused to see Karl, as she felt that he had abandoned her while she was pregnant, but she allowed him to see Melissa, in her mother's presence. Since then Karl only saw Melissa during the university vacations. When Melissa was three years old, Lauren met Neil. They moved in together six months later and recently married. Karl has just returned to the area, having completed his university degree and secured a job with a large local business. He now wants to see Melissa regularly and wants to be involved in decisions regarding her upbringing. He feels that Neil should play no part in important decisions relating to Melissa, as he is not her biological or legal father. Lauren and Neil are happy for Karl to see more of Melissa, who knows that he is her father, but do not want him interfering with their decision-making.

Advise Karl in relation to this matter.

CAUTION!

- To answer this question you need to be able to advise Karl as to whether he has parental responsibility and if not, whether he can acquire it.
- In order to properly advise Karl, you need to be able to explain Neil's position.
- You also need to be able to discuss the scope and limits of parental responsibility.

DIAGRAM ANSWER PLAN

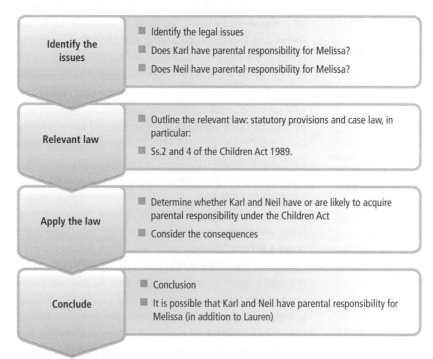

Identify the issues	■ Identify the legal issues ■ Does Karl have parental responsibility for Melissa? ■ Does Neil have parental responsibility for Melissa?
Relevant law	■ Outline the relevant law: statutory provisions and case law, in particular: ■ Ss.2 and 4 of the Children Act 1989.
Apply the law	■ Determine whether Karl and Neil have or are likely to acquire parental responsibility under the Children Act ■ Consider the consequences
Conclude	■ Conclusion ■ It is possible that Karl and Neil have parental responsibility for Melissa (in addition to Lauren)

SUGGESTED ANSWER

Karl is Melissa's legal father, which means that he has certain rights and responsibilities. For example, he has the right to apply for orders under **s.8** of **the Children Act 1989** and is liable for child support under **the Child Support Act 1991**. But this does not necessarily mean that he has the right to make decisions relating to her upbringing, as the latter depends upon whether he has parental responsibility. **Section 3(1)** defines parental responsibility as 'all the rights, duties, powers, responsibilities and authority which by law a parent of a child has in relation to the child and his property'. It includes the right to make decisions regarding the child's residence, education, medical treatment and religious upbringing.

Who has Parental Responsibility?

[1] **Section 2(1)** also applies if the parents married after the birth.

If Karl and Lauren had been married when Melissa was born, both parents would have had parental responsibility under **s.2(1)**.[1] But as they were not, **s.2(2)** applies, which provides that 'the mother shall have parental responsibility for the child' and that 'the father shall

[2] This provision makes it clear that acquired PR can be terminated (by the court). In contrast, automatic PR under **s.2(1)** cannot be terminated.

[3] Consider the impact that **the Registration of Births (Parents Not Married And Not Acting Together) Regulations 2010** would have had, if it had come into force.

[4] Consider why these formalities are required.

[5] See chapter 8 for more detail.

have parental responsibility for the child if he has acquired it (and has not ceased to have it).[2] **Section 4** indicates that a father can acquire parental responsibility in three ways. First, a father will acquire parental responsibility by being 'registered as the child's father' under **the Births and Deaths Registration Act 1953**. This provision was inserted by **the Adoption and Children Act 2002** and came into effect on 1 December 2003. In 2011, only 6 per cent of births were registered by the mother alone, which means that the vast majority of fathers who are not married to their child's mother have parental responsibility (ONS, 2013). It is unlikely that Karl acquired parental responsibility under **s.4(1)(a)** given that he and Lauren had separated at this point. This is because joint registration of a birth requires the mother's cooperation[3] and the case study indicates that Lauren refused to see Karl when Melissa was born.

The second means of acquiring parental responsibility is by the father and mother entering into a parental responsibility agreement under **s.4(1)(b)**. The agreement must be in the form prescribed by regulations made by the Lord Chancellor (**s.4(2)(a)**) and filed in the Principal Registry of the Family Division.[4] As Karl and Lauren separated before Melissa was born and Karl saw Melissa infrequently, it is highly unlikely that Lauren would have agreed to Karl acquiring parental responsibility in the past. As she is now married to Neil and they do not want Karl to interfere with their decision-making, Lauren is even less likely to enter into a parental responsibility agreement with him.

Parental Responsibility Orders

The only option available to Karl is to apply to the court for a parental responsibility order under **s.4(1)(c)**. When the court hears an application it will consider whether the father has demonstrated commitment to the child, his reasons for seeking the order and whether parental responsibility would be misused. However, 'the child's welfare shall be the court's paramount consideration' under **s.1** of the Act, as the court emphasised in *Re M (Contact: Parental Responsibility)* **[2001] 2 FLR 342**. As the application is likely to be opposed by Lauren, **s.1(4)** requires the court to have regard to the circumstances mentioned in **s.1(3)**.[5] This is known as the welfare checklist and includes matters such as the needs of the child and the capability of each of the parents in terms of meeting those needs. The 'non-intervention principle' contained in **s.1(5)** also applies, which means that the court will only make an order if 'doing so would be better for the child than making no order at all'. A parental responsibility order has been refused in cases where the father was violent towards the mother (*Re G (Domestic Violence)* **[2000]**

1 FLR 865 FD), where contact was very limited (*Re D (Parental Responsibility: IVF baby)* [2001] FLR 230 CA) and where the father lacked the mental capacity to exercise parental responsibility (*M v M (Parental Responsibility)* [1999] 2 FLR 737). However, hostility between the parents (*Re J-S (Parental Responsibility Order)* [2003] 1 FLR 399) and non-payment of regular maintenance (*Re H (Parental Responsibility: Maintenance)* [1996] 1 FLR 867 CA) have not prevented the making of an order. It is thus possible that the court would make a parental responsibility order in Karl's favour as he has maintained contact with Melissa and there was a genuine reason why it could not be more frequent.

If the court refuses to grant the order, Karl will not be entitled to make decisions regarding Melissa's upbringing. But if he disagrees with a decision that Lauren has made or wishes to make he can apply for a prohibited steps order or specific issue order under **s.8** of **the Children Act 1989**.[6] Applications for such orders should be made to resolve one-off issues, rather than on-going issues. In *Re N (Section 91(14) Order)* [1996] 1 FLR 356, the court used **s.91(14)** of **the Children Act 1989** to bar the father from making further applications without leave, because he was continually initiating proceedings regarding his child and often the application related to trivial matters. In extreme cases involving continual litigation, a judge might make the child a ward of the court and treat the parents as forfeiting their parental responsibility, as in *Wardship: T v S (Wardship)* [2011] EWHC 1608 (Fam).

Other Options

It should be noted that an application for a parental responsibility order constitutes family proceedings, which means that the court could make any **s.8** order instead of a parental responsibility order if the interests of the child so requires. In this case, the court might make a child arrangements order granting residence to Lauren,[7] in addition to making a parental responsibility order in favour of Karl, if it was concerned that Karl might interfere with day-to-day parenting. This is because **s.2(8)** provides that 'the fact that a person has parental responsibility for a child shall not entitle him to act in any way which would be incompatible with any order made with respect to the child under this Act'. For example, Karl could not remove Melissa from the country without the consent of Lauren or take steps to remove Melissa from the nearby school.

Exercising Parental Responsibility

Section 2(7) of **the Children Act 1989** provides that 'where more than one person has parental responsibility for a child, each of them may act alone and without the other (or others) in meeting that responsibility'.[8]

[6] A MIAM would be required, but whether mediation would be successful is questionable.

[7] A child arrangements order is made under **s.8** of **the Children Act 1989**—it replaced residence orders and contact orders.

[8] It should also be noted that there are enactments that require the consent of all persons with parental responsibility, for example **s.3** of **the Marriage Act 1949**.

This means that when Melissa is with Karl he can make decisions relating to her without having to consult Lauren and vice versa. Despite this, case law has suggested that certain steps should not be taken without consulting the other parent with parental responsibility, for

example education (*Re G (Parental Responsibility: Education)* **[1994] 2 FLR 964 CA**).[9] If the parents cannot reach consensus, an application may be made to the court for a specific issue order.

Neil's Position

Karl needs to be advised that Neil may already have or may acquire parental responsibility for Melissa, as he is her step-father.

[10] Inserted by **the Adoption and Children Act 2002.**

Section 4A(1) of **the Children Act 1989**[10] provides that 'where a child's parent ('parent A') who has parental responsibility for the child is married to or a civil partner of, a person who is not the child's parent ('the step-parent')—parent A or, if the other parent of the child also has parental responsibility for the child, both parents may by agreement with the step-parent provide for the step-parent to have parental responsibility for the child' (**s.4A(1)(a)**). Lauren can therefore enter into a parental responsibility agreement with Neil and as Karl does not currently have parental responsibility, his consent is not necessary. Indeed, Lauren may have already have done so. Alternatively, Neil can acquire parental responsibility by order of the court under **s.4A(1)(b)** but such an application is unlikely, given the fact that Neil can readily acquire PR by entering into an agreement with Lauren. Neil will also acquire parental responsibility if a child arrangements order is made providing that Melissa should reside with Lauren and Neil (**s.12(2)**).

As explained above, an application for a parental responsibility order constitutes family proceedings, which means that the court can make any **s.8** order, such as a child arrangements order, as an alternative to or in addition to the requested order. The court hearing an application from Karl might therefore grant a child arrangements order with residence in favour of Lauren and Neil, which will mean that Neil has parental responsibility for Melissa. It should be noted that it is possible for the court to grant parental responsibility to Neil and Karl, which would mean that both Melissa's parents and her step father have parental responsibility for her. This occurred in *T v T* [2010] **EWCA Civ 1366.**[11]

Conclusion

The answer above has demonstrated that parental responsibility is a complex legal issue, particularly in cases where the parents were not married when the child was born and where the child has a step-parent. It is possible that Lauren, Karl *and* Neil could have parental responsibility for Melissa, in which case they will have to manage decision-making on an on-going basis and if disputes arise, they may have to resort to litigation.

LOOKING FOR EXTRA MARKS?

- Utilise the IRAC method to ensure that you answer this problem question properly.
- Gain extra marks by including statistics regarding joint registration of births, etc.

TAKING THINGS FURTHER

- Bainham and Gilmore, S. *Children—The Modern Law* (2013) Jordans Publishing.
  Contains a thorough review of the law relating to children including, parenthood, parental responsibility and surrogacy.

- Brown, A. 'Re G; Re Z (Children: sperm donors: Leave to apply for Children Act orders); essential "biological fathers" and invisible "legal parents"' (2014) Child and Family Law Quarterly 26 (2) 237.
  Considers the case of Re G; Re Z *and in the light of the decision argues that the model of the traditional nuclear family, involving gendered roles continues to be applied by the courts.*

- Fenton-Glynn, C. 'The regulation and recognition of surrogacy under English law: An overview of case-law' (2015) Child and Family Law Quarterly 27 (1) 83.
  Argues that case law demonstrates that there is a conflict between the enforcement of statutory provisions and the welfare of the child (when deciding whether to authorise surrogacy arrangements).

- Gheera, M. 'Parental responsibility' (2014) House of Commons Standard Note SN/SP/2827.
  Explains the current law relating to the attribution and acquisition of parental responsibility under the Children Act 1989.

- Smith, L. 'Tangling the web of legal parenthood: Legal responses to the use of known donors in lesbian parenting arrangements' (2013) Legal Studies 33 (3) 355.
  Explores cases involving disputes between lesbian parents and known donors and considers some of the possible legal responses.

- Stoll, J. *Surrogacy and Legal Parenthood* (2013) Uppsala Universitet.
  Compares the law of surrogacy in Sweden with the law in a variety of jurisdictions, including England and Wales.

- Welstead, M. 'The battle for parenthood—lesbian mothers and biological fathers', in Atkin, B. (ed.), *International Survey of Family Law 2014 Edition*, International Society of Family Law 97.
  Explores recent case law relating to disputes between lesbian parents and the male biological fathers of their children.

Online Resource Centre   http://www.oxfordtextbooks.co.uk/orc/qanda/

Go online for extra essay and problem questions, a glossary of key terms, online versions of all the answer plans and audio commentary on how selected ones were put together, and a range of podcasts which include advice on exam and coursework technique and advice for other assessment methods.

The Law Relating to Children: Children's Rights and Private Law

ARE YOU READY?

In order to attempt the four questions in this chapter you will need to have covered the following topics:

- the rights of the child: **Gillick** competence; restrictions on the capacity of children to make decisions and the voice of the child in legal proceedings;
- the general principles of **the Children Act 1989**: the welfare principle, the no-order principle, the no-delay principle and the presumption of involvement;
- **Section 8** orders: child arrangements orders, prohibited steps orders, specific issue orders;
- the inherent jurisdiction of the High Court.

KEY DEBATES

Debate: The rights of the child in England and Wales

Does the law in England and Wales have sufficient regard to the rights of the child? The United Kingdom has ratified the United Nations Convention on the Rights of the Child (UNCRC), but has not incorporated it into UK law. However, in 2011 the Welsh Assembly passed the Rights of Children and Young People (Wales) Measure, which requires Welsh Ministers to have regard to the rights and obligations in the UNCRC. Should the UK incorporate the Convention? What difference would this make?

Debate: The legislative presumption of parental involvement and shared care

The introduction of a legislative presumption of parental involvement was the subject of much debate. Do you think it was appropriate to include a presumption in **the Children Act 1989**? Will it result in more instances of shared care and should shared care be the norm?

QUESTION | 1

Analyse the rights of a child to make his or her own decisions and to participate in private law proceedings under **the Children Act 1989**.

CAUTION!

- Do not attempt the question unless you have sufficient knowledge and understanding of both areas, i.e. decision-making and participation in private law proceedings under **the Children Act 1989**.

- You do not have to consider public law proceedings in the second part of the question.

DIAGRAM ANSWER PLAN

> Define a child

> ▼

> Discuss *Gillick* competence

> ▼

> Explain the limitations placed on the right of a child to make his/her own decisions

> ▼

> Explain the right of a child to initiate private law proceedings and the part the child plays in proceedings that concern him

> ▼

> Discuss the importance of the child's views and consider how they are communicated during private law proceedings

> ▼

> Conclusion

SUGGESTED ANSWER

[1]The UN Convention on the Rights of the Child defines a child as a person under the age of 18, unless majority is reached earlier.

Since **the Family Law Reform Act 1969,** a child is a person under the age of 18[1] and those with parental responsibility technically retain 'authority' until majority is reached. But in *Gillick v West Norfolk and Wisbech Area Health Authority* [1986] 1 FLR 224, the House of Lords held that a child will have the right to make his own decisions when 'he reaches a sufficient understanding and intelligence to be capable of making up his own mind' (Lord Scarman at p.186). The case concerned contraceptive advice and treatment,[2] which according to a Department of Health Notice, could be provided to girls under 16 in exceptional circumstances. The House of Lords declared that if a doctor felt that such advice was in the child's best interests and she was of sufficient intelligence and maturity, then the doctor could provide treatment without the parent's consent. It should be noted that s.8(1) of **the Family Law Reform Act 1969** provides that a minor who has attained the age of 16 can consent to medical treatment[3] and in such cases, it is not necessary to also obtain parental consent. However, children under 16 would have to establish *Gillick* competence to consent to medical treatment. In *An NHS Trust v A, B and C and A Local Authority* **[2014] EWHC 1445 (Fam)**, a 13-year-old girl was competent to consent to an abortion.

[2] It is worth pointing out that *Gillick* was applied in *R (Axon) v Secretary of State for Health and the Family Planning Association* [2006] 2 FLR 206.

[3] Although **s.44(7) Children Act 1989** provides that a competent child may 'refuse to submit' to an examination or assessment, this does not extend to treatment itself.

Refusing Medical Treatment[4]

[4] Emma Cave discusses the issues associated with the *Gillick* decision (see Taking Things Further).

Gillick and **s.8(1)** enable children to consent to medical treatment, but can they refuse it? Medical treatment can be provided against the will of a mature minor, if a person with parental responsibility consents, and in such cases it is not necessary to bring the matter before the court (*Re K, W and H (Minors) (Medical Treatment)* **[1993] 1 FLR 854**). However, a doctor may prefer to obtain the court's authorisation before treating a minor in such circumstances. If a child requiring treatment does not consent to it and those with parental responsibility for him do not consent either, it is essential to bring the matter before the court if treatment is to proceed. In both cases, the court can override a minor's refusal to consent. For example, in *Re M (Medical Treatment: Consent)* **[1999] 2 FLR 1097** the court authorised a life-saving heart transplant to be performed on a 15-year-old, intelligent girl, despite the fact that she did not wish to have the operation. Urgent life-saving medical treatment is usually authorised by the High Court exercising inherent jurisdiction. As the Court of Appeal pointed out in *Re W (A Minor) (Medical Treatment: Court's Jurisdiction)* **[1993] Fam 64**, neither *Gillick* nor **s.8** provide a right to veto medical treatment. According to Hedley J in *L v P (Paternity Test: Child's Objection)* **[2011] EWHC 3399 (Fam)**, a refusal of consent 'triggers the issue of welfare' (at para. [17]). The judge will therefore have to decide whether treatment is in the child's best interests.

Other Restrictions on Decision-making[5]

[5] Try to consider why these restrictions are in place.

There are further statutory restrictions on a child's ability to make decisions. For example, **s.7** of **the Wills Act 1857** provides that a person must normally have reached the age of 18 to make a will. In addition, a child cannot make an enforceable contract (**Minors Contracts Act 1987**) and cannot purchase tobacco (**Children and Young Persons (Sale of Tobacco etc.) Order 2007 (SI 2007/767)** or alcohol (**Licensing Act 1964**). Furthermore, 16- and 17-year- olds require parental consent to marry (**s.3 Marriage Act 1949**). *Gillick* competence does not apply to situations where a statute expressly restricts the ability of a child to do something.

The Child's Right to Initiate Proceedings

[6] Rule16.6 of the Family Procedure Rules 2010 allows competent children to commence proceedings without a litigation friend.

If there is a disagreement between a child and his parents, it is possible for the child to instruct a solicitor to make an application under **s. 8 of the Children Act 1989** to have the matter resolved.[6] A child does not have an automatic right to apply for **s.8** orders (i.e. specific issue, prohibited steps and child arrangements orders), but can do so with leave of the court (**s.10)(1)(a)(ii)**). **Section 10(8)** provides that where an application is made by a child, the court must be satisfied that he is of sufficient understanding, which is assessed in the light of the complexity and gravity of the particular issue. Even if a child is of sufficient understanding, the court has a discretion to refuse leave (*Re C (A Minor) (Leave to Seek Section 8 Order)* [1994] 1 FLR 26 FD) and the court will consider the likelihood of the substantive application succeeding when determining the matter (*Re J (Leave to issue application for residence order)* [2002] EWCA Civ 1346). In *Re C (A Minor) (Leave to Seek Section 8 Order)* [1994] 1 FLR 26 FD, a 15-year-old girl requested leave to apply for a **s.8** order to allow her to go on holiday with her friend's family. The court rejected the application because the nature of the substantive application was too trivial to litigate and because a child should not be given the impression that she has won a victory over her parents.

[7] This paragraph explains the role a child plays in proceedings that concern him. Only in exceptional cases will a child be party to proceedings and separately represented.

Participation in Proceedings[7]

In proceedings under **s.8** the child concerned is not normally party to the proceedings and will not be separately represented. However, in *Re C (A Child)* [2011] EWCA Civ 261 the Court of Appeal held that the 12-year-old child should be joined as party[8] and separately represented to ensure that someone put forward the child's views independently of both parents, but this is an exceptional case.

[8] Rule16.2 of the Family Procedure Rules 2010 allows the court to make a child party if it is in the best interests of the child to do so.

Despite this, the Family Justice Review Final Report recommends greater involvement in family proceedings. Children and young people should 'be given age appropriate information which explains what is happening when they are included in disputes' and should 'as early as possible in a case be supported to be able to make their views known and older children should be offered a menu of options, to lay out the ways in which they could—if they wish—do this' (2011, p. 45).

The Child's Views

Section 1(1) of **the Children Act 1989** states that when a court determines a question regarding the upbringing of a child, 'the child's welfare shall be the court's paramount consideration'. If a private law application under **s.8** is opposed, as many are, **s.1(4)** requires the court to have regard to the welfare checklist. The first factor is the ascertainable wishes and feelings of the child considered in the light of his age and understanding (**s.1(3)(a)**). This is consistent with **art. 12** of **the UN Convention on the Rights of the Child 1989**, which proclaims the right 'of the child who is capable of forming his or her own views to express those views freely in all matters affecting the child, the views of the child being given due weight in accordance with the age and maturity of the child'. Although the child's wishes are the first factor on the list, it does not have priority over other factors, which include: the child's needs, the likely effect of change and his age, sex and background. Ultimately, the court's decision will be based on the child's welfare rather than his wishes.[9]

When determining how much weight to attach to a child's wishes, his age will clearly be crucial. In *Re S (Contact: Children's Views)* **[2002] EWHC 540**, a father sought contact with his three children aged 16, 14 and 12. It was held that it would be pointless to order contact with the eldest child as he was opposed to it, but contact with the middle son was ordered by common agreement. In relation to the youngest boy, who had maintained most contact with his father, the order allowed him some choice, commensurate with his age, about the form it should take. But the age and maturity of the child is not the only factor to consider when deciding how much weight should be given to the child's views. The court must also take into account the importance of the issue, the possibility that pressure has been placed on the child by a parent and the harm that may be caused if a child is asked to choose between parents.

Communicating the Child's Views

In private law proceedings the court will usually learn of the child's views through a welfare report, which can be ordered under **s.7** of **the Children Act 1989**. The court can ask the local authority[10] or CAFCASS[11] to prepare a report and in the latter case, the report is prepared by a Children and Family Reporter. The duty of the reporter is to comment on the child's welfare, but this will involve an investigation of the child's views. Although it is possible for the judge to interview the child, many cases are resolved without this happening. The judge

[9] Do you agree with this?

[10] It is not common practice for the local authority to be asked in private law proceedings.

[11] CAFCASS is the Children and Family Court Advisory and Support Service. In Wales it is CAFCASS (Cymru).

has discretion as to whether to meet the child, but when exercising this discretion he must consider the '*Guidelines for Judges Meeting Children who are Subject to Family Proceedings*' issued by the Family Justice Council in 2010. In 2014, the Minister of State for Justice and Civil Liberties announced that children aged ten should have the opportunity to communicate their views to a judge (or in another way if they prefer). Ewing et al. consider the Government's interest in the voice of the child in private law proceedings to be 'somewhat ironic' given that its policies discourage court proceedings in private law matters (2015, p. 44).

Conclusion

The discussion above has demonstrated that the law recognises the rights of mature children to make *certain* decisions and to have their views taken into account during private legal proceedings that relate to them, but they are not determinative.

➕ LOOKING FOR EXTRA MARKS?

- Refer to international law instruments such as **the UN Convention on the Rights of the Child**.
- Gain extra marks by considering the reasons for enforcing or restricting children's rights.

ⓠ QUESTION | 2

'In private law we of course believe strongly that most children benefit from a relationship with both parents post separation.'

David Norgrove, Chair of the Family Justice Review, Foreword to the Final Report, 2011, p. 4.

Discuss how the Children Act 1989 (as amended) helps to ensure that children have a relationship with both parents post separation.

❗ CAUTION!

- You do not need to know a great deal about the Family Justice Review to answer this question in an examination—the purpose of the question is to assess whether the law reflects the viewpoint expressed in the question.
- You need to discuss child arrangements orders as they enable children to have a relationship with their parents.

DIAGRAM ANSWER PLAN

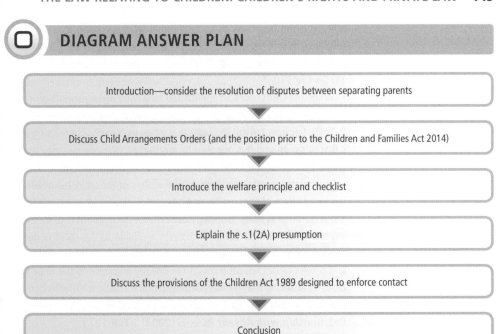

Introduction—consider the resolution of disputes between separating parents

⬇

Discuss Child Arrangements Orders (and the position prior to the Children and Families Act 2014)

⬇

Introduce the welfare principle and checklist

⬇

Explain the s.1(2A) presumption

⬇

Discuss the provisions of the Children Act 1989 designed to enforce contact

⬇

Conclusion

A) SUGGESTED ANSWER

[1] **Section 41 MCA 1973**, which required divorcing parents to present a statement of arrangements to the court, was repealed by **the Children and Families Act 2014**.

When parents separate, arrangements will need to be made relating to their children.[1] If they cannot determine this amicably, an application may be made to the court under **s.8** of **the Children Act 1989**, but first, the applicant must attend a Mediation Information and Assessment Meeting (unless exempt from doing so). The matter may be referred to the court if mediation is unsuitable or unsuccessful. A parent can apply for a **s.8** order without the need to obtain leave of the court, which recognises the significance attached to the parent/child relationship (**s.10(4)**).

Child Arrangements Orders

[2] This implemented the recommendations of the Family Justice Review.

Prior to **the Children and Families Act 2014** arrangements relating to children were determined by contact and residence orders,[2] but these have been replaced by the child arrangements order. **Section 8(1)** of **the Children Act 1989** (as amended) defines a child arrangements order as an order regulating 'a) with whom the child is to live, spend time or otherwise have contact, and b) when a child is to live, spend time or otherwise have contact with any person'. Making a child arrangements order is thought to be less emotive than granting residence to one parent and contact to the other. In addition, if a child is to spend some nights with one parent and some nights with the

[3] In *Re W*, the Court of Appeal held that an order that provided that the child would spend 25 per cent of his time with his father was a shared residence order.

other, it is not necessary to consider whether this constitutes shared residence or sole residence to one parent with staying contact, as was previously the case (see *Re W (Shared Residence Orders)* [2009] **EWCA Civ 370**).[3]

When the court hears an application for a child arrangements order 'the child's welfare shall be the court's paramount consideration' (**s.1(1)**). **Section 1(4)(a)** indicates that when the court is considering a **s.8** application and it is opposed by any party to the proceedings, the welfare checklist, contained in **s.1(3)** must be considered. The checklist contains seven factors, namely; the wishes of the child; his needs; the likely effect of change; his age, sex and background; any harm he has suffered or is likely to suffer; how capable each parent is of meeting his needs; and the range of powers available to the court under the Act.

[4] The data and case law demonstrate that the courts considered it important for a child to have a relationship with both parents prior to **the 2014 Act**.

When applying the welfare principle and checklist to contact and residence disputes the courts continually emphasised the importance of ensuring that a child has a continuing relationship with both parents.[4] As Butler-Sloss P explained in *Re S (Contact: Promoting Relationship with Absent Parent)* [2004] 1 FLR 1279:

no parent is perfect but 'good enough parents' should have a relationship with their children for their own benefit and even more in the best interests of the children. It is therefore, most important that the attempt to promote contact between a child and the non-residential parent should not be abandoned until it is clear that the child will not benefit from the continuing attempt (at 32).

In 2010, contact orders were made in relation to 95,460 children. Contact was refused in relation to 300 children and a no-contact order was made in relation to 840 (Judicial and Court Statistics, 2011, p. 52). It is therefore unusual for the court to prohibit any form of contact. The approach of the courts is consistent with that of the European Court of Human Rights, which has emphasised that contact between parent and child is a fundamental element of family life (*Kosmopolou v Greece* [2004] 1 FLR 800).

In addition, the courts have stressed that there is no presumption that children should live with their mother, as *Re H (A Child)* [2011] **EWCA Civ 762** demonstrates. In this case, a residence order was made in favour of the 11-year-old girl's father, because she wanted to live with him. The order ensured that the child would continue to have a relationship with both parents, because the girl indicated that she was only prepared to have contact with her mother if she lived with her father.

The s.1(2A) Presumption

Following **the Children and Families Act 2014**, **s.1(2A)** of **the Children Act 1989** states that when the court is considering making a parental responsibility order or a contested **s.8** order the court must 'presume, unless the contrary is shown, that involvement of [each relevant] parent in the life of the child concerned will further the child's welfare'. Involvement means 'involvement of some kind, either direct or indirect, but not any particular division of a child's time' (**s.1(2B)**). The sentiment expressed by David Norgrove has thus been encapsulated into a legislative presumption; however, the Family Justice Review Final Report did not actually recommend this. But because of the 'alleged' bias against fathers,[5] the Government felt the need to clarify the law and thus issued the Consultation Paper: 'Co-operative Parenting Following Family Separation: Proposed Legislation on the Involvement of Both Parents in a Child's Life' (TSO, 2012). The Government came to the conclusion that the best way to achieve the aim expressed by Norgrove was to include a presumption to this effect in **the Children Act 1989.** Whether a legislative presumption is appropriate has been the subject of much debate.[6] For example, there is a fear that the presumption of involvement will be interpreted by parents as a right to involvement. This seems to have occurred in Australia and may impact on children's welfare (see Kaspiew et al., 2006).[7]

The presumption contained in **s.1(2A)** only applies in relation to a relevant parent, which is defined as a parent that 'can be involved in the child's life in a way that does not put the child at risk of suffering harm' (**s.1(6)**). Cases such as *Re T (A Child: Murdered Parent)* **[2011] EWHC B4 (Fam)**, would not therefore be decided differently today. In *Re T*, the father had caused the death of the child's mother when she was two years old. The child lived with her maternal aunt who opposed contact, as did the child, who was eight when the application was heard. Contact was refused and the court also imposed a **s.91(14)** restriction on further applications without the leave of the court until the child reached 16. It should be noted that prior to the presumption of involvement, the courts had declared that there was no presumption for or against contact between a child and a violent parent (*Re L (A Child), Re V (A Child), Re H (A Child) (Contact: Domestic Violence)* **[2011] Fam 260**).

Annex A to **the Children and Families Act 2014** contains a flow chart and five examples of how the presumption will work. Each of the examples deals with contact issues. It is therefore uncertain how the presumption will work in relation to parental responsibility orders and relocation outside of the jurisdiction.[8] In relation to **s.8** applications, Kanagas suggests 'that the change will have little impact in the courts' (2013, p. 271).

Enforcing Contact

In *Sylvester v Austria* **[2003] 2 FLR 210**, the European Court of Human Rights indicated that authorities should take all necessary

[5] Do you think the law was biased against fathers?

[6] The House of Commons Justice Committee supported the principle of involvement but had concerns about the inclusion of a legislative presumption.

[7] Australia introduced legislation to promote shared parenting in 2006.

[8] See chapter 9 for a question on relocation.

steps to facilitate contact between parents and their children. It is therefore important that child arrangements orders that grant contact to parents are actually enforced. **Sections 11A–11G** of **the Children Act 1989** (inserted by **the Children and Adoption Act 2006**) contain provisions that are designed to promote contact. For example, **s.11A(3)** enables the court to make 'a contact activity direction' when an application for contact is made. The activities that the residential parent could be required to engage in take the form of classes and counselling designed to convince the residential parent of the benefits of contact with the other parent. Contact activity 'conditions' can be made during the latter stages of proceedings under **s.11C**.[9] Even if the parent participates in the activities, their intended purpose may not be achieved as the person with whom the child lives may continue to frustrate contact.

[9] Contact activity directions and conditions may be monitored by CAFCASS officers.

In cases where the residential parent refuses to allow contact in breach of an order, the court has various options available in terms of enforcement. Prior to **the Children and Adoption Act 2006**, breach of a contact order was punished as contempt of court. The residential parent could thus face a fine or imprisonment, but the courts were reluctant to impose either, due to the impact that such penalties would have on the child concerned[10] (see *V v V (Contact: Implacable Hostility)* [2004] 2 FLR 851). **Section 11J** of **the Children Act 1989** now provides that the court can make an enforcement order imposing on the person an unpaid work requirement. Such an order will not be made if the person had a reasonable excuse and will only be made if the individual concerned was warned of the consequences of non-compliance (see **s.11L**). The person with an order for contact can also seek compensation from the recalcitrant party for financial losses caused by the failure to comply (**s.11O**). Ultimately residence could be transferred from the residential parent to the other parent, but in *Re W (Residence: Leave to Appeal)* [2010] **EWCA Civ 1280** the Court of Appeal stressed that this cannot be done to punish the parent in breach of the order: it must be in the best interests of the child.

[10] Consider what the impact on the child might be.

Conclusion

This essay has demonstrated that the provisions of **the Children Act 1989** (as amended) and the courts that apply the legislation implement the sentiment expressed by David Norgrove, that children should have a relationship with both parents post separation. But this will only be encouraged where it is safe for the child concerned.

LOOKING FOR EXTRA MARKS?

- Emphasise the reforms enacted by **the Children and Families Act 2014**.
- Gain extra marks by comparing the recommendations of the Family Justice Review with the provisions of **the Children and Families Act 2014**.
- Try to consider whether the reforms were necessary and desirable.

QUESTION | 3

Olga and Patrick divorced three years ago after 12 years of marriage. They have two children: Quentin, aged ten and Ruth, aged seven. When the couple separated they agreed that the children should live with Olga and spend every weekend with Patrick. The children currently attend the local Roman Catholic primary school. Patrick and the children are Roman Catholics, but Olga is not. Olga has recently inherited some money and wants to move the children to a non-religious private school near their home. Patrick objects to this, as he is concerned about their religious education. He is also concerned because Olga's boyfriend, Stephen has moved into the house. Stephen has told the children that there is no such thing as God. Because of this Patrick wants the children to live with him.

Advise Patrick.

CAUTION!

- Although **the Children and Families Act 2014** abolished residence and contact orders, case law relating to these orders can be applied to child arrangements orders.
- In order to advise Patrick properly, you need to discuss the fact that Olga might apply to the court for permission to change the children's school.

DIAGRAM ANSWER PLAN

Identify the issues	▪ Identify the legal issues
	▪ Can Patrick prevent Olga from changing the children's school?
	▪ Should Patrick apply to the courts for the children to live with him?

Relevant law	▪ Outline the relevant law:
	▪ Orders under s.8 Children Act 1989: child arrangements, specific issue and prohibited steps
	▪ Principles of the Children Act 1989: the Welfare Principle (s.1(1)), the Welfare Checklist (s.1(3))

Apply the law	▪ Apply the factors in the welfare checklist to the problem in particular: the child's needs, the child's background, the impact of change and the risk of harm

Conclude	▪ Conclusion
	▪ Advise Patrick as to whether his (or Olga's) applications will be successful

SUGGESTED ANSWER

As Olga and Patrick were married when the children were born, both had parental responsibility under **s.2(1)** of **the Children Act 1989** and both continue to do so, as parental responsibility is unaffected by divorce. Olga *and* Patrick therefore have the right to make decisions regarding the upbringing of their children. **Section 2(7)** provides that where more than one person has parental responsibility, each of them may act alone and without the other in meeting that responsibility.[1] This means that when the children are with Patrick he can make decisions without having to consult Olga and vice versa, but decisions regarding a child's education are not made on a daily basis. Although no enactment requires both parents to consent to a change of school, case law has suggested that certain important issues, such as decisions regarding education, should be determined by both parents with parental responsibility (*Re G (Parental Responsibility: Education)* **[1994] 2 FLR 964 CA**). In practice, schools and education authorities are likely to require the consent of both parents with parental

[1] Unless an enactment specifies otherwise.

responsibility to admit a child to a new school. If the parents cannot agree, an application will need to be made to the court under **s.8**, but first, the applicant will be required to attend a Mediation Information and Assessment Meeting. If mediation is unsuitable or unsuccessful legal proceedings may be initiated.[2]

[2] Even if mediation is pursued, the parties may require legal advice to inform the negotiation process.

Specific Issue and Prohibited Steps Orders[3]

[3] Prohibited Steps Orders and Specific Issue Orders have many common characteristics.

Olga might apply for a specific issue order, which is defined in **s.8(1)** as 'an order giving directions for the purpose of determining a specific question which has arisen, or which may arise, in connection with any aspect of parental responsibility for a child'. Specific issue orders are designed to deal with one-off disputes and in *M v M (Specific Issue: Choice of School)* **[2005] EWHC 2769 (Fam)** this type of order was applied for, to adjudicate on a dispute regarding schooling. Patrick could also apply for a specific issue order, or alternatively he could apply for a prohibited steps order to prevent Olga from changing the children's school. A prohibited steps order is 'an order that no step which could be taken by a parent in meeting his parental responsibility for a child, and which is of a kind specified in the order, shall be taken by any person without the consent of the court' (**s.8(1)**). A PSO is therefore entirely negative, whereas an SIO can require someone to refrain from acting in a particular way *or* act positively. Patrick could also apply for a prohibited steps order to prevent Stephen from telling the children that there is no such thing as God because such orders can restrain third parties, as well as parents[4] (*Re H (Children) (Residence Order: Condition)* **[2001] 2 FLR 1277**). As Olga and Patrick are parents, they have the right to apply for a **s.8** order without leave of the court (**s.10(4)**).

[4] You could point out that a prohibited steps order cannot prohibit Olga from living with Stephen, as it is not an aspect of parental responsibility.

Child Arrangements Order

Patrick has indicated that he wishes the children to live with him because he does not approve of Olga's partner. Prior to **the Children and Families Act 2014** Patrick would have applied for a residence order, but now he will need to apply for a child arrangements order. **Section 8(1)** of **the Children Act 1989** (as amended) defines a child arrangements order as an order regulating 'a) with whom the child is to live, spend time or otherwise have contact, and b) when a child is to live, spend time or otherwise have contact with any person'.

The Welfare Principle and Checklist[5]

[5] The purpose of this paragraph is to indicate the general principles that the court considers when hearing an application under **s.8**. They are contained in **s.1** of the Act.

'When a court determines any question with respect to the upbringing of a child or the administration of the child's property or the application of any income arising from it, the child's welfare shall be the court's paramount consideration' (**s.1(1)**).[6] As the application will be opposed by the other party, **s.1(4)(a)** requires the court to consider

[6] You may consider the meaning of 'welfare' and 'paramount', particularly in a coursework question.

the welfare checklist, contained in **s.1(3)** and discussed below. The court will also have regard to the 'no-order principle', which means that the court will only make an order if 'doing so would be better for the child than making no order at all' (**s.1(5)**). As there is a specific dispute that requires resolution, an order is necessary in this particular case (*Re P (Parental Dispute: Judicial Intervention)* [2003] 1 FLR 286). In addition, the court will consider the no-delay principle contained in **s.1(2)**. The presumption that 'the involvement of [each relevant] parent in the life of the child concerned will further the child's welfare' also applies, but in this particular case neither parent is attempting to prevent the other from being involved with the children (**s.1(2A)**).

The Wishes of the Children

The first factor in the checklist is the 'ascertainable wishes and feelings of the child concerned (considered in the light of his age and understanding)' (**s.1(3)(a)**). In *Re R (A Child) (Residence Order: Treatment of Child's Wishes)* [2009] 2 FCR 572, a judge was criticised for failing to attach sufficient weight to the wishes of a ten-year-old child, whilst in contact cases, the courts have considered the views of younger children. For example, in *Re U (A child)* [2003] EWCA Civ 27 the court declared that the eight-year-old child 'had a perfectly clear perception of whether or not she wanted to receive communication from her father' Quentin and Ruth are ten and seven, respectively and should therefore be asked for their views on moving schools, but of course, these are not determinative. Whether it is appropriate to ask a seven-year-old child who she wants to live with is another matter entirely.[7]

[7]What are your views? And what approach have the courts taken?

The Children's Needs, Background and the Impact of Change

[8]Consider whether emotional and educational needs include religion.

The 'physical, emotional and educational needs'[8] of the children should be considered under **s.1(3)(b)**. There is nothing in the case study to suggest that the children have any particular educational needs, nor is there any indication that the children's current school does not meet their needs. Changing schools will have an impact on the children and under **s.1(3)(c)** the court must take into account the likely effect of any change in circumstances. Given that the vast majority of children have to change schools at least once in their lifetime and that many regularly move schools, the courts may be more willing to interfere with the status quo in relation to schooling than they have been in cases concerning residence (see later). However, the change of school may impact upon their religious education as the children currently attend a Catholic school. **Section 1(3)(d)** requires the court to have regard to the children's age, sex, background and any characteristics which the court considers relevant, which includes cultural and religious background. In *Re T and M* **[1995] FLR 1**, the two children concerned were baptised as Roman Catholics, but the mother later converted to Islam. A PSO was made to prevent the mother from moving the children from a Christian school to an Islamic school, although the mother was permitted to discuss her religion with them. In this case, the PSO had to be made to maintain the children's religion, but Olga is not attempting to change the children's religion and they spend every weekend with their father, who is therefore able to take them to Mass on Sunday. It is uncertain whether the court would prohibit the change of school.[9]

[9]Do you think it is in the children's best interests?

Change of Residence

In relation to the children's residence, the likely effect of any change (**s.1(3)(c)**) is particularly significant as a change of residence can be traumatic (see *Re B (Residence Order: Status Quo)* **[1998] 1 FLR 368**). The children have lived with Olga for three years post separation, which is a considerable period of time for a young child, particularly Ruth, who is only seven years old. When determining residence disputes the court would consider how capable each parent is of meeting the children's needs, but also the capability of any other person that the court considers relevant, i.e. Stephen (**s.1(3)(f)**). There is nothing in the case study to suggest that either parent cannot meet the children's needs and although Stephen has made inappropriate comments, there is no evidence that he is incapable of otherwise meeting the children's needs. Patrick may argue that the children are suffering harm due to the comments Stephen has made regarding the existence of God. The court is required to consider any harm the children have suffered or are at risk of suffering under **s.1(3)(e)**, and although the definition of harm is broad[10] (see **ss.105(1)** and **31(9)**), it is unlikely to cover the 'harm' that might result from not believing in God. Even if it does, such 'harm' could be dealt with by prohibiting Stephen from discussing religious issues with the children: it would not be necessary to remove them from the home they are settled in. Although Patrick may not be successful in his application for a child arrangements order, the court could nonetheless make an order confirming that the children should live with Olga, as **s.1(3)(g)** requires the court to consider the range of powers available to it under the Act. Alternatively, the court may make no order at all.

[10]In a coursework question, you would have time to consider the definition of harm in more depth.

Conclusion

Patrick should be advised that he is unlikely to be successful in his application for a child arrangements order specifying that the children should live with him. His case in relation to changing the children's school is, however, stronger.

LOOKING FOR EXTRA MARKS?

- Utilise the IRAC method to ensure that you answer this problem question properly.
- Consider whether children as young as ten and seven should be asked which parent they would prefer to live with.
- Gain extra marks by considering whether Stephen is causing the children harm.

QUESTION | 4

Teresa is consultant heart surgeon in a large hospital. One of her patients, Ursula, aged five, suffers from a congenital heart defect, which is currently being treated with drugs. Teresa has explained to Ursula's parents, Victoria and William, that the drugs are no longer working effectively. Teresa has indicated that Ursula needs a life-saving operation, but Victoria and William are opposed to the operation as it will involve a blood transfusion and they are Jehovah's witnesses.

Advise Teresa. [25 marks]

What would the legal position be if Ursula was 16 and refusing medical treatment? [25 marks]

CAUTION!

- Although the marks awarded for each section are the same, you may find that your answer to the second part is slightly shorter, as it is not necessary to repeat information that you have included in the first part of your answer, for example the explanation of inherent jurisdiction.

DIAGRAM ANSWER PLAN

Identify the issues	■ Identify the legal issues ■ Can Teresa apply to the court to overrule the parents' refusal to consent to treatment or the child's refusal to consent to treatment?
Relevant law	■ Outline the relevant law: ■ The Children Act 1989, the Inherent Jurisdiction of the High Court
Apply the law	■ Apply the case law to the scenario ■ *Re A (Minors) (Conjoined Twins: Medical Treatment)* **[2001]** ■ *Re P (Medical Treatment: Best Interests)* **[2004]**
Conclude	■ Conclusion ■ Decide if the court will overrule the refusal of the parents or the child to consent to the treatment

SUGGESTED ANSWER

Ursula requires a life-saving heart operation but her parents are opposed to the procedure, because it will involve a blood transfusion. If Victoria and William were married when Ursula was born, both would automatically have parental responsibility (**s.2(1) Children Act 1989**). This is likely to be the case, given that Jehovah's Witnesses do not believe in sexual relations outside of marriage. Even if they were not married when Ursula was born, William was probably registered as her father, which has conferred parental responsibility on the father since 1 December 2003 (**s.4(1)(a)**). Both parents would therefore have the right to make decisions relating to Ursula, including decisions regarding medical treatment.[1] In this case, Victoria and William have refused to consent to an operation, which according to the consultant heart surgeon, is required to save Ursula's life. Given that Ursula is not capable of consenting herself, the matter will have to be brought before the court. If the medical treatment is not required as a matter of urgency an application can be made for a

[1] It is worth pointing out that parental responsibility involves a duty to obtain medical treatment for a child.

specific issue order under **s.8** of **the Children Act 1989** (see *Re R (A Minor)(Blood Transfusion)* **[1993] 2 FLR 757**). The hospital or health authority treating Ursula can make an application to the court for leave to apply for a specific issue order **(s.10(1)(a)(ii))**. The need to seek leave lengthens the duration of the proceedings and as a result, an application for a specific issue order is inappropriate in cases of urgency.[2]

[2] It is worth pointing out that specific issue orders are more commonly utilised where the parents are in dispute regarding the medical treatment of their child.

Inherent Jurisdiction[3]

[3] The procedure is governed by **the Family Procedure Rules 2010** (and the accompanying **Practice Direction 12D**).

Cases concerning urgent life-saving medical treatment can be dealt with by the High Court exercising its inherent jurisdiction. Any person can make an application[4] but a local authority requires leave of the court **(s.100(3) the Children Act 1989)**. Inherent jurisdiction refers to the automatic, non-statutory powers that the High Court can exercise on behalf of the Crown. The Crown, as *'parens patriae'* or father of the nation, has a special duty to protect its subjects, particularly those who cannot protect themselves, such as children. Often the court invokes its powers by making a child a ward, which means that no important step can be taken in relation to the child without leave of the court. However, inherent jurisdiction can also be utilised to determine one-off issues relating to a child, such as medical treatment. In such cases, the hospital authorities will submit an application for authorisation to treat the child. *Re A (Minors) (Conjoined Twins: Medical Treatment)* **[2001] 1 FLR 1** concerned an application to separate conjoined twins, which would inevitably result in the death of the weaker child, but would preserve the life of the stronger child. If the operation did not go ahead, both twins would die. The court thus authorised the operation because the stronger twin should have the opportunity to receive life-saving treatment. There are several examples of cases where the court has ordered a life-saving operation on a child whose parents refused to consent because they are Jehovah's Witnesses, for example *Re E (A Minor) (Wardship: Medical Treatment)* **[1993] 1 FLR 386** and *Re S (A Minor) (Consent to Medical Treatment)* **[1994] 2 FLR 1065**.[5] This is because 'it is the duty of the court under its inherent jurisdiction to ensure that a child who is the subject of proceedings is protected and properly taken care of' (**Practice Direction 12D—Inherent Jurisdiction (Including Wardship) para. 1.1**). In *Re P (Medical Treatment: Best Interests)* **[2004] 2 FLR 1117**, the court authorised the hospital to administer blood or blood products against the will of the child and parents, provided that no other treatment was available. The court's decision will thus be influenced by the evidence provided by medical professionals as to whether the treatment is essential.

[4] The advantage of inherent jurisdiction over a specific issue order is speed.

[5] In a coursework question, you would be expected to explain the cases in more depth.

[6] Consider whether overriding a parental decision constitutes a breach of **art. 8** of **the European Convention on Human Rights**.

The Views of the Parents[6]

The court's duty is to decide what is in the best interests of the child: the parent's religious views will not therefore take priority over the child's welfare. But this does not mean that the parents' wishes will be ignored. In *Re T (A Minor) (Wardship: Medical Treatment)* [1997] 1 FLR 502, a baby had a life-threatening liver complaint, which meant that he would not live beyond the age of two-and-a-half unless he had a transplant. The parents refused to consent and the court did not order the transplant to take place for several reasons. First, the child had previously undergone unsuccessful surgery, which had caused him much pain and distress. Secondly, the parents were health care professionals who fully understood the consequences of their decision. Thirdly, the parents had moved to a distant Commonwealth country: an order would therefore require them to return to the UK for the operation. The parents did, in fact, return to the UK and eventually consented to the transplant. Ursula's situation is quite different from the position in *Re T* as she has not previously undergone surgery and there are no practical reasons why the operation cannot go ahead. It is therefore likely that the court will sanction the operation.

[7] This paragraph sets the context—it explains the right of a child to consent to medical treatment.

The Position if Ursula is 16[7]

If Ursula is 16 years old, she is technically a child (**s.1** of **the Family Law Reform Act 1969**). Her parents retain parental responsibility for her until she reaches the age of 18, which means that they can consent to medical treatment on her behalf. **Section 8(1)** of **the Family Law Reform Act 1969** provides that a minor who has attained the age of 16 can consent to medical treatment, and in such cases it is not necessary to also obtain parental consent. However, Ursula is refusing to consent. In *Gillick v West Norfolk and Wisbech Area Health Authority* [1986] 1 FLR 224, the House of Lords held that a child will have the right to make his own decisions when he or she reaches a sufficient understanding and intelligence to be capable of making up her own mind on the matter requiring decision (Lord Scarman at p. 186). In this particular case, the House of Lords declared that if a doctor felt that a child was of sufficient intelligence and maturity to understand the issues, then the doctor could provide contraceptive treatment without the parent's consent. The question is whether **s.8(1)** and *Gillick* enable a child, such as Ursula, to refuse medical treatment.

Refusing Medical Treatment

Medical treatment can be provided against the will of a mature minor, if a person with parental responsibility consents, and in such cases it is not necessary to bring the matter before the court

(*Re K, W and H (Minors) (Medical Treatment)* [1993] 1 FLR 854). However, a doctor may prefer to obtain the court's authorisation before treating a minor in such circumstances, particularly in a case such as this, where the child has reached the age of 16. If a child requiring medical treatment does not consent to it *and* those with parental responsibility refuse to consent, it is essential to bring the matter before the court if treatment is to proceed. In both cases, the court can override a minor's refusal to consent (and that of the parents) if medical treatment is considered to be in the child's best interests. As explained earlier, the application may be made under **the Children Act 1989** or, in urgent cases, under the Inherent Jurisdiction of the High Court.[8]

[8]It is not necessary to repeat the information you have provided on specific issue orders and inherent jurisdiction in the first part of the answer.

[9]See the answer to question one for more details.

Relevance of the Child's Views[9]

When the court considers an application for authorisation for medical treatment, the child's views are relevant, as exemplified by **s.1(3)(a)** of **the Children Act 1989**. In addition, **art. 12** of **the UN Convention on the Rights of the Child 1989** provides for the right 'of the child who is capable of forming his or her own views to express those views freely in all matters affecting the child, the views of the child being given due weight in accordance with the age and maturity of the child'. But ultimately, the court's decision is based on the child's welfare, rather than his or her wishes.

As the Court of Appeal pointed out in *Re W (A Minor) (Medical Treatment: Court's Jurisdiction)* [1993] **Fam 64**, neither *Gillick* nor **s.8** of **the Family Law Reform Act 1969** provide children with a right to veto medical treatment.

In *Re M (Medical Treatment: Consent)* [1999] **2 FLR 1097**, the court authorised a life- saving heart transplant to be performed on a 15-year-old, intelligent girl, despite the fact that she did not want to have the operation because she did not wish to have someone else's heart. In *Re P (Medical Treatment: Best Interests)* [2004] **2 FLR 1117**, the court overrode the refusal of a 16-year-old Jehovah's Witness to consent to a blood transfusion provided that no other treatment was available.[10] As explained earlier, the court's decision will be heavily influenced by medical professionals that provide evidence to the court.

[10]Remember—when the child reaches majority he or she will be able to refuse medical treatment.

Conclusion

Whether Ursula is five or 16 years old, Teresa (or more specifically, the hospital or health authority that is treating her) can make an application to the court for authorisation to perform the operation. The court can overrule parental refusal and refusal of the child herself if the operation is considered to be in the child's best interests.

LOOKING FOR EXTRA MARKS?

- Utilise the IRAC method to ensure that you answer this problem question properly.
- Gain extra marks by referring to the **UN Convention on the Rights of the Child**.
- Consider whether overriding parental decisions constitutes a breach of **art. 8** of **the European Convention on Human Rights**.

TAKING THINGS FURTHER

- Cave, E. 'Goodbye Gillick? Identifying and resolving problems with the concept of child competence' (2014) Legal Studies 34(1) 103.
  Discusses the problems associated with assessing a child's competence and argues that the Mental Capacity Act 2005 is not suited to protecting the minor from harm.

- Ewing, J., Hunter, R., Barlow, A. and Smithson, J. 'Children's voices: Centre-stage or sidelined in out-of-court dispute resolution in England and Wales' (2015) Child and Family Law Quarterly 27(1) 43.
  Argues that the Government proposal to allow children to be consulted during court mediation would require a major cultural shift and increased training for the professionals involved.

- Family Justice Council 'Guidelines for Judges Meeting Children who are Subject to Family Proceedings' (2010).
  Sets out the guidelines that judges must have regard to when considering whether to meet a child that is subject to proceedings and the guidelines to be followed if the meeting goes ahead.

- Hale, B. 'New Families and the welfare of children' (2014) Journal of Social Welfare and Family Law 36(1) 26.
  Argues that there is confusion regarding the balance between the rights of parents or would-be parents and the welfare of the children affected in relation to 'new families'.

- Herring, J. 'The welfare principle and the Children Act: Presumably it's about welfare?' (2014) Journal of Social Welfare and Family Law 36(1) 14.
  Explains why presumptions appeal to lawyers involved in Children Act cases but supports the move away from the use of presumptions by the courts in recent years.

- HM Government 'Co-operative parenting following family separation: Proposed legislation on the involvement of both parents in a child's life' (2012) TSO.
  Sets out the proposals for a legislative statement regarding the importance of involvement of both parents in the child's life.

- Kanagas, F. 'A presumption that "involvement" of both parents is best: Deciphering the law's message' (2013) Child and Family Law Quarterly 25(3) 270.
  Considers the rationale for introducing a presumption of involvement and argues that the presumption has a largely symbolic function.

■ Kaspiew, R., Gray, M., Weston, R., Malony, L., Hand, K. and Qu, L. and the Family Law Evaluation Team 'Evaluation of the 2006 Family Law Reforms' (2012) Melbourne: Australian Institute of Family Studies.

Evaluates the 2006 Australian law reforms, which introduced a presumption of involvement of both parents and identifies the problems with the introduction of the presumption.

Online Resource Centre   www.oxfordtextbooks.co.uk/orc/qanda/

Go online for extra essay and problem questions, a glossary of key terms, online versions of all the answer plans and audio commentary on how selected ones were put together, and a range of podcasts which include advice on exam and coursework technique and advice for other assessment methods.

International Relocation and Child Abduction

9

ARE YOU READY?

In order to answer the questions in this chapter you will need to have covered the following topics:

- applications for leave to relocate outside of the jurisdiction under **the Children Act 1989**;
- **The Hague Convention on the Civil Aspects of International Child Abduction 1980** (implemented in the UK by **the Child Abduction and Custody Act 1985 (Part I)**);
- **The European Council Regulation on the Jurisdiction, Recognition and Enforcement of Judgments in Matrimonial Matters and Matters of Parental Responsibility 2201/2003** (implemented in the UK by **the European Communities (Jurisdiction and Judgments in Matrimonial and Parental Responsibility Matters) Regulations 2005**);
- the use of inherent jurisdiction in abduction cases.

KEY DEBATES

Debate: Adopting a uniform approach to international relocation

The **Washington Declaration** (see 'Taking Things Further' section) indicates that decisions regarding international relocation should be based on the principle that the best interests of the child should be the paramount (primary) consideration and that there should be no presumption for or against relocation. It then contains a list of factors that courts should consider when hearing applications to relocate. It can be argued that the declaration should be incorporated into an international convention in order to ensure a uniform approach to international relocation.

Debate: The concept of habitual residence for the purpose of international child abduction

The concept of habitual residence is central to **the Hague Convention on Civil Aspects of International Child Abduction**, but it is not defined within it. As a consequence, there is a significant number of cases that have considered the meaning of habitual residence. Indeed, the Supreme Court heard three cases in close succession: *A v A (Children: Habitual Residence)* [2013] UKSC 60; *Re KL (A Child) (Abduction: Habitual Residence: Inherent Jurisdiction)* [2014] 1 FLR 772; *Re LC (Reunite International Child Abduction Centre Intervening)* [2014] UKSC 1. Do you think that the concept of habitual residence should be defined at an international level in order to prevent inconsistent interpretations?

QUESTION 1

Analyse how the courts have dealt with applications by one parent to relocate outside of the jurisdiction.

CAUTION!

- Do not attempt this question unless you are aware of the provisions of **the Children Act 1989** that are utilised in international relocation cases.
- It is essential that you discuss the leading case: ***Payne v Payne* [2001] 1 FCR 425**, but you are also expected to consider several post-*Payne* cases, for example ***K v K* [2011] EWCA Civ 793**.

DIAGRAM ANSWER PLAN

Introduction—consider relocation applications under the Children Act 1989

Discuss the principles upon which the decision is based

Explain *Payne v Payne*—the leading case

Consider criticisms of the *Payne v Payne* approach

Discuss cases where permission to relocate has been refused

Conclusion

[1] In a coursework question, you would have time to consider why the courts are hearing so many applications.

[2] Previously, a residence order.

The English family courts hear numerous applications[1] each year from parents wishing to relocate outside of the jurisdiction. **Section 13(1)(b)** of **the Children Act 1989** provides that if there is a child arrangements order[2] in force which includes arrangements specifying with whom the child is to live and/or when the child is to live with any person, no person can remove the child from the UK unless there is written consent from every person with parental responsibility or leave of the court. The person named in the child arrangements order as the person with whom the child lives can remove the child for up to one month without permission (**s.13(2)**).

If the parent with whom the child lives wants to relocate permanently outside of the UK with the child, he or she will require the approval of every person with PR or the court. If the latter is required, the application may be made under **s.13(3)**. If no child arrangements order is in force an application would be made for a specific issue order under **s.8(1)**.[3] In principle, the non-residential parent could apply for a specific issue order to relocate with the child, but this would be unusual and unlikely to succeed given that the child does not live with that parent. A relocation case may also reach the courts if the non-residential parent makes an application for a prohibited steps order under **s.8(1)**[4] to prevent the residential parent from relocating. This would be essential if the non-residential parent is the child's father and he does not have PR.

[3] See chapter 8.

[4] See chapter 8.

Principles Upon Which the Decision is Based

[5] See chapter 8.

[6] Include case law on the wishes of the children in relocation cases.

The court hearing an application to relocate will base its decision on the welfare principle[5] contained in **s.1(1)** of **the Children Act 1989**. The court must therefore be satisfied that the move would promote the child's welfare. As applications for permission to relocate are opposed, the court will have regard to the welfare checklist, which contains seven factors, namely; the wishes of the child; his needs; the likely effect of change; his age, sex and background; any harm he has suffered or is likely to suffer; how capable each parent is of meeting his needs; and the range of powers available to the court (**s.1(3)**). In relation to relocation, the views of older children will be given due weight[6] and the effect that change will have on them will be particularly relevant. The harm a child is likely to suffer if permission is granted—for example, by the reduction of contact with the other parent—will have to be balanced against the harm the child is likely to suffer if permission is refused—for example, because of the impact that this will have on the primary carer. Since **the Children and Families Act 2014**, the

[7] Consider whether this infringes the **art. 8** rights of the non-residential parent.

[8] It is worth noting that none of the examples of how the presumption will work that were attached to the Act related to relocation.

presumption that the involvement of both parents in the life of the child will further the child's welfare[7] also applies (**s.1(2A) Children Act 1989**). As Lowe and Douglas point out, it is unclear how this will impact upon relocation cases (2015, p. 435).[8]

Payne v Payne

The leading case relating to relocation is **Payne v Payne [2001] 1 FCR 425**, which concerned a mother's application to remove her four-year-old daughter to New Zealand. At first instance, permission was granted and so the father appealed. The Court of Appeal indicated that the first question that the court should ask is whether the proposed relocation is genuine. A move that is calculated to exclude the other parent from the child's life will not be approved (**H v F [2005] 1 FLR 687**), whereas a move prompted by a genuine wish to return to the home country or to join a new partner (**Re A (Leave to Remove: Cultural and Religious Considerations) [2006] EWHC 421 (Fam)**) will be considered. The desire to pursue a career or educational opportunity (**W v A [2004] EWCA Civ 1587**) or to enable a partner to do so (**L v L (Leave to remove children from the jurisdiction: Effect on children) [2002] EWHC 2577**) also constitutes a genuine motive to relocate. The court will then ask if the proposal is realistic, i.e. well researched and practical. If the answer to this question is no, the application will be dismissed, but if the move is realistic, the court must then explore the position of the non-resident parent, in this case, the father. The court will consider whether his opposition to the move is caused by concern that contact with his child will diminish or whether there is an ulterior motive. It will also ask whether the adverse impact that the move will have on his relationship with the child will be offset by the benefits of relocation, for example contact with the residential parent's family. The court will then consider the impact that refusing the application will have on the mother. The results of these appraisals must then be 'brought into an overriding review of the child's welfare as the paramount consideration, directed by the statutory checklist insofar as appropriate' (para. 40). Thorpe LJ pointed out that 'refusing the primary carer's reasonable proposals for the relocation of her family life is likely to impact dramatically on the welfare of her dependent children. Therefore her application to relocate will be granted unless the court concludes that it is incompatible with the welfare of the children' (para. 26). However, Thorpe LJ did point out that this statement did not create a legal presumption in favour of approving the reasonable plans of the primary carer.

[9] This paragraph indicates how **Payne** has been applied in subsequent cases.

The emphasis placed on the impact that a refusal would have on the primary carer meant that leave to relocate was usually granted[9]— see **Re H (Children) [2011] EWCA Civ 529** and **Re C (A child)**

[2011] EWCA Civ 72 for examples. The approach has been subject to much criticism from academics and the judiciary because it prioritises one factor over the others and does not focus on the best interests of the child (see Wall LJ in *Re D (Leave to Remove: Appeal)* [2010] EWCA Civ 50). But as George points out, critics should look at what *Payne* actually says: 'the central point of the case is that the child's welfare is paramount, with all other considerations being merely factors that contribute to the analysis' (2012, p. 112)

Where approval is granted the court order often contains provision for the child to return to the UK for holidays. For example, in *Re H (Leave to Remove)* [2010] EWCA Civ 915 leave to relocate to the Czech Republic was granted to the mother on the basis that the father had four to five weeks of staying contact in the UK, a further one week of staying contact in the Czech Republic and frequent indirect contact.

Unsuccessful Applications

Since *Payne*, there have been instances where permission to relocate outside of the jurisdiction has been refused. For example, in *Re Y (Leave to remove from Jurisdiction)* [2004] 2 FLR 330 the mother's application to take the child to America was refused because the child's home was in Wales and he lived with both parents. The move would not only cause disruption and a reduction in contact with the child's father, but would result in the loss of his bicultural and bilingual life. The decision thus focused more on the child's welfare and the welfare checklist, which expressly requires the judge to have regard to the child's age, sex and background (**s.1(3)(d)**) and the latter includes cultural heritage (*Re M (Child's Upbringing)* [1996] 2 FLR 441). See also *Re AR (A Child: Relocation)* [2010] EWHC 1346 (Fam) and *C v C (International Relocation-Shared Care arrangement)* [2011] EWHC 335, where the mothers' applications were rejected because the children concerned spent a significant amount of time with their fathers (although no shared residence order was in place at the time of the application). In both cases, the relocation would have a considerable impact on the children's fathers and would not be in the children's best interests.

[10] *K v K* is the most important post-*Payne* case and should therefore be included in your answer.

In *K v K* [2011] EWCA Civ 793,[10] the Court of Appeal unanimously overturned the decision which granted the mother permission to relocate to Canada. A shared residence order had been made, whereby the children spent five nights (six days) with their father and nine nights with their mother in a 14-day period. The mother was assisted by a nanny, whereas the father cared for the children himself. The time each spent with the children was therefore equal and the CAFCASS officer did not recommend relocation. Thorpe LJ declared that the guidance in *Payne* did not apply to cases of shared care, such as this, whereas Moor-Bick LJ and Black LJ stated that the only binding principle that comes from *Payne* is that the welfare of the child is paramount. The rest is guidance to be applied or distinguished, depending on the circumstances. Black LJ warned against classifying cases as '*Payne*' cases or '*Re Y*' cases depending upon the amount of time the child spends with the parents: a sentiment which was endorsed by Munby J in *Re F (Relocation)* [2013] 1 FLR 645.

Conclusion

The case law discussed above demonstrates how difficult relocation cases are to determine. Ultimately the court has to base its decision on the welfare principle and will consider the guidance issued by judges in cases such as *Payne* and *K v K*. Whether the approach adopted by the courts changes following the introduction of the presumption of involvement of both parents remains to be seen.

LOOKING FOR EXTRA MARKS?

- Utilise the PEA method to ensure that you answer this essay question well.

- Gain extra marks by considering whether the presumption of parental involvement, introduced by **the Children and Families Act 2014**, will change the approach taken to relocation cases.

- In a coursework question, you would be expected to include more academic criticism of *Payne v Payne*.

QUESTION | 2

Xena and Yunus met in Canada when they were both studying at University. Yunus is Canadian, whereas Xena is English: her parents still live in London, where she grew up. Xena and Yunus are married and have a child, Zander, who is now five years old. Since Zander was born, their relationship has deteriorated and last month Xena returned to England with Zander. She intends to divorce Yunus. Yunus has contacted Xena in England and demanded that she return with Zander, otherwise he will take legal action.

a) Advise Yunus. [20 marks]

b) What would the position be if Xena and Yunus had met in France, Zander was born there and the family lived there until Xena returned to England? [10 marks]

c) What would the position be if Xena and Yunus had met in Thailand, Zander was born there and the family lived there until Xena returned to England? [20 marks]

CAUTION!

- You are not expected to memorise the countries that have ratified the Hague Convention but you should be aware that western jurisdictions, such as Canada and the UK have done so.

- Although you may not know whether Thailand has ratified the Convention, you should be able to work out that it has not, otherwise the answer to part c) would be exactly the same as part a), which would be pointless.

DIAGRAM ANSWER PLAN

Identify the issues
- Identify the legal issues
- Advise Yunus as to whether Zander will be returned to his home country

Relevant law
- Outline the relevant law:
- The Hague Convention on the Civil Aspects of International Child Abduction 1980, BIIR, the Children Act 1989 and Inherent Jurisdiction

Apply the law
- Canada—apply the provisions of the Hague Convention to the case
- France—apply the additional provisions of BIIR to the case
- Thailand—apply the provisions of the Children Act 1989 and case law relating to inherent jurisdiction e.g. *Re J (Child Returned Abroad: Convention Rights)* [2005]

Conclude
- Conclusion
- In each case, decide whether Zander will be returned to his home country

SUGGESTED ANSWER

[1] You are expected to know that the UK and Canada are party to the Hague Convention.

a) Canada to the UK[1]

As Zander has been brought to the UK from Canada, **the Hague Convention on the Civil Aspects of International Child Abduction 1980** is applicable, which was implemented in the UK by the Child Abduction and Custody Act 1985 (Part I). The aims of the Convention are 'to secure the prompt return of children wrongfully removed to or retained in any contracting state' and 'to ensure that rights of custody and access under the law of one contracting state are effectively respected in the other contracting states' (**art. 1**).

A removal/retention is wrongful if it is in breach of rights of custody attributed to a person under the law of the state in which the child was habitually resident[2] immediately before the removal/retention and at the time those rights were actually exercised or would have been but for the removal/retention (**art. 3**). Rights of custody include 'rights relating to the care of the person of the child and the right to determine the child's place of residence' (**art. 5**). As Baroness Hale explained in *Re D (Abduction: Rights of Custody)* [2006] UKHL 51, the courts are not concerned with domestic law but 'with the effect given domestically to autonomous terms in an international treaty which are meant to be applied consistently by all member states' (para. 44). The Convention can only be utilized if the child is under 16 (**art. 4**). Zander is under 16, was habitually resident in Canada and his removal is wrongful, as Yunus would have rights of custody under Canadian law.

Each contracting state is required to designate a central authority to discharge the duties imposed by the Convention: they must cooperate with each other to promote the Convention's objectives (**art. 7**). **Article 8** indicates that Yunus can apply to the Canadian central authority or the central authority of any contracting state for assistance, i.e. the International Child Abduction and Contact Unit (ICACU), which is the Central Authority in England and Wales. It is likely that Yunus will apply to the Canadian central authority, which will contact ICACU under **art. 9**. ICACU must take or cause to be taken all appropriate measures in order to obtain the voluntary return of the child (**art. 10**). If this is not possible judicial or administrative proceedings must be commenced and **art. 11** requires the authorities to act expeditiously.[3]

Article 12 provides that if less than one year has elapsed from the date of the wrongful removal/retention, the authority concerned *shall* order the return of the child *forthwith*. Even if proceedings were commenced after one year, the authorities should order the return of the child, *unless* it is demonstrated that the child is settled in its new environment (see *Re N (Minors) (Abduction)* [1991] 1 FLR 413). If Yunus contacts the Canadian central authority and Xena does not voluntarily return with Zander, the court must order her to do so unless one of the defences outlined in **art. 13** apply. The first is that Yunus was not exercising rights of custody, consented to the removal or acquiesced to it (*A v T* [2011] EWCA 3882 (Fam)). The second is

[2] Habitual residence is a question of fact. Refer to cases such as *Re LC (Reunite International Child Abduction Centre Intervening)* [2014] UKSC 1 for the meaning.

[3] If they have not reached a decision within six weeks of commencement of proceedings, the applicant or central authority of the requested state can ask for the reasons for the delay under **art. 11**.

that there is a grave risk of harm if the child is returned to his/her country of habitual residence. The third is that the child objects to being returned (*Re G (Abduction: Children's Objections)* [2010] **EWCA Civ 1232**). None of these appear to apply in Zander's case, which means that Xena should return him to Canada.[4]

[4]Each section of the answer ends with its own conclusion.

b) France to the UK[5]

[5]France and the UK also ratified the Council of Europe Convention (1980), known as the Luxembourg Convention, but its application is restricted by BIIR.

As France is a member of the EU the additional provisions contained in **the European Council Regulation on the Jurisdiction, Recognition and Enforcement of Judgments in Matrimonial Matters and Matters of Parental Responsibility 2201/2003, (BIIR)** apply.[6]. It was implemented in the UK by **the European Communities (Jurisdiction and Judgments in Matrimonial and Parental Responsibility Matters) Regulations 2005.** BIIR gives directions as to how **the Hague Convention** should be applied between member states and governs the position if a return order is refused.

[6]BIIR takes precedence over **the Hague Convention**.

If Zander was habitually resident in France, Yunus would apply to the French central authority, which will make contact with ICACU in order to attempt to secure a voluntary return. If this is not possible, proceedings will be initiated and **art. 11(3)** requires a court to use the most expeditious procedures available in national law. It goes on to provide that the court should 'issue judgement no later than six weeks after the application is lodged' 'except where exceptional circumstances make this impossible'. **BIIR** thus attempts to make six weeks an obligation, rather than a target, as it is under **the Hague Convention.**[7]

[7]You could refer to *Shaw v Hungary* [2012] 2 FLR 1314, where the ECHR held that Hungary violated **art. 8** of **the European Convention** for failing to deal with a case expeditiously.

Article 11(2) indicates that when a court is applying **arts 12** and **13** of **the Hague Convention**, the child should be 'given an opportunity to be heard during the proceedings unless this appears inappropriate having regard to his or her age or degree of maturity' (see *Abduction: WF v RJ, BF and RF* [2010] **EWHC 2909 (Fam)**). As Zander is only five years old, this provision is unlikely to be relevant. In addition, a court cannot refuse to return a child on the basis of **art. 13(b)** of **the Hague Convention** if it is established that adequate arrangements have been made to secure the protection of the child after his or her return (**art. 11(4) BIIR**).[8] Nor can the court refuse to order the return of a child unless the person requesting recovery is given an opportunity to be heard (**art. 11(5)**). If the court does make a judgement of non-return, the court in the applicant's state must be sent a copy within one month (**art. 11(6)**). The parties must be invited to make submissions: if none are received, the case is closed (**art. 11(7)**) but if the court in the applicant's state makes an order

[8]As there appear to be no **art. 13** defences in this case, it is not necessary to discuss this in depth.

requiring the return of the child, that order is enforceable under **art. 11(8)** of **BIIR**.

The primary benefit of **BIIR** in this case would be the duty for the court to reach a judgment within six weeks.

c) Thailand to the UK

Thailand is not a signatory to **the Hague Convention**, which means that its provisions are not applicable in this case. As Baroness Hale indicated in *Re J (Child Returned Abroad: Convention Rights)* [2005] **UKHL 40**, 'there is no warrant, either in case law or in statute for the principles of the Hague Convention to be extended to countries which are not parties to it' (para. 22). Applications for the return of children to a country which is not party to **the Hague Convention** are often decided by the High Court exercising inherent jurisdiction, but can also be decided under **the Children Act 1989**. For example, in *Re J (Child Returned Abroad: Convention Rights)* the father applied for a specific issue order[9] for the return of his child to Saudi Arabia from the UK. Whichever jurisdiction is used, the decision will be based on the principle that the welfare of the child is the court's paramount consideration. Sometimes this requires the dispute to be settled in a court that has direct knowledge of the child's state of domicile and so a peremptory return order may be made (*Re Z (Non-Convention Country)* [1999] **1 FLR 1270**). However, there is no presumption of prompt return when abduction cases are heard using inherent jurisdiction or **the Children Act 1989**. The court may decide to undertake a full investigation of the case, which will prevent the speedy return of the child. At the end of this, the court may decide that returning the child is in his best interests, but equally, it may find that making a return order would be contrary to the child's welfare. In *Re J (Child Returned Abroad: Convention Rights)*, the House of Lords indicated that the following factors should be considered when deciding whether a child should be returned: the degree of connection with each country; the length of time spent in each country; the approach taken to determining issues in the foreign country;[10] and the effect of the decision on the primary carer. In *Re J* itself, the court refused to order the return of the children because the father had made allegations about the mother's association with another man and there was concern as to how she would be treated in Saudi Arabia, and because there was no jurisdiction in the home country which would enable the mother to apply to the court for permission to relocate to England. It was not therefore possible for the relocation issue to be resolved by a court in Saudi Arabia.

In contrast, the court in *Re U (Abduction: Nigeria)* [2010] **EWHC 1179** ordered the child's return to Nigeria, despite the fact that the

[9] Section 8(1) Children Act 1989.

[10] The English courts will be concerned as to whether foreign courts will treat the child's welfare as paramount.

mother made allegations of domestic violence because: it was the children's home country; there was domestic violence legislation in the state within which the parties resided; the father had made undertakings not to molest the mother and to pay for separate accommodation for her; the father had made an undertaking to pay for a lawyer to represent the mother in court; the Nigerian courts were capable of resolving the dispute as to relocation; and because the courts would have treated the mother and father equally and apply the welfare principle. The situation in Nigeria was therefore quite different from the situation in Saudi Arabia.

In this case, we would need to know whether the law in Thailand enables Xena to apply for relocation and whether the courts in Thailand treat the child's welfare as paramount.

LOOKING FOR EXTRA MARKS?

- Utilise the IRAC method to ensure that you answer this problem question properly.
- Include the recent case law of the Supreme Court regarding habitual residence, for example *Re LC (Reunite International Child Abduction Centre Intervening)* [2014] UKSC 1.

QUESTION | 3

Does the Hague Convention on the Civil Aspects of International Child Abduction 1980 ensure that the child's best interests are protected in child abduction cases?

CAUTION!

- This question requires detailed knowledge of the aims and key provisions of the Hague Convention—do not answer this question unless you possess such knowledge.
- Do not write all you know about the Convention—you must apply your knowledge to the question set.
- Ensure that you include some recent case law relating to the application of the Convention.

DIAGRAM ANSWER PLAN

Introduction to the Hague Convention—consider aims and principles

▼

Explain when the Hague Convention applies

▼

Discuss article 12—summary return—does it protect the child's best interests?

▼

Discuss the article 13 defences and whether they protect the child's best interests

▼

Consider whether a return order might breach article 8 of the ECHR

▼

Conclusion

 # SUGGESTED ANSWER

The Hague Convention on the Civil Aspects of International Child Abduction 1980 is a global treaty adopted by the Hague Conference on Private International Law. It has 93 contracting parties, including the United Kingdom, which implemented it by passing **the Child Abduction and Custody Act 1985 (Part I)**.

The Aims of the Convention[1]

[1] It is important to set out the aims of the Convention in order to contextualise the specific provisions of the Convention discussed later.

The preamble to the Convention states that 'the interests of children are of paramount importance in matters relating to their custody'. **Article 1** then proceeds to state that the aims of the Convention are: 'to secure the prompt return of children wrongfully removed to or retained in any contracting state' and 'to ensure that rights of custody and access under the law of one contracting state are effectively respected in the other contracting states'. The Convention is based on the premise that it is in a child's best interests not to be abducted, but this does not mean that an individual child's welfare is paramount when an application for return is being considered.

[2] Consider why the age is set at 16.

[3] See *A v A and another (Children: Habitual Residence)* [2013] UKSC 60 and other Supreme Court judgements for the meaning of habitual residence.

When the Convention Applies

The Convention can be utilised to secure the return of a child under 16[2] **(art. 4)** who was habitually resident[3] in a contracting state and has been removed to or retained in another contracting state. Habitual residence is a question of fact and Schuz argues that the approach used to determine habitual residence should be child-centric. She also indicates that recent case law demonstrates that the UK Supreme Court has now adopted a child-centric approach (Schuz, 2014, p. 342).

The removal/retention must have been wrongful, which means that it is in breach of rights of custody attributed to a person under the law of the state in which the child was habitually resident immediately before the removal/retention and at the time of removal/retention those rights were actually exercised, either jointly or alone, or would have been so exercised but for the removal/retention (**art. 3**). 'Rights of custody' is a broad term, which includes 'rights relating to the care of the person of the child and the right to determine the child's place of residence' (**art. 5**).[4]

[4]In *K (A Child) (Northern Ireland)* [2014] UKSC 29, inchoate or de facto rights of custody were recognised.

Summary Return

Article 12 of the Convention provides that if less than one year has elapsed from the date of the wrongful removal/retention, the authority concerned *shall* order the return of the child *forthwith*. The primary obligation of contracting states is therefore, to order the summary return of an abducted child. The authorities are not required to investigate the merits of the case and the interests of the particular child are not the paramount consideration.[5] **Article 12** goes on to state that where proceedings are commenced after one year, the authorities should order the return of the child, *unless* it is demonstrated that the child is now settled in its new environment. It is assumed that the child will be returned, but the authorities can refuse to do so if the child has settled in the new state, which clearly considers the child's interests. In *Re N (Minors) (Abduction)* [1991] 1 FLR 413, the court indicated that the relevant date is when proceedings were commenced rather than the date of the hearing, and that 'new environment' encompasses home, school, friends, activities and opportunities. The term 'settled' refers to emotional and psychological, as well as physical settlement (*Re M (A Minor) (Abduction: Acquiescence)* [1996] 1 FLR 315).

[5]This is an example of how to apply the information to the question set.

[6]There is also a defence in **art. 20**—a child's return can be refused if 'it would not be permitted by the fundamental principles of the requested state relating to the protection of human rights and fundamental freedoms'.

Article 13 Defences[6]

The judicial and administrative authorities in contracting states can also refuse to order the return of a child if one of the limited circumstances set out in **art. 13** apply. First, the authorities of the requested state are not bound to order the return of the child if the parent who removed or retained the child can establish that the other parent 'was not actually exercising the custody rights at the time of removal or retention, or had consented to or subsequently

[7] But the removal of the child may be contrary to the child's welfare.

acquiesced in the removal or retention' (**art. 13(a)**). In such cases, the removal/retention is not, strictly speaking, wrongful, as it is not in breach of the rights of custody of the other parent.[7] *A v T* **[2011] EWCA 3882 (Fam)** is a recent example where the English courts refused to order the return of a child because the father had expressly agreed to it.

Secondly, the judicial or administrative authorities can refuse to order the return of a child if 'there is a grave risk that his or her return would expose the child to physical or psychological harm or otherwise place the child in an intolerable situation' (**art. 13(b)**). Although **art. 13(b)** prioritises the welfare of the specific child that has been abducted, it can be difficult to establish a grave risk of harm because the harm must result from being returned to the home state, not from the other parent. Thus, in *Re H (Children) (Abduction)* **[2003] EWCA Civ 355** the court ordered the return of the children to Belgium despite the father's violence, because the children would not be living with the father and Belgian authorities could take action to protect them.

[8] The purpose of this paragraph and the paragraph that follows is to consider the relationship between **art. 13 Hague Convention** and **art. 8 ECHR**.

In *Neulinger and Shuruk v Switzerland (Application No 41615/07)* **[2011] 1 FLR 122**,[8] the European Court of Human Rights considered the relationship between **art. 13(b)** of **the Hague Convention** and **art. 8 ECHR**. The case concerned a Swiss couple who moved to Israel and had a child. After the father became involved with an extreme religious group, the mother abducted the child to Switzerland. The Swiss Federal court ordered the child's return under **art. 12** of **the Hague Convention**, following which, the mother and child brought the matter before the European Court of Human Rights, arguing that their rights under **art. 8** would be violated if the child was returned to Israel. The case was based on the fact that the mother would have to return with the child, as the father was only permitted limited supervised contact due to his extreme behaviour. She would then face a criminal prosecution for abducting the child, which would mean that she would be separated from him, causing both of them intolerable harm. The ECHR held that to enforce the Federal Court's return order would violate the **art. 8** rights of the applicants and pointed out that 'the child's best interests must be the primary consideration' under **art. 8** (para. 134). The Court then explained that 'the same philosophy is inherent in the Hague Convention, which in principle requires the prompt return of the abducted child unless there is a grave risk that the child's return would expose it to physical or psychological harm or otherwise place it in an intolerable situation. In other words the concept of the child's best interests is also an underlying principle of the Hague Convention' (para. 137).

[9] In this case, the Supreme Court considered the decision of the ECHR in *Neulinger*. It concluded that the proper application of **the Hague Convention** will not involve a breach of **art. 8**.

[10] This is an example of how to apply the information to the question set.

Following this, in *Re E (Children) (Abduction: Custody Appeal* **[2011] UKSC 27**[9] the mother and half-sister of a child were given permission to appeal against a return order so that the uncertainty created by *Neulinger* could be resolved. The Supreme Court emphasised that **the Hague Convention** and **BIIR** were devised for the benefit of children *generally* and with the aim of serving the interests of the individual child, but they did not expressly make the best interests of the specific child a primary consideration. The justices also declared that the proper application of **the Hague Convention** would not involve a violation of **art. 8** of **the European Convention** and that *Neulinger* did not require a departure from the normal summary process. The Supreme Court upheld the trial judge's order to return the children to Norway. Although it is now clear that the best interest of the individual child is not the court's paramount consideration, it will of course refuse to order the return of a child on the basis of **art. 13(b)**. Indeed, shortly after its decision in *Re E*, the Supreme Court upheld a trial judge's refusal to order the return of a child to Australia in *Re S (A child)* **[2012] UKSC 10**.

The third ground upon which a return order may be refused is if the child objects and has attained an age and degree of maturity at which it is appropriate to take account of its views (**art. 13**). This provision is clearly child-focused, but the judicial or administrative authorities are not actually required to respond to the child's wishes.[10] Thus in *Zaffino v Zaffino (Abduction: Children's Views)* **[2005] EWCA Civ 1012** a 13-year-old girl was returned to Canada, despite her objections. But, in *Re G (Abduction: Children's Objections)* **[2010] EWCA Civ 1232** the return order was set aside by the Court of Appeal as it was made in the face of objections from the children aged 13 and nine. In addition, *W v W* **[2010] EWHC 332 (Fam)** demonstrates that the courts will take into account the views of very young children, in this case, children aged eight and five. Mrs Justice Black pointed out that **the Hague Convention** does not stipulate an age at which a child's views should be taken into account. The decision of the High Court was upheld in the Court of Appeal.

Conclusion

This essay has demonstrated that although the interest of the individual child is not the paramount consideration when an application for return is being considered under **the Hague Convention**, the importance of children's welfare underlies the entire Convention.

LOOKING FOR EXTRA MARKS?

- Utilise the PEA method to ensure that you answer this essay question well.
- Consider the difference between the child's interests being the 'paramount consideration' and the interests of the child being an 'underlying principle' of the Convention.
- Gain extra marks by discussing the relationship between **the Hague Convention** and **art. 8** of **the European Convention on Human Rights**.

TAKING THINGS FURTHER

- George, R. 'Reviewing relocation? *Re W (Relocation: Removal Outside Jurisdiction)* [2011] EWCA Civ 345 and *K v K (Relocation: Shared Care Arrangement)* [2011] EWCA Civ 793' (2012) Child and Family Law Quarterly 24(1) 110.

  Considers three questions raised by the two cases referred to above, namely: the role of precedent in family law cases; the significance of shared care in relocation disputes; and the use of research evidence to review the law.

- George, R. 'Children's state of mind and habitual residence in abduction cases' (2014) Journal of Social Welfare and Family Law 36(3) 311.

  Examines the judgment of the Supreme Court in Re LC (Children) *[2014] UKSC 1, which considered habitual residence for the purpose of the Hague Convention.*

- George, R. *Relocation Disputes: Law and Practice in England and New Zealand* (2014) Hart Publishing.

  Compares the law in England and Wales with the law in New Zealand and the approach taken by the courts in each jurisdiction to resolving relocation disputes.

- Hill, D. 'Habitual residence in the Supreme Court' (2014) Journal of Social Welfare and Family Law 36(2) 211.

  Considers the recent case law of the Supreme Court regarding habitual residence for the purpose of the Hague Convention.

- International Judicial Conference 'Washington Declaration' (2010) (set out in full in International Family Law (2010) 211).

  The Washington Declaration is a non-binding declaration adopted by the international community in an attempt to promote a uniform approach to international relocation. It sets out 13 factors to be considered when dealing with international relocation disputes.

- Schuz, R. 'Habitual residence of the child revisited: A trilogy of cases in the Supreme Court' (2014) Child and Family Law Quarterly 26(3) 342.

  Examines recent case law of the Supreme Court, which has adopted a more child-focused model to determine habitual residence in international child abduction cases.

■ Trimmings, K. *Child Abduction within the European Union* (2013) Hart Publishing.

Explores the background to and the impact of the European Council Regulation on the Jurisdiction, Recognition and Enforcement of Judgments in Matrimonial Matters and Matters of Parental Responsibility 2201/2003. The book considers case law relating to BIIR and examines return applications made under the Regulations.

Online Resource Centre

www.oxfordtextbooks.co.uk/orc/qanda/

Go online for extra essay and problem questions, a glossary of key terms, online versions of all the answer plans and audio commentary on how selected ones were put together, and a range of podcasts which include advice on exam and coursework technique and advice for other assessment methods.

10 The Law Relating to Children: Public Law and Adoption

ARE YOU READY?

In order to attempt the four questions in this chapter you will need to have covered the following topics:

- emergency protection for children—**the Children Act 1989** and inherent jurisdiction;
- care and supervision orders under **the Children Act 1989**;
- **The Adoption and Children Act 2002**;
- the difference between adoption and special guardianship.

KEY DEBATES

Debate: The threshold criteria for supervision and care orders

The criteria that must be satisfied for the court to make a supervision order are the same as the criteria for a care order (**s.31(2) Children Act 1989**). Is this appropriate given that a supervision order is far less intrusive and more temporary than a care order? It can be argued that the courts should be able to make a supervision order if the child concerned is suffering, or is likely to suffer *any form* of harm.

Debate: The role of adoption in modern family law

The role of adoption in modern family law has been the subject of much debate. One of the key issues is whether 'forced adoption'—i.e. adoption without parental consent—should be possible. It can be argued that this violates the parents' human rights. Whether we still need 'adoption' has also been questioned—are special guardianship orders better for the children and their birth parents?

QUESTION | 1

Discuss the steps that can be taken to protect a child in situations of urgency and explain the consequences of taking such steps.

CAUTION!

- As the question focuses on emergency protection you do not need to consider long-term orders—i.e. care and supervision orders—or the threshold criteria that must be satisfied for such orders to be made.
- Ensure that you consider the consequences of an emergency protection order/police protection, for example the duty to make enquiries under **s.47 Children Act 1989**.

DIAGRAM ANSWER PLAN

Explain police protection—s.46 Children Act 1989

Discuss when police protection should be used and the consequences of police protection

Explain Emergency Protection Orders—s.44 Children Act 1989

Explain the court's decision to make an EPO and the impact of an EPO

Consider enquiries under s.47 Children Act 1989

Consider the use of inherent jurisdiction in emergency cases

Conclusion

¹ Consider what is meant by 'in need of immediate protection'. Examples are given in the paragraph below.

If a child is in immediate need of protection¹ various steps can be taken. For example, if the police are called to respond to a situation, a constable can 'remove a child to suitable accommodation and keep him there' if he has 'reasonable cause to believe that a child would otherwise be likely to suffer significant harm' (**s.46(1)(a) Children Act 1989**). The police do not acquire parental responsibility, but must do what is reasonable in the circumstances to promote the child's welfare (**s.46(9)(b)**). As soon as is reasonably practicable, the designated police officer must inform the local authority within whose area the child was found of the steps that have been taken and are proposed to be taken with respect to the child (**s.46(3)(a)**). Usually, the police officer will take a child to local authority accommodation or a refuge. It should be noted that local authorities have a duty to 'provide accommodation for any child in need within their area who appears to require accommodation' (**s.20(1)**). In addition, if a child is taken into police protection, the local authority must make enquiries under **s.47** of the Act (see later).

² The purpose of this paragraph is to discuss when police protection should be utilised. The evidence is provided by the cases such as *Re M*, but the paragraph ends by indicating that police protection has been legitimately utilised in less urgent situations.

'Working Together to Safeguard Children' indicates that police powers 'should be used only when necessary.² Where possible the decision to remove a child from a parent or carer should be made by a court' (2015, p. 58). This reiterates the decision of the Court of Appeal in *Langley v Liverpool Council* **[2005] EWCA Civ 1173**, which held that the removal of children should usually be effected by an emergency protection order (EPO) and that **s.46** should only be utilised if it is impracticable to obtain an EPO. In *Re M (A Minor) (Care Threshold Conditions)* **[1994] 2 FLR 577**, the police exercised their powers under **s.46** when they were called to a house to find that a husband had murdered his wife in front of the children. In *Re B (Care Proceedings: Interim Care Order)* **[2010] 1 FLR 1211**, a boy was removed under **s.46** when the police and a social worker discovered him in a darkened room with no toys, just a potty. However, the removal of a child has been held to be legitimate in less extreme circumstances (see *A v East Sussex County Council and Chief Constable of Sussex Police* **[2010] EWCA Civ 743**).

If the child's parent appears whilst the child is in police protection, he must be handed to her unless there are grounds to believe that he is likely to suffer significant harm if released (**s.46(5)**). In any event, the child can only be kept in police protection for 72 hours (**s.46(6)**) and so an application for an EPO would need to be made if a child requires protection beyond 72 hours. **Section 46(7)** enables the designated officer to apply on behalf of the appropriate authority for an EPO.

Emergency Protection Orders

An EPO can be made by the court under **s.44** of **the Children Act 1989** if it is satisfied 'that there is reasonable cause to believe that the child is likely to suffer significant harm if he is not removed to accommodation provided by or on behalf of the applicant' (**s.44(1) (a)**). Anyone can make an application but usually, the local authority applies and in such cases, the court will only make the EPO if it is satisfied that enquiries in respect of a child are being made and that 'those enquiries are being frustrated by access to the child being unreasonably refused to a person authorised to seek access and that the applicant has reasonable cause to believe that access to the child is required as a matter of urgency' (**s.47(1)(b)**). If someone other than the local authority applies for the order, the authority would be informed and would be obliged to commence enquiries under **s.47(1) (a)(i)**. As EPOs are supposed to be used in urgent cases, they are usually made on an ex parte basis.[3]

[3] It is useful to explain the meaning of ex parte.

The Court's Decision

In *X Council v B and Others (Emergency Protection Orders)* **[2004] EWHC 2015,** Munby J declared that 'summarily removing a child from his parents, is a terrible and drastic remedy' (para. 34).[4] The court must therefore give careful consideration to the circumstances, before making such an order. As McFarlane J indicated in *Re X* **[2006] 2 FLR 701,** 'mere lack of information or a need for assessment can never of themselves establish the existence of a genuine emergency sufficient to justify an EPO' (para. 101). As Lowe and Douglas point out, emergency protection orders provide a means of protecting children from immediate threats of harm but 'they are more in the nature of back-up powers should other means of protection not be sufficient' (2015, p. 589). If it is not a genuine emergency, the rights of the parents under **the European Convention** may be infringed (*Haase v Germany* **[2004] 2 FLR 39**).[5] Even if the court can make an emergency protection order, it is not obliged to do so. The child's welfare is the court's paramount consideration under **s.1(1)** of the Act and the court must be satisfied that to make an order is better than no order at all (**s.1(5)**).

[4] It is useful to include some quotes from key cases. In a coursework question, you are expected to do so.

[5] Consider which rights may have been infringed.

Impact of the Order

If the court makes an EPO, the applicant acquires parental responsibility for the duration of the order. The order can last up to eight days (**s.45(2)(a)**), but can be extended by a further seven days (**s.45(4)**).[6] Its precise contents will depend upon the circumstances existing at the time; for example, it can include a direction for medical assessments to take place and for contact to be arranged with the child's

[6] This buys the local authority enough time to decide what action to take next.

parent, etc. EPOs can also contain an exclusion requirement under **s.44A(1)**.

Section 47 Enquiries

Where the local authority is informed that a child who lives or is found in their area is subject of an EPO or is in police protection the authority shall make such enquiries as they consider necessary (**s.47(1)(a)**). In addition, if an EPO is applied for but not granted, the local authority should consider whether to commence enquiries, as **s.47(1)(b)** provides that where a local authority has reasonable cause to suspect that a child is suffering or likely to suffer significant harm, it must investigate the situation. Once the local authority has completed its enquiries under **s.47**, it will have to decide what action, if any, to take. It may apply for an EPO (if this has not already been applied for), a child assessment order, a care order or supervision order. In urgent situations, the local authority may consider applying for an interim care or supervision order under[7] **s.38**. Under **s.47(6)** the local authority should apply for an order unless the child's welfare can be safeguarded without doing so. If the local authority concludes that it should take action to safeguard or promote the child's welfare, **s.47(8)** requires the authority to take action (so far as it is both within their power and reasonably practicable for them to do so). It should be noted that a child assessment order is not suitable for emergency situations[8] as it is designed to ensure that a child is assessed, rather than protected (**X Council v B (Emergency Protection Order) [2004] EWHC 2015**).

Inherent Jurisdiction

In addition to the provisions of **the Children Act 1989**, inherent jurisdiction, and in particular, wardship, can be utilised if a child is in need of urgent protection. If a child is made a ward of the court, the court takes responsibility for the child and 'no important steps can be taken without the court's consent' (Cross J in **Re S (Infants) [1967] 1 WLR 396 at 407**). Any person with a genuine interest can apply and the child becomes a ward immediately on application (**s.41(2) Senior Courts Act 1981**). Wardship should not be used if the provisions of **the Children Act** can be utilised. There are, however, situations where emergency and long-term protection is required, but the provisions of **the Children Act** would not be appropriate. For example, in **London Borough of Tower Hamlets v M and others [2015] EWHC 869** children at risk of travelling to countries such as Syria to support ISIS were made wards of the court and passport orders were made. According to the local authorities that initiated the applications, the families of the children were unlikely to prevent them

[7] See **Re G (Minors) (Interim Care Order)** [1993] 2 FLR 839.

[8] **Section 43(4)** expressly provides that if the grounds for an emergency protection order are established, the court should make an EPO rather than a CAO.

from travelling overseas. As Gilmore and Glennon explain, 'inherent jurisdiction is usually used to fill any gaps where otherwise there may be no jurisdiction to intervene' (2014, p. 542).

Conclusion

The Children Act 1989 contains two key provisions that can be utilised to protect children in emergency situations, namely **s.44**, which enables the court to make emergency protection orders, and **s.46**, which enables the police to remove a child at risk of significant harm. The latter is only to be used when necessary, as it is preferable for the court to authorise a child's removal. If either provision is utilised the local authority must make enquiries and must consider whether to apply for a more long-term order. In cases where the provisions of **the Children Act 1989** are not appropriate, wardship can be used.

LOOKING FOR EXTRA MARKS?

- Gain extra marks by discussing the use of inherent jurisdiction/wardship in an emergency situation.
- Gain extra marks by referring to the guidelines contained in 'Working Together to Safeguard Children' (2015, Department for Education).

QUESTION 2

Annie is 15 years old. She lives with her mother Bella, her stepfather Cliff and her half-brothers, Daniel who is 12 years old and Evan, who is nine. Her father, Fred, died when she was two years old. Annie has just told one of her teachers, Miss Gregson, that she has been sexually abused by Cliff and does not want to go home. Miss Gregson immediately contacted the local authority and Annie stayed with her best friend, Helena that night. Cliff denies the allegations and claims that Annie has always had a problem with him. Bella confirms that Annie and Cliff have never got on well and cannot believe that Cliff would abuse Annie. Miss Gregson also informed the local authority that she is concerned about Daniel as he is a regular truant, rude to teachers and disruptive in class. As a result, he has fallen behind his classmates. Evan's teacher has reported no problems with Evan's attendance, behaviour or development. Cliff is currently working away from home on a two-month-long project. Annie returned to the family home after he left.

Advise the local authority as to the orders it could apply for and whether they are likely to be granted.

CAUTION!

- As Cliff is currently away from home, you do not need to explain emergency protection orders, but should discuss care and supervision orders.

- As the question requires you to discuss the orders the court could make and whether it is likely to do so, it is not necessary to consider the precise contents of the order, for example contact.

DIAGRAM ANSWER PLAN

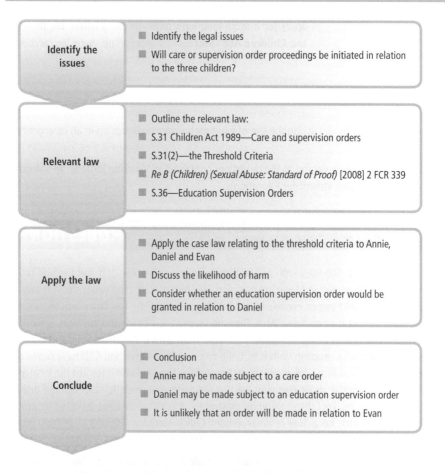

Identify the issues
- Identify the legal issues
- Will care or supervision order proceedings be initiated in relation to the three children?

Relevant law
- Outline the relevant law:
- S.31 Children Act 1989—Care and supervision orders
- S.31(2)—the Threshold Criteria
- *Re B (Children) (Sexual Abuse: Standard of Proof)* [2008] 2 FCR 339
- S.36—Education Supervision Orders

Apply the law
- Apply the case law relating to the threshold criteria to Annie, Daniel and Evan
- Discuss the likelihood of harm
- Consider whether an education supervision order would be granted in relation to Daniel

Conclude
- Conclusion
- Annie may be made subject to a care order
- Daniel may be made subject to an education supervision order
- It is unlikely that an order will be made in relation to Evan

SUGGESTED ANSWER

Annie has made an allegation against her stepfather, Cliff and as the local authority has been informed, presumably enquiries have commenced under **s.47** of **the Children Act 1989**. As Cliff is working

[1] See question one for further information on emergency protection orders and child assessment orders.

away from home, an emergency protection order[1] is not currently required. In addition, there is nothing to suggest that Bella is being uncooperative, which means that a child assessment order would not be necessary.

Care and Supervision Orders[2]

[2] As a result of **s.14** of **the Children and Families Act 2014** proceedings should normally take no longer than 26 weeks.

[3] Interim orders can also be considered.

The local authority must consider whether to apply for a care or supervision order.[3] A care order places the child concerned in the care of the local authority (**s.31(1)(a)**), whose duty it is to receive the child into their care and to keep him in their care while the order remains in force (**s.33(1)**). Most children reside with local authority foster parents, but it is possible for the child to live with a parent, relative or friend, if appropriate. **Section 22C(8)** (inserted by **the Children and Young Persons Act 2008**) requires the local authority to make arrangement for the child to live with his family or friends unless it is not practicable or consistent with his welfare. The local authority has parental responsibility for the child while the care order is in force and has the power to determine the extent to which the parents can exercise their parental rights (**s.33(3)(a)**). If a supervision order is made, the local authority does not acquire parental responsibility and the child is not normally removed from the home. A supervision order puts the child under the supervision of a designated local authority (**s.31(1)**), who appoints a supervisor to 'advise, assist and befriend the supervised child' (**s.35(1)(a)**).

The Threshold Criteria

'A court may only make a care or supervision order if it is satisfied that the child concerned is suffering, or is likely to suffer, significant harm; and that the harm or likelihood of harm is attributable to, the care given to the child or likely to be given to him if the order were not made, not being what it would be reasonable to expect a parent to give to him or the child's being beyond parental control' (**s.31(2)**). Harm is defined as 'ill treatment or the impairment of health or development including, for example, impairment suffered from seeing or hearing the ill-treatment of another' (**s.31(9)**). Ill-treatment includes sexual abuse and thus covers Annie's allegation. Development means physical, intellectual, emotional, social or behavioural development, which in Daniel's case will be impeded by his truancy (**Re O (A Minor) (Care Order: Education: Procedure) [1992] 2 FLR 7**). Both would be considered 'significant' forms of harm.

It is necessary to establish that the child *is* suffering or *is likely to* suffer significant harm. In relation to the former, the relevant time is when the local authority intervened, rather than the date of the hearing, as the child may have been removed from the home by the time the court hears the application (*Re M (A Minor) (Care Order: Threshold Conditions)* **[1994] 2 FLR 577**). In this case, it would need to be proved on the balance of probabilities that Cliff abused Annie, prior to leaving the family home. In relation to Daniel, it will be easy to establish that he has not attended school. In *Re B (Children) (Sexual Abuse: Standard of Proof)* **[2008] 2 FCR 339**, the House of Lords made it clear that the seriousness of the allegation does not affect the standard of proof.[4]

[4]Previously it had been suggested that the more serious the allegation, the greater the evidential requirement.

An order can also be made if a child is *likely* to suffer significant harm, i.e. it is a real possibility that cannot sensibly be ignored (*Re H (Minors) (Sexual Abuse: Standard of Proof)* **[1996] AC 563**). In this case, the court will need to consider whether Daniel and Evan are likely to be abused in the future. In *Re H*, a 15-year-old girl alleged that she had been abused by her mother's partner and so the local authority initiated care proceedings in relation to the girl's younger sisters. The House of Lords held that in order to find that harm was likely, it was first necessary to prove certain primary facts on the balance of probabilities. The court must then decide whether these facts demonstrate that significant harm is a real possibility. In *Re H*, it had not been established that the mother's partner had abused the girl, and so it could not be shown that it was likely that the younger girls would be abused. Even if it is established that Cliff abused Annie, the court might not find that significant harm to the younger children is likely. In *Re D (A Child: Care Order)* **[2011] EWCA Civ 34**, a father was convicted of offences involving indecent photos of children and attempting to procure an underage girl for sex. A care order made in relation to his child was overturned because expert evidence suggested that he posed a low risk to his own daughter. In *Re MA (Care Threshold)* **[2009] EWCA Civ 853**, the couple had three children and also housed a 'mystery girl' who they treated extremely badly. The judge did not find that it was likely that the couple's own children would suffer significant harm on the basis of the abuse of the mystery girl. However, in *Re B (Care Proceedings: Interim Care Order)* **[2010] 1 FLR 1211** an order was made in relation to half-siblings, where one was treated badly and the other perfectly well, because the latter would suffer psychological damage due to the poor treatment of the former. If the court does not find that significant harm to Daniel and Evan is likely, it can nonetheless conclude that the threshold criteria is satisfied in relation to Daniel due to his truancy.[5]

[5]You cannot assume that the court will find that harm to Daniel and Evan is likely.

Cause of the Harm

The local authority must establish that the harm is attributable to the care given or likely to be given (not being what it would be reasonable to expect) or the child is beyond parental control. Harm will be attributable to parental care where a parent's act harms the child or s/he fails to protect the child from harm. Assuming that it is proven that Cliff abused Annie, the harm she has suffered is clearly attributable to the care she has received. In *Re O (A Minor) (Care Order: Education: Procedure)* **[1992] 2 FLR 7**, the court indicated that where a child is suffering harm because he or she is not attending school and that child is living at home, it follows that the child is either beyond parental control or that they are not giving the child the care that it would be reasonable to expect a parent to give. The local authority will therefore be able to establish the threshold criteria in relation to Daniel.

The Court's Decision

If the threshold criteria is met, the court will have to decide whether to make an order, based on the welfare principle (**s.1(1)**) and the non-intervention principle (**s.1(5)**).[6] Where an order is deemed to be in the child's best interests, the court will have to determine whether to make a care *or* supervision order. A care order would be required in relation to Annie as she would need to be removed from the home.[7] The court will only make a care order if the local authority has prepared a care plan which sets out what will happen to the child while in care (**s.31A**). **Section 22(4)** imposes a duty on the local authority to consult the child and her parents and give due consideration to their wishes. If a care order is made it will last until Annie is 18, unless it is discharged or replaced with another order before this point.[8]

Daniel and Evan

If the court finds that there is a real possibility that Cliff will abuse Daniel and Evan, they too would need to be removed from the home under a care order, but as explained above, this is by no means certain. If it does not do so, Evan would remain with his parents, unsupervised, but an order could be made in relation to Daniel due to his truancy. This would not necessitate removal from the home and so a supervision order[9] may be appropriate. Given that Daniel's problems are associated with his schooling, an education supervision order may be the most suitable course of action (**s.36**).[10] The order is only available if the child concerned is of compulsory school age and is not being properly educated (**s.36(3)**). The court will make the order if it is in the child best interests (**s.1(1)**) and if it is satisfied that making the order is better than making no order at all (**s.1(5)**). The designated local education authority will then appoint a supervisor 'to advise, assist, befriend and give directions to the supervised child and his parents in such a way as will, in the opinion of the supervisor, secure that he is properly educated' (**Schedule 3 Para. 12(1)**). The order

[6] See chapter 8 for more detail on the welfare principle and the no-order principle.

[7] It is possible that Annie could live with her mother under a care or supervision order, with the threat that Annie will be removed if Cliff does not leave.

[8] The care order would come to an end if an adoption order was made or a child arrangements order specifying who a child should live with.

[9] A supervision order lasts up to one year, but can be extended to last up to three years on the application of the supervisor (**Schedule 3 para. 6**).

[10] The local education authority applies for an ESO (**s.36(1)**)—it should consult with the social services department of the local authority under **s.36(8)**.

normally lasts one year, but can be extended in appropriate cases (**Schedule 3 Para. 15**).

Conclusion

If the court finds on the balance of probabilities that Cliff abused Annie, a care order would be made and she would be removed from the home. But it does not follow that Daniel and Evan will also be made subject to a care order. Evan is likely to remain in the family home, unsupervised but Daniel may be subject to an education supervision order.

LOOKING FOR EXTRA MARKS?

- Utilise the IRAC method to ensure that you tackle this problem question correctly.
- To gain extra marks, discuss the education supervision order, available under **s.36 of the Children Act**, which may be appropriate for Daniel.

QUESTION | 3

Analyse the differences between adoption and special guardianship in terms of:
a)   the availability of the orders; and
b)   the effect of the orders.

CAUTION!

- This question requires you to discuss the eligibility criteria for and impact of special guardianship orders and adoption orders.
- It is not necessary to discuss the adoption process in detail—for example, the role of adoption agencies, matching and adoption placements—as the question asks candidates to focus on availability and effect.

DIAGRAM ANSWER PLAN

Explain who can be adopted and who can be the subject of a special guardianship order

Discuss the eligibility criteria under the Adoption and Children Act 2002 and the Children Act 1989

Identify the proceedings during which orders can be made

▼

Discuss the effect of the orders in relation to parenthood and parental responsibility

▼

Discuss links with the birth family

▼

Conclusion

SUGGESTED ANSWER

[1]Ensure that you refer to 'special guardians' in this essay and not simply 'guardians', which are different.

Adoption and special guardianship orders[1] are both designed to ensure that a child is provided with a secure, stable home. Adoption was formally introduced by **the Adoption of Children Act 1926** and is currently regulated by **the Adoption and Children Act 2002**. It severs the legal link between the child and his birth parents, and in almost all respects, the child is treated as the child of the adoptive parents. In 2012, 5,206 adoptions were registered on the Adopted Children Register, most of which involved children who had been looked after

[2]British Association for Adoption and Fostering—see http://www.BAAF.org.uk.

by the local authority (BAAF, 2015)[2]. Special guardianship orders are not designed to cut the tie between the child and the birth family, but provide the special guardians with enhanced parental responsibility. They were introduced by **the Adoption and Children Act 2002** and are now regulated by **s.14A–F** of **the Children Act 1989**. In 2011, 2,973 orders were made during public law proceedings, whilst 1,288 orders were made in private law proceedings (Judicial and Court Statistics, 2012). As Lowe and Douglas explain, 'special guardianship orders are intended to meet the needs of children for whom adoption is not appropriate (e.g. older children who do not wish to be adopted)' (2015, p. 730). Selwyn and Masson's research findings demonstrate that special guardianship orders are most frequently used where children are placed with relatives, for example grandparents. In contrast, adoption orders are rarely made to family members as 'in family adoption is viewed as distorting legal relationships' (2014, p. 1711) but see **N v B and Ors [2013] EWHC 820**.

[3]I have taken each issue and discussed special guardianship and adoption. You could have one section on all aspects of adoption and one section on special guardianship.

Availability[3]

An application for either order must be made before the child reaches 18. A special guardianship order can only be made if the child has not attained adulthood at the date of the order, but an adoption order can be made in relation to an 18-year-old, provided that the application was submitted beforehand (**s.49(4)** and **(5) Adoption and Children Act 2002**). This is because adoption creates a permanent relationship between the adopter and adoptee, whereas a special guardian is only required during minority. An adoption order cannot be made in relation to a child who has been married (**s.47(8)**) or in a civil partnership (**s.47(8A)**), and although **the Children Act** does not contain equivalent provisions, special guardianship orders would not be made in relation to a child who had been married or a civil partner.[4]

[4] Consider why this is the case.

Eligibility to Adopt/Be a Special Guardian

A special guardian must be aged 18 or over and must not be a parent of the child in question (**s.14A(2) Children Act 1989**). An order can be made in favour of a single person, a couple, two persons who are not in an intimate relationship or more than two persons. For example, in *Re A and B* **[2010] EWHC 3824** an order was made in favour of the maternal and paternal grandparents after the father had killed the mother. **Section 49** of **the Adoption and Children Act 2002** indicates that an application for adoption can be made by one person or by a couple who may be married, civil partners or cohabiting, and may include the natural parent of the child to be adopted. Domicile and residence requirements apply (**s.49(2)** and **(3)**) and in the case of a couple, both adopters must be 21 (**s.50(1)**) unless one of them is the natural parent, in which case s/he only needs to be 18 years of age (**s.50(2)**). If an adoption order is to be made in favour of one person, s/he must be 21 and must not normally be married or in a civil partnership (**s.51(1)**). In addition to this, the adopters must have lived with the child for a set period of time. For example, if the child has been placed with the potential adopters by an adoption agency, one or both of them must have lived with the child at all times for ten weeks preceding the application (**s.42(2)**). If the adopters are the child's current foster parents, the residence requirement is one year (**s.42(4)**).

Certain persons can apply for a special guardianship order without leave: i.e. the child's guardian; a person named in a child arrangements order as a person with whom the child is to live; foster parents or relatives with whom the child has lived for one year; a person with whom the child has lived for three years; a person who has the consent of those named in a child arrangements order as persons with whom the child should live; a person who has consent of the local authority (if the child is in care); and any person who has consent of all those with parental responsibility (**s.14A(5)**). This demonstrates that a special guardianship order can be made even if the child has not lived with the applicant, which is not possible in the case of an adoption order. *Re A and B* is an example of this, for the maternal grandparents were made special guardians even though the children did not live with them. **Section 14(A)(5)** also indicates that a special guardianship order may be made with or without the consent of the parents or persons with parental responsibility. The position in relation to adoption is different as an adoption order can only be made if the parent or guardian consents or if the court is satisfied that consent should be dispensed with[5] because the parent or guardian cannot be found or lacks mental capacity or because the welfare of the child requires the consent to be dispensed with (**s.52(1)**).

[5] The need to obtain consent or for the court to dispense with it, also applies to the placement of a child for adoption, which occurs earlier in the process (**ss.19** and **21**).

Proceedings

[6] The applicant must give three months' written notice to the local authority of intention to apply under **s.14A(7) CA 1989**.

A special guardianship order can be made following a specific application[6] or during other family proceedings (**s.14A(6)**). In *Re T (A Child: Murdered Parent)* **[2011] EWHC B4**, a special guardianship order was made during care proceedings, whilst in *Re L (A Child) (Special Guardianship Order and Ancillary Orders)* **[2007] 1 FCR 804** the couple had applied for adoption but the judge made a special guardianship order.[7] In contrast an adoption order cannot be made during other family proceedings. In both cases, the order will only be made if it is in the child's best interests (**s.1(1) Children Act 1989** and **s.1(2) Adoption and Children Act 2002**).

[7] If a special guardianship order is made instead of adoption, a local authority report on suitability is required under **s.14A(8) CA 1989**.

The Effect of the Order

Section 46(1) of **the Adoption and Children Act 2002** provides that an adoption order gives the adopters parental responsibility for the child. It also operates to extinguish the parental responsibiity which any person (other than the adopter) had for the child immediately before the order was made (**s.46(2)**). Furthermore, any orders that had previously been made under **the Children Act** would be terminated by the adoption order (**s.46(2)**). **Section 67(1)** indicates that 'an adopted person is to be treated in law as if born as the child of the adopters or adopter'. The child therefore takes on the nationality of the adopter, can inherit from the adopter and the adopter acquires the duty to support the child financially. However, the child remains within prohibited degrees of relationship in relation to his or her birth family, for the purpose of marriage (**s.74(1)**).

In contrast, a special guardianship order does not transfer legal parenthood from the natural parents to the special guardians, which means that the child's nationality and succession rights are unaffected and the birth parents remain liable for child support. In addition, the natural parents do not lose parental responsibility, although their ability to exercise it is extremely limited, as the special guardians acquire enhanced parental responsibility. This means that the special guardians make the day-to-day decisions regarding the child[8] and only have to consult the birth parents in limited circumstances, for example to

[8] Special guardians are entitled to local authority support services.

change the child's surname (**s.14C(3)(a) Children Act 1989**). Thus, in **Re L** the special guardians had to apply to the court for leave to change the child's name because the parents did not consent. The court refused because the child should know that she is being brought up by her grandparents. This reflects the fact that special guardianship is intended to be 'open' (as some adoptions are) and is not intended to 'transplant' the child into a new family (as traditional adoptions are). If the couple had adopted the child, they would have been entitled to change her name. Similarly, a special guardian cannot remove the child from the UK for more than three months without the consent of those with parental responsibility or the court (**s.14C(3)(b)**), whereas an adoptive parent does not require permission to take the child abroad for any length of time.

Post-order Contact

A significant distinction between adoption and special guardianship exists in relation to post-order contact with the birth family. Before making a special guardianship order, the court has to decide whether contact should be ordered and whether existing **s.8** orders should be varied or discharged (**s.14B(1)**). This emphasises that maintaining contact is not unusual when a special guardianship order is made.[9] **Section 46(6)** of **the Adoption and Children Act 2002** requires the court to consider whether any arrangements for contact should be made before making an adoption order and although post-adoption contact is not uncommon, it is highly unusual to impose it on the adopters (**Re R (Adoption: Contact) [2005] EWCA Civ 1128**). Consequently, in **Re T (Adoption: Contact) [2010] EWCA Civ 1527** the maternal grandmother's application for contact was refused because the adoptive parents were not in favour. Even indirect contact has been denied because the adopters opposed it (see **Oxfordshire County Council v X, Y and J [2010] EWCA Civ 581**)

[9] In **Re L,** the court ordered direct contact with mother and indirect contact with father.

Conclusion

This answer has emphasised the distinctions between adoption and special guardianship, which in turn reveal that each order will be appropriate in different circumstances.

LOOKING FOR EXTRA MARKS?

- Utilise the PEA method to ensure that you answer this essay question appropriately.
- Demonstrate the currency of your knowledge by citing recent cases on post-adoption contact, for example **Re T (Adoption: Contact) [2010] EWCA Civ 1527** and **Oxfordshire County Council v X, Y and J [2010] EWCA Civ 581**.

Isaac and Joanna are in their forties, have been married for 15 years and have lived in England all their lives. They have no children of their own but are close to all their nieces and nephews. Isaac's niece, Katy has one child, Libby, who is five years old. Katy has had a drug problem for the past few years and just over a year ago, Libby was taken into care by the local authority. Since then Libby has lived with Isaac and Joanna, who were approved as local authority foster parents. Katy is allowed to see Libby once a week. Libby's father disappeared shortly after she was born and cannot be found.

Joanna's niece, Michelle, who is 21, has a child, Nicola, who has just turned three years old. Michelle suffered with post-natal depression after the birth of Nicola and found it difficult to cope. When Nicola was two months old Michelle left her with Isaac and Joanna, while she went travelling. Isaac and Joanna sent Michelle regular photographs of Nicola and kept her informed about Nicola's progress, but no direct contact occurred. Michelle does not know who Nicola's father is.

Isaac and Joanna want to adopt Libby and Nicola. Katy does not object to this as she feels that Isaac and Joanna will provide a much better home for Libby. She does want to remain in contact with Libby, though. Michelle has just returned from her travels and objects to Nicola being adopted. Michelle wants Nicola to live with her once she has found herself a job and a suitable home. Isaac and Joanna do not believe that Michelle will be able to find a job, a home and look after Nicola.

Advise Isaac and Joanna as to whether they will be able to adopt Libby and Nicola.

CAUTION!

- This question asks you to advise a couple as to whether they can adopt two children. To do this, you must explain the rules on eligibility, notice of intention to adopt, the qualifying residence periods and the requirements for making an adoption order.

- It is not necessary to discuss the effect of an adoption order in any depth.

DIAGRAM ANSWER PLAN

Identify the issues	■ Identify the legal issues ■ Will Isaac and Joanna be able to adopt Libby and Nicola? ■ What alternatives to adoption are available?
Relevant law	■ Outline the relevant law: ■ Paramountcy principle—s.1(2) Adoption and Children Act 2002 ■ Requirements for adoption—ss.42–50 ■ Dispensing with consent—ss.51–52 ■ Special Guardianship orders—s.14A–F Children Act 1989
Apply the law	■ Assess whether Isaac and Joanna are eligible to adopt ■ Consider whether Michelle's consent will be dispensed with ■ Consider whether adoption is in the children's best interests
Conclude	■ Conclusion ■ Decide whether adoption orders will be made in respect of Libby and Nicola

SUGGESTED ANSWER

Isaac and Joanna wish to adopt Libby and Nicola. Both children are under 18, which means that they can be adopted (**s.49(4) Adoption and Children Act 2002**). Isaac and Joanna are eligible to adopt, as both are over 21 (**s.50(1)**) and are domiciled and habitually resident in the British Isles (**s.49(2) and (3)**). Whenever a court or adoption agency comes to a decision relating to the adoption of a child, the paramount consideration 'must be the child's welfare, throughout his life' (**s.1(2)**). The court or adoption agency[1] is also required to bear in mind that any delay is likely to prejudice the child's welfare (**s.1(3)**) and must have regard to the matters contained in the welfare check-list (**s.1(4)**).

[1] In 'stranger' adoptions, the adoption agency places children with potential adopters. The latter are vetted for suitability and matched to an appropriate child.

Procedure

The couple would have to give the local authority notice of their intention to adopt because the children have not been placed with them as potential adopters. When a court makes a care order, it can make a placement order at the same time if the care plan provides that the child should be adopted (**ss.21–22**).[2] The case study does not suggest that a placement order was made when Libby was taken into care: she was therefore accommodated with Isaac and Joanna as foster parents rather than potential adopters. The arrangement in relation to Nicola is even less formal, as Michelle left her with Isaac and Joanna while she went travelling. The couple must give no less than three months' notice to the local authority before making the application (**s.44**). The local authority will then conduct an investigation and report to the court (**s.44(5)**).[3]

[2]**Section 22** of **the Children Act 1989** *requires* the local authority to apply for a placement order if it thinks that the child should be adopted.

[3]The report will consider the appropriateness of adoption and alternatives to adoption.

Residence Requirements

Before an application for adoption can be made, the child must have lived with the potential adopters for a set period of time. If the child has been placed with the potential adopters by an adoption agency, one or both must have lived with the child for ten weeks preceding the application (**s.42(2)**). As explained above, Libby and Nicola were not placed by an adoption agency and as a result the qualifying residence period is longer. In relation to Libby, the residence requirement is one year, as Isaac and Joanna are her foster parents (**s.42(4)**). In relation to Nicola, the residence requirement is three years (during the period of five years preceding the application) (**s.42(5)**).

Nicola has resided with the couple for almost three years and so they would have to wait a few months before they can make an application or they can apply for leave to adopt (**s.42(6)**). They can give notice of intention to adopt immediately: Michelle will not be permitted to remove Nicola from them once they have given notice of intention to adopt, applied for adoption or applied for leave to make an application for adoption (**s.36(1)**).

Consent

Section 47(1) states that an adoption order cannot be made if the child has a parent or guardian unless one of three conditions is met. The first is that the parent or guardian consents to the making of the adoption order (**s.47(2)(a)**), *or* the parent or guardian consented under **s.20** (i.e. gave advanced consent), has not withdrawn it and does not oppose the order (**s.47(2)(b)**) *or* the parent or guardian's consent should be dispensed with under **s.52** (**s.47(2)(c)**). The second condition is that the child has been placed for adoption by an adoption agency and either the parent consented to the placement or the child was placed under a placement order and no parent or guardian opposed the adoption order (**s.47(4)**). Alternatively, the court must be satisfied that the child is free for adoption under Scottish or Northern Irish legislation (**s.47(6)**).

194 THE LAW RELATING TO CHILDREN: PUBLIC LAW AND ADOPTION

Libby

It seems that Katy will consent to the adoption, but this must be given 'unconditionally and with full understanding of what it involves' (**s.52(5)**). Katy should therefore be aware that adoption will terminate the legal tie between her and Libby and will extinguish her parental responsibility (**s.46(1)**). Katy must understand that she will not be able to change her mind after the adoption order has been made, as an order will only be revoked in exceptional circumstances (see *Re W (Adoption Order: Set aside and Leave to Oppose)* **[2010] EWCA Civ 1535**). **Section 52(6)** indicates that 'parent' refers to a parent with parental responsibility. It is unclear whether Libby's father has parental responsibility,[4] but if he does, the court will dispense with the need to obtain his consent under **s.52(1)(a)**, as he cannot be found (*KK v FY* **[2014] EWHC 3111 (Fam)**).

The fact that Katy will consent to adoption does not mean that the court is required to make an adoption order, as the decision will be based on the welfare principle (**s.1(2)**) and the welfare checklist (**s.1(4)**). The factors contained in the welfare checklist are:[5] the child's ascertainable wishes and feelings; the child's particular needs; the likely effect on the child (throughout his life) of having ceased to be a member of the original family and become an adopted person; the child's age, sex, background and any other relevant characteristics; any harm which the child has suffered or is at risk of suffering; and the relationship which the child has with relatives or other relevant persons. This final factor requires the court or adoption agency to consider the likelihood of any such relationship continuing, the value to the child of its doing so, the ability and willingness of any child's relatives, or of any such person to provide the child with a secure environment in which the child can develop and otherwise to meet the child's needs and the wishes and feelings of any of the child's relatives or of any such person regarding the child. Adoption may be in Libby's interests, particularly if it is open and she continues to have contact with her mother.

The court must consider the whole range of powers available to it under **the Adoption and Children Act 2002** and **the Children Act 1989** and must not make any order under the former, unless 'it considers that making the order would be better for the child than not doing so' (**s.1(6) Adoption and Children Act 2002**). The court could therefore make a special guardianship order, a child arrangements order or no order at all,[6] in which case Libby would remain in the care of the local authority, with Isaac and Joanna continuing to act as foster parents. Although the White Paper that preceded **the Adoption and Children Act 2002** indicated that special guardianship will sometimes be more appropriate for children being cared

[4] See chapter 7 for an explanation of the law relating to parental responsibility.

[5] The checklist is similar to that contained in **s.1(3) Children Act 1989**.

[6] These orders are made under **the Children Act 1989** and so the welfare principle under **s.1(1)** applies.

for on a permanent basis by members of the wider birth family (Adoption—a new approach, 2000, para. 5.8), there is no presumption in favour of this order over adoption. As Wall L.J. emphasised in *Re M-J (Adoption Order or Special Guardianship Order)* **[2007] EWCA Civ 56**, the decision 'depends on the order which in all the circumstances of the case best meets the welfare needs of the child or children concerned' (para. 17). It is likely that an order will be made, rather than no order at all, as it will be in Libby's interests to formalise the relationship with Isaac and Joanna. Whichever order the court makes, it is probable that contact with Katy will be maintained and this is unlikely to be problematic.[7]

[7] This sentence concludes the position relating to Libby.

Nicola

Michelle will not consent to Nicola being adopted, which means that Isaac and Joanna can only adopt her if Michelle's consent is dispensed with.[8] Consent can be dispensed with 'if the welfare of the child *requires* the consent to be dispensed with'(**s.52(1)(b)**). As Wall L.J. explained in *Re P (Placement Orders: Parental Consent)* **[2008] EWCA Civ 535**, the court must be satisfied that 'the child's welfare requires adoption as opposed to something short of adoption' (paras 124–125), which will be difficult to establish. The court will base its decision on the welfare principle (**s.1(2)**), the welfare checklist (**s.1(4)**) and **s.1(6)**, which requires the court to consider alternatives to adoption. In *Re B (Adoption Order)* **[2001] EWCA Civ 347**, an adoption order made in favour of the child's foster mother was overturned as the Court of Appeal considered a residence order[9] to be more appropriate because adoption would terminate the legal relationship between the boy and his father, with whom he had a very good relationship. The position in relation to Michelle and Nicola is different as Nicola has had no direct contact with Michelle since she was two months old. Nonetheless, adoption against the will of a parent is considered an extreme step (see *Re B-S (Children)* **[2013] EWCA 963**). The court might therefore prefer to grant a special guardianship order or child arrangements order, particularly if the local authority has made a specific recommendation. In *A Local Authority v Y, Z and others* **[2006] 2 FLR 41**, a special guardianship order was made in favour of the children's aunt and uncle, with whom they lived. The court felt that this was preferable to an order granting them mere residence as it would not cement the relationship between the children and their aunt and uncle and was more appropriate than adoption, which would be harsh on the mother and skew relationships within the family. It also held that making no order at all was not appropriate, as the children and their uncle and aunt would have no security. In relation to Nicola, the court should therefore make an order, rather than no

[8] As Michelle does not know who the father is, there cannot be a father with parental responsibility whose consent is required.

[9] This would now be a child arrangements order, specifying who the child should live with.

[10] This sentence concludes the position relating to Nicola.

order at all, so that the matter can be formally settled. The court is likely to conclude that Nicola should not be removed from Isaac and Joanna and the court may grant a special guardianship order so that the relationship between them can be formalised. Whichever order the court makes in relation to Nicola, it is likely to provide for contact between her and her mother.[10]

LOOKING FOR EXTRA MARKS?

■ Ensure that you consider alternatives to adoption, namely special guardianship and child arrangements orders.

■ Gain extra marks by considering post-order contact with the birth mother.

TAKING THINGS FURTHER

■ Cooper, P. 'Speaking when they are spoken to: Hearing vulnerable witnesses in care proceedings' (2014) Child and Family Law Quarterly 26 (2) 132.
Considers how vulnerable witnesses are heard during care proceedings and recommends steps that the family justice system should take to protect such witnesses.

■ Doughty, J. 'Care proceedings—Is there a better way?' (2014) Child and Family Law Quarterly 26 (2) 113.
Considers alternatives to care proceedings identified by the Family Justice Review 2011 and the steps that have been taken to implement them.

■ Hedley, Sir M. 'Family life and child protection: Cleveland, Baby P et al' (2014) Child and Family Law Quarterly 26 (1) 7.
Sir Mark Hedley, retired judge of the High Court, reflects on his experience of child protection cases. He argues that neither parents nor professionals are perfect and that there is a risk of wrong decisions being made.

■ Heenan, A. 'Step-parent adoption and proportionality' (2015) Journal of Social Welfare and Family Law 37 (2) 244.
Examines the decision in Re P (Step-parent Adoption) *[2014] EWCA Civ 1774, where the Court of Appeal overturned the High Court's refusal to dispense with the requirement to obtain the consent of the father, who had not had contact with the child for nine years.*

■ Holt, K. and Kelly, N. 'When adoption without parental consent breaches human rights: Implications of Re B-S (Children) [2013] EWCA 963' (2015) Journal of Social Welfare and Family Law 37 (2) 228.
Examines the decision of the Court of Appeal in Re B-S, *which emphasised that adoption without parental consent is extremely draconian and stressed that courts must weigh up all the options available for a child.*

- Masson, J. 'Third (or fourth) time lucky for care proceedings reform?' (2015) Child and Family Law Quarterly 27 (1) 3.

  Considers the implementation of the Public Law Outline 2010 and discusses the views of practitioners about the likely success of the scheme.

- Selwyn, J. and Masson, J. 'Adoption, special guardianship and residence orders: A comparison of disruption rates' (2014) Fam Law 1709.

  Focuses on the duration of adoption, special guardianship and residence orders but also discusses the differences in the use of each type of order.

Online Resource Centre

www.oxfordtextbooks.co.uk/orc/qanda/

Go online for extra essay and problem questions, a glossary of key terms, online versions of all the answer plans and audio commentary on how selected ones were put together, and a range of podcasts which include advice on exam and coursework technique and advice for other assessment methods.

11 Mixed Topic Questions

In real life a client is likely to require advice in relation to a number of family issues. For example, a person seeking a divorce may need advice relating to the ground for divorce, financial relief, arrangements for children and protection from domestic violence. As a consequence, family law assessments sometimes require students to demonstrate knowledge and understanding of a variety of topics. Mixed questions usually take the form of problem questions: this chapter therefore contains five problem questions that cover more than one area of family law. The list below indicates the topics covered by each question.

Question 1
Forced marriage: forced marriage protection orders, inherent jurisdiction, wardship, emergency protection orders, prohibited steps orders
Nullity: annulment of a voidable marriage, non-existent marriage

Question 2
Divorce: the ground for divorce, fact (b)—behaviour
Domestic violence: non-molestation orders and occupation orders

Question 3
Legal parenthood: IVF treatment, the Human Fertilisation and Embryology Act 2008
Child Maintenance: liability under the Child Support Act 1991

Question 4
Children Act 1989: Private law, s.8 orders, welfare principle, welfare checklist, presumption of parental involvement
Resolution of family disputes: mediation and litigation

Question 5
Financial relief: on divorce, periodical payments, orders for sale, pension sharing orders, property adjustment orders
Family property: claiming a beneficial ownership in the family home, joint bank accounts

---

Omana is 16 and has just started her A levels. She was born in England but her parents were born in India. She has just told one of her teachers that she is worried that her parents will force her to marry her cousin from India. Her parents have been discussing it with her for some time. Omana told them that she did not feel ready for marriage, that she wants to stay in school to finish her A levels and then study at university. Omana's parents have said that it is her duty to obey them and that if she does not do so, they will disown her. Omana told the teacher that her parents are currently arranging a 'holiday' to India and Omana is concerned that when she gets there she will be forced to marry her cousin.

a) **What can be done to prevent Omana from being forced to marry? [40 marks]**

b) **If Omana is required to marry her cousin, what can she then do? [10 marks]**

CAUTION!

■ You should notice that Omana is 16 and therefore still a child. You should therefore discuss child protection measures in addition to **the Forced Marriage (Civil Protection) Act 2007**.

■ The second part of your answer should focus on nullity, which is the primary remedy for forced marriage. You cannot consider divorce, as you are not given any information to enable you to discuss it.

DIAGRAM ANSWER PLAN

Identify the issues
- Identify the legal issues
- What steps can be taken to prevent Omana from being forced to marry?
- What can be done if Omana is forced to marry?

Relevant law
- Outline the relevant law:
- The Forced Marriage (Civil Protection) Act 2007 and Family Law Act 1996
- Inherent jurisdiction and wardship
- The Children Act 1989: emergency protection orders, prohibited steps orders and police protection

Apply the law
- Apply the provisions of the Family Law Act 1996, the Children Act 1989 and the Matrimonial Causes Act 1973 to Omana's situation
- E.g. the definition of force, discussion of who would apply for orders, the definition of duress

Conclude
- Conclusion
- The local authority should be informed as soon as possible and an application made for a FMPO or EPO
- If the marriage goes ahead it is voidable and can be annulled

SUGGESTED ANSWER

Omana appears to be at risk of being forced to marry. A forced marriage is one 'conducted without the valid consent of one or both parties where duress is a factor' (Forced Marriage: A Wrong not a Right, FCO/Home Office, 2005, p. 1). It must be distinguished from an arranged marriage,[1] which is one where the families of one or both parties take a leading role in choosing the spouse, but the bride and groom provide free and full consent. Clearly, Omana will not provide free and full consent and, as a result, she requires protection.

It should be noted that forced marriage is a criminal offence punishable by up to seven years in prison as a result of **s.121(1)** of **the Anti-social Behaviour, Crime and Policing Act 2014**. In addition, **s.121(3)** makes it an offence to practise deception with the intention

[1] Do not confuse forced and arranged marriages.

of causing another person to leave the UK for the purpose of forced marriage. Omana's parents may, therefore, be prosecuted for their actions, but as the focus of the question is the protection of Omana, this will not be considered further.[2]

[2]Do not waste time discussing the criminalisation of forced marriage. Focus on the steps that can be taken to protect Omana and what she can do if she is forced to marry.

Preventing a Forced Marriage

Although it is possible to apply for a non-molestation order under **the Family Law Act 1996** or an injunction under **the Protection from Harassment Act 1997** to protect Omana, this is unlikely. Neither statute was passed with forced marriage or child protection in mind: they are not the most appropriate means of dealing with this situation.[3] In contrast, **the Forced Marriage (Civil Protection) Act 2007** was passed in order to provide specific protection for those at risk of being forced to marry. The Act inserted 19 provisions into **the Family Law Act 1996**, which can be used to protect adults and children. **Section 63A** of **the Family Law Act 1996** provides that the courts can make an order for the purpose of protecting a person from being forced into a marriage or for the purpose of protecting a person who has been forced into a marriage. Force includes coercion 'by threats or other psychological means' (**s.63A(6)**), which reflects the fact that threats of social exclusion are common in forced marriage cases. The pressure being exerted on Omana would thus fall within the definition of force.

[3]You could point out the problems with each of these statutes.

An application for a forced marriage protection order (FMPO) can be made by the person to be protected or a relevant third party[4] without the need for leave of the court (**s.63C(2)**). **The Family Law Act 1996 (Forced Marriage) (Relevant Third Party) Order 2009** designates local authorities as relevant third parties. In this case, it is likely that Omana's teacher would contact the local authority and it would submit an application to the court. Any other interested person, such as Omana's teacher or friends, would require leave to apply for an order.

[4]This is an advantage of FMPOs, compared to non-molestation orders and injunctions to prohibit harassment.

The order can be made against those who force, attempt to force or may force a person to marry (**s.63B(2)**) and those who encourage or assist them (**s.63B(3)**). Where necessary, the application can be made without notice (**s.63D**). The order itself may contain 'any such prohibitions, restrictions or requirements and such other terms as the court considers appropriate' (**s.63B(1)**). For example, an order might prohibit the respondents from organising a marriage for the victim and oblige them to surrender the victim's passport to the court, which would be appropriate in Omana's case. If the victim has been removed from the jurisdiction the order can require the respondent to allow the victim to attend the British High Commission. This obligation was imposed by the High Court in the much-publicised case of Dr Humayra Abedin, who was held captive by her family in Bangladesh.

Following the order, Dr Abedin was released into the custody of the British High Commission and returned to the UK.

Failure to comply with a protection order constitutes contempt of court, which is punishable by up to two years in prison (**s.630**). It is also a specific criminal offence punishable by up to five years in prison as a result of **s.120(1)** of **the Anti-social Behaviour, Crime and Policing Act 2014**.

Inherent Jurisdiction

[5] The High Court can transfer cases to the Family Court.

In addition to the above, the High Court can use its inherent jurisdiction to protect those at risk of forced marriage.[5] Inherent jurisdiction means the automatic, non-statutory powers that the Court can exercise on behalf of the Crown. The Crown, as 'parens patriae' or father of the nation, has a special duty to protect its subjects, particularly those who cannot protect themselves, such as children and vulnerable adults. The High Court has employed its inherent jurisdiction to protect adults and children at risk of forced marriage. In relation to the latter, the High Court is likely to invoke its inherent jurisdiction by making the child a ward of the court. A child becomes a ward of the court on the issue of a summons making the application (**s.41(2)** of **the Senior Courts Act 1981**), which means that it is immediate. The effect of wardship is that no important step can be taken in respect of the ward without the leave of the court. It can therefore be used to prevent parents from arranging a marriage for their child and to prevent them from taking the child overseas. Omana could therefore be made a ward of the court, as she is 16 years old. The court would order the surrender of her passport.

The Children Act 1989

The provisions of **the Children Act 1989** can also be utilised to protect a child at risk of forced marriage. In urgent cases, an emergency protection order (EPO) can be made by the court under **s.44** of **the Children Act 1989** if it is satisfied 'that there is reasonable cause to believe that the child is likely to suffer significant harm if he is not removed to accommodation provided by or on behalf of the applicant' (**s.44(1)(a)**). The police, the local authority, the NSPCC or even Omana's teacher can apply for the order, as anyone can make an application. Usually, it is the local authority that applies for the order and in such cases, the court will only make the EPO if it is satisfied that enquiries in respect of a child are being made and that 'those enquiries are being frustrated by access to the child being unreasonably refused to a person authorised to seek access and that the applicant has reasonable cause to believe that access to the child is required as a matter of urgency' (**s.47(1)(b)**). If someone other than the local authority applies for the order, the authority would be informed and would be obliged to commence enquiries under **s.47(1)(a)(i)**.[6] As EPOs are supposed to be used in urgent cases, they are usually made on an ex parte basis. The order can last up to eight days (**s.45(2)(a)**), but can be extended by a further seven days (**s.45(4)**). In less urgent circumstances, an application can be made under **s.8** for a prohibited steps order, but the provisions contained in **the Family Law Act 1996** are more appropriate. In extreme situations, the police could be telephoned and Omana could be taken into police protection under **s.46** of **the Children Act 1989**.

[6] Consider what the local authority might do after conducting enquiries.

The Position if Omana is Forced to Marry

If Omana is taken to India and required to marry her cousin, inherent jurisdiction or **the Forced Marriage (Civil Protection) Act 2007** can be used to secure her return to this jurisdiction. Omana can then petition for an annulment under **s.12(1)(c)** of **the Matrimonial Causes Act 1973**, which provides that a marriage is voidable if either party 'did not validly consent to it whether in consequence of duress, mistake, unsoundness of mind or otherwise'. As explained above, a forced marriage is one conducted without the valid consent of one or both parties where *duress* is a factor. In *Hirani v Hirani* **[1982] 4 FLR 232**, the court indicated that the test for duress is whether the threats were such as to destroy the reality of the consent given by the petitioner. In this case, the 19-year-old girl was told by her parents to marry the person that they had chosen or pack her bags and leave. This pressure meant that the girl's consent to marry was not given freely and as a result, a decree of nullity was granted. The ability to annul, rather than dissolve a marriage due to lack of consent is important in cases of forced marriage. In *P v R (Forced Marriage: Annulment: Procedure)* **[2003] 1 FLR 661**, the court heard evidence that a lesser stigma is attached to a woman who obtains a decree of nullity than a woman who obtains a divorce.[7] Omana would need to act relatively quickly as **s.13(4)** of **the Matrimonial Causes Act 1973** imposes a three-year bar on petitions for annulment of marriage. After three years have expired, the victim can petition for divorce or apply for a declaration that the marriage never existed[8] under **s.55** of **the Family Law Act 1986**, as in *B v I* **[2010] 1 FLR 1721**.

[7] There is no information in the case study to enable you to discuss the ground and facts for divorce.

[8] You could explain the difference between this and a decree annulling a voidable marriage.

Conclusion

The local authority should be contacted as soon as possible and an application submitted for an FMPO or an EPO. Alternatively, inherent jurisdiction can be utilised. If Omana is taken overseas before steps can be taken to protect her, an application should be made to the court to secure her return, following which she can apply for a decree of nullity.

LOOKING FOR EXTRA MARKS?

■ You can briefly mention non-molestation orders and injunctions to prohibit harassment, but should explain that Omana is unlikely to apply for such orders.

■ Gain extra marks by explaining that Omana's marriage could be declared non-existent under **the Family Law Act 1986**.

QUESTION | 2

Poppy and Quinn have been married for three years. Six months ago Quinn lost his job at the local factory and started drinking heavily. When Quinn is drunk he is aggressive: he regularly shouts at Poppy, throws things across the room and smashes glasses and plates, etc. Last month, when Quinn was drunk he punched Poppy. Afterwards he said that he was very sorry and that he would not do it again. As Poppy wanted to believe Quinn, she stayed in the house, but last week when he was drunk he attacked her again. A neighbour called the police, as he could hear Poppy screaming. When the police arrived, they called an ambulance and Poppy was taken to hospital. She had several broken ribs and severe bruising. Poppy has not returned to the family home: she is currently staying with her sister, Rachael, but cannot remain there indefinitely as there is not enough room. Poppy has decided that she wants to divorce Quinn and to return to her house but she is worried that Quinn will be violent towards her.

Advise Poppy.

N.B. You do not need to discuss the financial aspects of the divorce.

CAUTION!

■ The question indicates that Poppy wishes to return to the family home, which means that occupation orders must be discussed. You should be aware that Poppy is an entitled applicant. You should also discuss non-molestation orders.

■ No specific marks have been allocated to the divorce and domestic violence elements of the question, but you will need to spend more time explaining the law relating to domestic violence.

DIAGRAM ANSWER PLAN

Identify the issues	■ Identify the legal issues ■ Can Poppy divorce Quinn? ■ What steps can be taken to protect Poppy from domestic violence?
Relevant law	■ Outline the relevant law: ■ S.1 Matrimonial Causes Act 1973—ground and facts for divorce ■ S.42 Family Law Act 1996—non-molestation orders ■ S.33 Family Law Act 1996—occupation orders
Apply the law	■ Apply s.1(2)(b) MCA 1973—behaviour to Poppy's situation ■ Discuss whether Poppy and Quinn are associated persons, whether Quinn has molested Poppy, whether Poppy is an entitled applicant, whether the balance of harm test has been satisfied
Conclude	■ Conclusion ■ Decide if Poppy can divorce Quinn and on what basis ■ Determine whether Poppy can apply for domestic violence orders

SUGGESTED ANSWER

Poppy wishes to divorce her husband Quinn, and as they have been married for three years, **s.3(1)** of **the Matrimonial Causes Act 1973**, which provides that 'no petition for divorce shall be presented to the court before the expiration of the period of one year from the date of the marriage' poses no problem.

Section 1(1) indicates that a petition for divorce can be presented 'on the ground that the marriage has broken down irretrievably'. Irretrievable breakdown of marriage can only be proved by estab- lishing one of the five facts[1] listed in **s.1(2)** (see ***Buffery v Buffery*** **[1988] 2 FLR 365**). If the court is satisfied that one of the facts has been established, it is assumed that the marriage has broken down irretrievably (**s.1(4) MCA 1973**) and although the court is required to enquire into facts alleged by the petitioner (**s.1(3) MCA 1973**), in reality the special procedure involves no testing of the evidence.

[1] Do not refer to the five facts as 'grounds' for divorce.

Under **s.1(2)(b)**, irretrievable breakdown occurs if 'the respondent behaved in such a way that the petitioner cannot reasonably be expected to live with the respondent'. The behaviour[2] may be an act, an omission or course of conduct, which has some reference to the marriage and has an effect on the petitioner (*Katz v Katz* **[1972] 3 ALL ER 219**). In *Livingstone-Stallard v Livingstone-Stallard* **[1974] Fam 47**, Dunn J indicated that the test is: 'would any right-thinking person come to the conclusion that this husband has behaved in such a way that this wife cannot reasonably be expected to live with him, taking into account the whole of the circumstances and the characters and personalities of the parties?' (p. 54). Quinn has clearly behaved in a way that Poppy cannot reasonably be expected to tolerate, as *Ash v Ash* **[1972] Fam 135**, which also concerned domestic violence, demonstrates.

The vast majority of divorces are undefended, which means that they are heard in the Family Court using the special procedure. If Quinn does not defend the divorce, the case is entered onto the special procedure list, the legal adviser reads through the documentation and if s/he is satisfied that the ground and fact for divorce have been established, the decree nisi will be pronounced. Six weeks later the petitioner can apply for the decree absolute, which finally dissolves the marriage.

Domestic Violence Protection[3]

The question indicates that the police were called to an incident at Poppy and Quinn's house. It is therefore possible that the police officer issued a Domestic Violence Protection Notice (DVPN),[4] which would prohibit Quinn from contacting Poppy or returning to the home and would enable the officer to apply to the court for a Domestic Violence Protection Order (DVPO)[5] within 48 hours. If this has happened, the order will only last 14–28 days, which means that Poppy requires a further order to provide more long-term protection.

Non-molestation Orders

Poppy should apply for a non-molestation order under **s.42** of **the Family Law Act 1996**, which is an order that prohibits 'a person (the respondent) from molesting another person who is associated with the respondent or a relevant child' (**s.42(1)**). Molestation is not defined in the statute but 'encompasses any form of serious pestering or harassment and applies to any conduct which could properly be regarded as such a degree of harassment as to call for the intervention of the court' (Law Commission, No. 207, 1992 Domestic Violence and Occupation of the Family Home para. 3.1). There is no question that Quinn has molested Poppy and it is clear that they are associated persons, as they are married to one another (**s.62(3)**).

---

[2] Do not refer to 'unreasonable behaviour'.

[3] The question focuses on protection for Poppy. It is possible that Quinn will face a criminal prosecution.

[4] Only senior police officers can issue notices.

[5] DVPNs and DVPOs were introduced as a result of **the Crime and Security Act 2010**.

Poppy should be advised that an application for a non-molestation order can be made ex parte[6] where the court considers it just and convenient to do so (**s.45(1)**). If an ex parte order is made, Quinn would have the right to a full inter partes hearing and would thus have the opportunity to apply to set the order aside.

When deciding whether to exercise its powers and if so, in what manner, the court must have regard to all the circumstances, including the need to secure the health, safety and well-being of the applicant (**s.42(5)**). As Quinn has attacked Poppy it is clear that the court needs to take action to ensure Poppy's safety, and although the court is able to accept an undertaking from the respondent, it will not normally do so 'in any case where it appears to the court that the respondent has used or threatened violence against the applicant' (**s.46(3A)**). The court should not therefore accept an undertaking and should make a

[7] You could consider the terms that the court will include in the order.

non-molestation order.[7] If Quinn does anything that he is prohibited from doing under the order, without reasonable excuse, he would be

[8] This provision was introduced by **the Domestic Violence, Crime and Victims Act 2004**.

guilty of a criminal offence (**s.42A**) and may face a prison sentence of up to five years.[8]

Occupation Orders

As Poppy wishes to return to the family home, she also needs to apply for an occupation order, as it can require Quinn to leave the property, enable Poppy to return to it and exclude Quinn from a defined area (**s.33(3)**). An occupation order can only be made in relation to a dwelling house that is, was, or was intended to be the family home. The applicant must be associated with the respondent *and* must have shared or intended to share a home with the respondent. These requirements are satisfied in this case.

[9] As Poppy is clearly an entitled applicant, it is not necessary to discuss non-entitled applicants.

Those who are in a position to make an application are categorised as 'entitled' or 'non-entitled' applicants.[9] Under **s.33** a person is an entitled applicant if s/he 'is entitled to occupy a dwelling house by virtue of a beneficial estate or interest or contract or by virtue of any enactment giving him the right to remain in occupation', or if s/he has home rights under **s.30**. A spouse or civil partner who is not entitled to occupy the home under the general law (i.e. because they do not have a beneficial interest in it or a contractual right to live in the property) has home rights. Although we do not know who owns the home, Poppy is an entitled applicant because she has home rights under **s.30**: she should therefore apply for an occupation order under **s.33**. The application can be made ex parte.

Section 33(7) provides that if it appears that the applicant or any relevant child is likely to suffer significant harm attributable to the conduct of the respondent if an order is not made, the court shall make the order unless it appears that 'the respondent or any relevant child is likely to suffer significant harm if the order is made' and 'the harm likely to be suffered by the respondent or child in that event is as great as or greater than, the harm attributable to conduct of the respondent which is likely to be suffered by the applicant or child if the order is not made'. This is known as the 'balance-of-harm test'. In this particular case, Poppy is likely to suffer significant harm if an occupation order is not made, as she cannot continue to reside with her sister and returning home without excluding Quinn would put her at risk. The question that follows is whether Quinn would suffer as great or greater harm than Poppy if the order is made (see *B v B* **[1999] 1 FLR 715**). There is nothing in the question to suggest that he would and so the court *must* make an occupation order. If the balance-of-harm test was not satisfied, the court could make a discretionary order and would consider the factors listed in **s.33(6)**.

A mandatory or discretionary occupation order can be made for a fixed term or unlimited length (**s.33(10)**). Under **s.40(1)** supplemental orders can be made relating to expenses associated with the property, but as we do not know whether the property is rented or subject to a mortgage, it is impossible to state what orders the court would make. It should also be noted that the court has an obligation to consider making a non-molestation order when making an occupation order. This means that if Poppy only applies for an occupation order, the court could actually make both orders.

Quinn may offer to make an undertaking to leave and stay away from the property. However, **s.46(3)** provides that the court shall not accept an undertaking where a power of arrest would be attached to the order. In this case, a power of arrest should be attached as Quinn has used violence towards Poppy (**s.47(2)**). The power of arrest gives the police the automatic power to arrest the respondent if he breaches the order. The respondent can then be prosecuted for contempt of court, which can be punished by a fine or prison sentence not exceeding two years. If the breach of the occupation order also constitutes a breach of the non-molestation order, a criminal offence is committed punishable by up to five years in prison.

Conclusion

Poppy should apply for ex parte non-molestation and occupations orders and petition for divorce on the basis of Quinn's behaviour.

LOOKING FOR EXTRA MARKS?

- Gain extra marks by pointing out that a DVPN and a DVPO may have been issued.
- Use the IRAC method to ensure that you tackle this problem question well.

Samantha and Timothy have been in a relationship for five years. Three years ago they moved into a flat owned by Samantha's parents and decided to start a family. After two years, the couple sought advice from a fertility specialist at a licensed clinic because Samantha had not become pregnant. They were advised to try *in vitro fertilization* (IVF) using Samantha's eggs and donated sperm. Timothy was present when the first embryo was implanted and the implantation was successful. Two months ago Samantha gave birth to a daughter, Uma. Last week Timothy told Samantha that he has been having an affair with Violet and that he was leaving her to live with Violet and her two children from a previous relationship, Willow, aged 15 and Xia, aged ten. Timothy has said that he does not want to see Uma, as she is not his biological child. Samantha has asked Timothy for child support but Timothy has refused to pay on the basis that he is not Uma's father. Timothy's gross income is £1,000 per week.

Advise Samantha.

CAUTION!

- To determine whether Timothy is liable for child support you need to decide whether he is the legal father of Uma.

- As the couple are not married, you should not discuss divorce or financial relief and there is no need to consider child arrangements orders.

- You should immediately realise that ownership of the family home is not an issue in this question.

DIAGRAM ANSWER PLAN

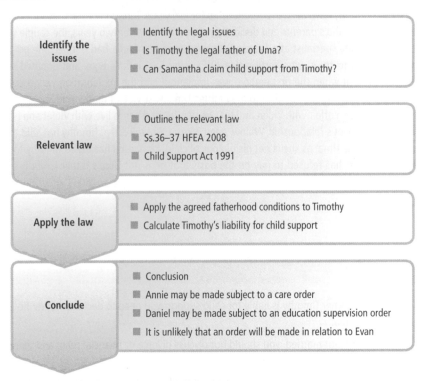

Identify the issues
- Identify the legal issues
- Is Timothy the legal father of Uma?
- Can Samantha claim child support from Timothy?

Relevant law
- Outline the relevant law
- Ss.36–37 HFEA 2008
- Child Support Act 1991

Apply the law
- Apply the agreed fatherhood conditions to Timothy
- Calculate Timothy's liability for child support

Conclude
- Conclusion
- Annie may be made subject to a care order
- Daniel may be made subject to an education supervision order
- It is unlikely that an order will be made in relation to Evan

SUGGESTED ANSWER

Samantha requires advice as to whether she can claim child support for her daughter, Uma from her former partner, Timothy. Liability for child support is primarily governed by **the Child Support Act 1991** (as amended). **Section 1(1)** of **the Child Support Act 1991** provides that 'each parent of a qualifying child is responsible for maintaining him'. A parent is defined as a person who is in the eyes of the law the mother or father of the child (**s.54**). The issue in this case, is therefore, whether Timothy is regarded as the legal father of Uma.

Legal Parenthood[1]

[1] It is not necessary to discuss motherhood, as this is not an issue in this problem question.

If a couple receive assisted reproduction services at a licensed clinic, utilising egg donations, sperm donations or donated embryos the provisions of **the Human Fertilisation and Embryology Act 2008** determine who is the legal father and mother of any child born as a result of the treatment. The 2008 Act replaced **the Human Fertilisation and Embryology Act 1990** and displaces the common law rules relating to parenthood in certain cases.

[2] Sperm donors protected by **s.41** cannot be pursued for child support.

The first point to note is that the sperm donor is not treated as the child's legal father (**s.41(1) HFEA 2008**).[2] This does not mean that children born as a result of sperm donor insemination will always be fatherless, as the Act enables the mother's husband or partner to be treated as the child's legal father. As Samantha and Timothy are not married, **s.36 HFEA 2008** is relevant. This provision enables a woman's male partner to be treated as the child's legal father if the requirements set out in **s.37** (the agreed fatherhood conditions) are satisfied. Under **s.37(1)(a)**, the man in question must give the person responsible at the licensed clinic a notice stating that he consents to being treated as the father of any child resulting from treatment provided to his partner and the woman in question must give notice that she consents to her partner being treated as her child's father (**s.37(1)(b)**). In both cases, the notice must be in writing and signed by the parties (**s.37(2)**) and must not have been withdrawn (**s.37(1)(c)**). The woman must not have given a further notice indicating that she consents to another man being treated as the father of any resulting child or that she consents to a woman being treated as the other parent of any resulting child (**s.37(1)(d)**) and the parties must not be within the prohibited degrees of relationship (**s.37(1)(e)**). This amended the position under **the 1990 Act, s.28(3)**, which provided that a male partner would be treated as the child's father if the woman was implanted/inseminated in the course of treatment services provided for her and the man together.[3]

[3] In this case, Timothy would have been treated as the father under the old Act, as well as the 2008 Act.

Given that Timothy attended the successful implantation, it is safe to assume that both parties gave the required written notices, as the clinic would not treat the couple without the requisite consents. It also assumed that Timothy did not withdraw consent before implantation, as he attended the implantation. There is nothing to suggest that Samantha has consented to anyone else being treated as Uma's father or other parent or that Samantha and Timothy are closely related. It can therefore be concluded that Timothy is Uma's legal father.

Child Support

As Timothy is Uma's legal father a claim can be made for child support under **the Child Support Act 1991**, as Uma is under the age of 16 (**s.55 CSA 1991**). Samantha can apply to the Child Maintenance Service (which replaced the Child Support Agency for new claims) for a maintenance calculation or she can additionally request that the Child Maintenance Service collects the maintenance from Timothy. A £20 application fee is payable for a maintenance calculation. If maintenance is also to be collected, the non-resident parent must pay a 20 per cent collection fee for every payment collected, whilst the recipient has 4 per cent deducted from the payments. It is not compulsory to utilise the Child Maintenance Service, as parents are permitted to make maintenance agreements under **s.9 CSA 1991**. In this case, a maintenance agreement seems unlikely, as Timothy is unwilling to support Uma.

The child must be a qualifying child, which means that one (or both) of his parents is in relation to him, a non-resident parent (**s.3(1)(a)**). A non-resident parent is one who is not living in the same household as the child and the child has his home with a person who is in relation to him a person with care (**s.3(2)(a)**). **Section 3(3)** defines a person with care as a person with whom the child has his home and who usually provides day-to-day care for the child (whether exclusively or in conjunction with any other person). Uma is a qualifying child as she is under 16, her father, Timothy, is a non-resident parent and she lives with her mother, Samantha, who is the person with care.

The Gross Income Scheme

Prior to the full implementation of **the Child Maintenance and Other Payments Act 2008**, child maintenance was based on the non-resident parent's net income. The net income scheme[4] has been replaced by a system based on the non-resident parent's gross salary, so that the Child Maintenance Service can easily obtain information from Her Majesty's Revenue and Customs. The amount payable will be based on the latest available tax year information and will therefore be automatically reviewed on a regular basis, which was not possible under the net income scheme. **Schedule 1 Para. 2(1) Child Support Act 1991** (inserted by **the Child Maintenance and Other Payments Act 2008**) indicates that if the non-resident parent earns over £200 per week, he or she must pay 12 per cent of his or her gross weekly salary to the parent with care for one qualifying child. If there are two qualifying children, 16 per cent of the gross weekly salary must be paid, and 19 per cent if there are three or more qualifying children. If the non-resident parent's weekly income exceeds £800, the amount payable is 12 per cent of the first £800 and 9 per cent of income in excess of £800 (**Schedule 1 Para. 2(2)**). The upper limit under the gross income scheme is £3,000 (**Schedule 1 Para. 10(1)**). If a parent earns more than £3,000 per week it is possible to apply for top-up maintenance under **Schedule 1** to **the Children Act 1989**.

Relevant Other Children

Under the gross income scheme, the non-resident parent's weekly income shall be treated as reduced by 11 per cent if he or she lives with one relevant other child.[5] A relevant child is one who lives with the non-resident parent. If the non-resident parent lives with two relevant other children, the gross weekly salary is reduced by 14 per cent and if

[4]In a problem question, you will not have to discuss the net income scheme as new claims are always based on the gross income scheme.

[5]The amount payable could be reduced if Uma regularly stayed with Timothy overnight—but that is highly unlikely in this case.

he or she has three or more relevant other children, the weekly salary is reduced by 16 per cent. Under the gross income scheme, Timothy's gross weekly salary will be reduced by 14 per cent as he currently lives with two relevant other children, but it should be noted that Willow is 15 and may not be 'relevant' after she has reached the age of 16.

[6]It is assumed that Timothy does not receive benefits that might affect his liability.

Calculation[6]

Timothy's income of £1,000 is reduced by 14 per cent (£140) as he lives with two relevant other children. His income for calculation purposes is therefore £860. The basic rate is 12 per cent of £800, which is £96. Timothy also has to pay 9 per cent of the income in excess of £800, i.e. 9 per cent of £60, which is £5.40. The total amount payable is £101.40, which is rounded down to the nearest pound. As explained earlier, the full amount will not be received if Samantha asks the Child Maintenance Service to collect the maintenance for her. The maintenance will be reduced by 4 per cent, i.e. £4.04. In total her maintenance would be reduced by £210.08 per year and she will have to pay the initial £20 application fee. In addition, Timothy will have to pay a weekly collection fee of 20 per cent, i.e. £20.20.

Liability and Enforcement

Once Timothy has been informed of his liability he must ensure that he pays promptly otherwise the Child Maintenance Service can take enforcement action if they have been asked to collect payments. The enforcement mechanisms currently available include: deduction from earnings (**s.31**); regular deduction from earnings (**s.32**); regular deductions from bank accounts (**s.32A**); lump sum deductions from bank accounts (**s.32E** and **F**); liability orders (**s.32M**); disqualification from driving or travel authorisation (**s.39B**); surrender of driving and travel documents (**s.39CA**); curfew orders (**s.39H**); and ultimately commitment to prison (**s.40**).

Conclusion

Timothy is the legal father of Uma and is therefore liable to pay child maintenance. He must accept the fact that he is required to support Uma or face the consequences.

 LOOKING FOR EXTRA MARKS?

■ Try to calculate exactly how much child support Timothy is required to pay each week and indicate the consequences of non-payment.

Yasmin and Zack have been living together for 12 years: they have never married. They have three children: Alex, aged 12, Bobby, aged nine and Claire, aged six. Yasmin has not worked since Alex was born and Zack works full time for an insurance company. Yasmin has just found out that Zack has been having an affair with a colleague, Don. When she confronted Zack about it, he admitted that he is bi-sexual. Yasmin told Zack to leave and said that she never wants to see him again. Zack has moved in with Don. Yasmin will not let Zack see the children. Zack says that if she does not let him see them, he will apply to the court for 'custody'.

Explain the law that applies in this situation and discuss whether the parties will be required to utilise mediation in an attempt to resolve the dispute.

CAUTION!

■ Yasmin and Zack are not married—you should not therefore discuss divorce or financial orders on divorce. There is no information regarding family property and so you should not discuss ownership of the home, etc.

■ Obviously, Yasmin would be able to claim child support from Zack, but the question does not ask you about this.

DIAGRAM ANSWER PLAN

Identify the issues	■ Identify the legal issues
	■ Is Zack entitled to see the children and if so, how can he enforce this?
	■ Should Zack apply for 'custody' as the case study suggests?
	■ Will the couple be required to attend mediation?

Relevant law	■ Outline the relevant law:
	■ S.8 Children Act 1989—child arrangements orders
	■ S.1(1) Welfare Principle
	■ S.1(2A) Presumption of parental involvement
	■ S.1(3) Welfare Checklist
	■ Children and Families Act 2014—use of mediation

Apply the law	■ Zack can apply for a child arrangements order to see the children or for the children to live with him
	■ Consider whether the presumption of involvement applies
	■ Discuss relevant aspects of the welfare checklist, e.g. wishes of the children, effect of change, potential harm
	■ Discuss whether the couple will be required to utilise mediation

Conclude	■ Conclusion
	■ If Zack wishes to initiate proceedings, a MIAM will be required
	■ The children may not be ordered to live with Zack but he would be involved in their lives

SUGGESTED ANSWER

Yasmin will not allow Zack to see their children and as a result he is threatening to sue for 'custody'. The first point to make is that 'custody' does not exist. Zack would therefore be applying for a child arrangements order,[1] which is defined by **s.8 of the Children Act 1989** as an order regulating 'with whom the child is to live, spend time or otherwise have contact and when a child is to live, spend time and otherwise have contact with any person'. A child arrangements order should be applied for if Zack wishes the children to live with him or if he wants contact with them.

[1] The child arrangements order replaced residence and contact orders, but you can still refer to old cases on residence and contact.

Zack is the biological and legal father of the children, which means that he has an automatic right to apply for any **s.8** order (**s.10(4)**). This is the case even if he does not have parental responsibility for the children,[2] which is a possibility, given that the couple were not married when the children were born (**s.2(2)**). But if a child arrangements order is made stating that the children should live with Zack, he will acquire parental responsibility if he does not already have it (**s.12**).

[2] It is not necessary to discuss the scope or limitations of parental responsibility as the question does not concern the making of decisions in relation to the three children.

Principles of the Children Act

When the court hears an application with respect to the upbringing of a child 'the child's welfare shall be the court's paramount considera-tion' (**s.1(1)**). Section 1(2A) and **s.1(6)** indicate that unless the con-trary is shown, it is presumed that the involvement of a parent who can be involved in a child's life without putting the child at risk of harm, will further the child's welfare.[3] It is therefore presumed that Zack should be involved in his children's lives as there is nothing to suggest that he will cause them harm. However, this does not mean that the court will order the children to live with him. In addition, **s.1(2B)** states that involvement means 'involvement of some kind, ei-ther direct or indirect but not any particular division of a child's time'.

[3] Inserted by **the Children and Families Act 2014**.

The Welfare Checklist

Section 1(4)(a) provides that when the court is considering a **s.8** app-lication and it is opposed by any party to the proceedings,[4] the wel-fare checklist, contained in **s.1(3)** must be considered. The checklist contains seven factors namely; the wishes of the child; his needs; the likely effect of change; his age, sex and background; any harm he has suffered or is likely to suffer; how capable each parent is of meeting his needs; and the range of powers available to the court under the Act.

[4] It is obvious that Yasmin would oppose any application made by Zack.

The children are 12, nine and six, which means that the views of (at least the older children) would be sought and may influence the court's decision. As we do not know their feelings, the potential significance of the children's opinions will not be considered further (**s.1(3)(a)**). The case study does not suggest that the children have any particu-lar needs that require discussion (**s.1(3)(b)**) but the likely effect of change will be a significant factor (**s.1(3)(c)**). Yasmin has always been the primary carer of the children and they currently live with her. If the children were ordered to live with Zack they would be removed from their mother to live with Zack and a man they do not know. This could cause the children psychological harm, which the court is required to consider under **s.1(3)(e)**. The fact that Yasmin has always looked after the children while Zack went to work might suggest that she is more 'capable' of meeting the children's needs. But there is no presumption that children should live with their mother, as *Re H (A Child)* [2011] **EWCA Civ 762** demonstrates, and in addition, **s.1(3)(f)** would require the court to consider the parents' attitudes to contact. Yasmin's refusal to allow the children to see their father diminishes her capability status and may be causing the children psychological harm, which the court will have regard to under **s.1(3)(e)**. However, Zack's sexual orientation would not be a factor that would influence the court's decision, as the attitude of the judiciary to same-sex relationships has changed in the past decade (see *Re G (Residence: Same-Sex Partner)* **[2005] EWCA Civ 462**). The court will take into account the age, sex and background of the children (**s.1(3)(d)**), but it should be noted that there is no presumption that older boys should live with their father and older girls with their mother. Finally, the court will consider the range of powers available under the act (**s.1(3)(g)**). It could, therefore make a child arrangements order stating that the children should live with Yasmin and that they should have contact with Zack. Given the importance of maintaining the status quo and the fact that it would be inappropriate for the children to live with a man whom they do not yet know, this seems probable.

Enforcing Contact

In this particular case, there is no good reason to deny Zack contact with his children. In the light of Yasmin's refusal to permit contact, the court would need to make an order because it will be 'better for the child than making no order at all' (**s.1(5)**). In addition, the court might include a 'contact activity condition'[5] under **s.11C** (inserted by **the Children and Adoption Act 2006**) requiring Yasmin to participate in activities designed to convince her of the benefits of contact. If she continues to frustrate contact in breach of a child arrangements order the court has various options available in terms of enforcement. Prior to **the Children and Adoption Act 2006**, breach of a contact order was punished as contempt of court. The resident parent could thus face a fine or imprisonment, but the courts were reluctant to impose either, due to the impact that such penalties would have on the child concerned. **Section 11J** of **the Children Act 1989** (inserted by **the Children and Adoption Act 2006**) provides that the court can make an enforcement order imposing on the person an unpaid work requirement. Such an order will not be made if the person had a reasonable excuse and will only be made if the individual concerned was warned of the consequences of non-compliance. The person in whose favour contact is made can also seek compensation from the resident parent for financial losses caused by the failure to comply (**s.110**). Ultimately, the court could transfer the children's residence from the resident parent to the other, but in *Re W (Residence: Leave to Appeal)* **[2010] EWCA Civ 1280** the Court of Appeal stressed that this cannot be done to punish the parent in breach of the order.

[5] Contact activity conditions can be included in the final order. At earlier stages of proceedings a contact activity direction can be made.

Residence can be transferred if it is in the best interests of the child, i.e. the harm caused by denying contact is greater than the harm caused by changing the child's residence.

Resolving the Dispute through Mediation

If Yasmin continues to deny Zack contact with his children, Zack will seek legal advice and may wish to initiate legal proceedings. Since **the Family Law Act 1996** the Government has promoted the use of mediation to resolve family disputes such as this.[6] The first point to note is that **the Legal Aid, Sentencing and Punishment of Offenders Act 2012** restricted the availability of legal aid for representation in the family courts to cases involving domestic violence, child abduction, etc. Legal aid for mediation is still available for disputes relating to children, such as this one. It is unlikely that Zack would be financially eligible for legal aid, but Yasmin would be, as she doesn't have a job. She could obtain legal aid for mediation to resolve this dispute, but she will not receive legal aid to cover legal proceedings if they are initiated.

Section 10(1) of **the Children and Families Act 2014** provides that before making a relevant family application, a person must attend a Mediation Information and Assessment Meeting. **Section 10(2)** of the Act states that Family Procedure Rules can make provision that s.10(1) does not apply in certain circumstances. **Rule 3.8** of **the Family Procedure Rules 2010 (SI 2010/2955)**[7] indicates that the MIAM requirement will not apply to cases involving domestic violence or child protection or urgent cases and cases involving financial remedies where the applicant is bankrupt. There are **additional** circumstances when the obligation to attend a MIAM will not apply[8], for example if either party has a disability that would prevent attendance, if there are no authorised mediators within 15 miles or if the applicant contacted three mediators and none were available within 15 days. If Zack wishes to initiate proceedings under **s.8** of **the Children Act 1989** for a child arrangements order he would be required to attend a MIAM, assuming that none of the circumstances that would exempt him from attendance apply. However, the mediator may conclude that the case is unsuitable for mediation if Yasmin refuses to co-operate. Zack may therefore have to initiate court proceedings, but as explained above, Yasmin would not be eligible for legal aid to pay for representation in court.

[6] In a problem question such as this, it is not necessary to discuss how the Government has promoted mediation over the years—you only need to know the current position.

[7] The Rules are supplemented by Practice Direction 3A Mediation Information and Assessment Meetings.

[8] Other examples are that the applicant or respondent are not habitually resident in England and Wales or if the applicant is a child, but these would not apply to Zack.

LOOKING FOR EXTRA MARKS?

■ Demonstrate the currency of your knowledge by discussing the changes made by **the Children and Families Act 2014**.

Emilia, who is 45, and Finlay, who is two years older, have been married for 25 years. They have one child, George, who is 22 and no longer lives with them. The couple have a joint bank account with £10,000 in it. Finlay works as an accountant and earns £80,000 per annum. Emilia has not worked since she gave birth to George. The family home, which was purchased after George was born, is worth £400,000. It is mortgage-free and is registered in Finlay's sole name. Finlay said that this was for tax reasons and that the house also belonged to Emilia. Finlay and Emilia have just separated and are about to divorce. Emilia is worried about her financial position.

a) **Advise Emilia as to her financial position in this case. [30 marks]**

b) **What would the position be if Emilia and Finlay had never married? [20 marks]**

NB. You do not need to consider the ground/facts for divorce.

CAUTION!

- In relation to married couples you must explain the powers of the court under **the Matrimonial Causes Act 1973** and the principles that guide the court when exercising its discretion.

- In relation to unmarried couples you must discuss ownership of property, in particular, funds in a joint bank account and the possibility of claiming a beneficial interest in the family home.

DIAGRAM ANSWER PLAN

Identify the issues	■ Identify the legal issues ■ What sort of financial settlement is Emilia likely to receive on divorce? ■ What is Emilia's financial position if the couple are unmarried?
Relevant law	■ Outline the relevant law: ■ Financial relief on divorce—Part II Matrimonial Causes Act 1973 ■ *White v White* [2001], *Miller v Miller; McFarlane v McFarlane* [2006] ■ Division of property when cohabitants separate—claiming a constructive trust—*Lloyds Bank v Rosset* [1991]
Apply the law	■ Identify the orders a court is likely to make on divorce ■ Apply s.25 factors to Emilia and Finlay ■ Apply *Lloyds Bank v Rosset*—is there an agreement to share the property, is there detrimental reliance?
Conclude	■ Conclusion

SUGGESTED ANSWER

a) Emilia's financial position

Emilia and Finlay are about to divorce. If they cannot reach an agreement, either of their own volition or during mediation sessions,[1] Emilia should make an application for financial relief under **Part II of the Matrimonial Causes Act 1973**. **Section 21** empowers the court to make an order for financial provision (which includes periodical payments and lump sum orders) or property adjustment (which includes transfers and settlements). **Section 21A** allows the court to make pension-sharing orders, whilst **s.24A** enables the court to make an order for sale. In this case, Emilia will require periodical payments. In addition, the matrimonial home may be subject to a transfer order, settlement or an order for sale may be made and a share of the proceeds paid to Emilia as a lump sum. The money in the joint bank account may be shared or transferred.

[1] A MIAM would be required under the Children and Families Act 2014.

When hearing an application for financial relief the court is required to consider whether to exercise its powers so 'that the financial obligations of each party towards the other will be terminated as soon after the grant of the decree as the court considers just and reasonable' (**s.25A(1)**). Clean break orders are sometimes inappropriate if the marriage is lengthy and if ongoing periodical payments are required to compensate one spouse for losses suffered as a result of the marriage (*McFarlane v McFarlane* [2006] **3 ALL ER 1**). Emilia will need periodical payments in the short-to-medium term, but a deferred clean break should be possible.

Section 25(1) MCA 1973 requires the court to 'have regard to all the circumstances of the case, first consideration being given to the welfare, while a minor of any child of the family who has not attained the age of 18'.[2] **S.25(2)** then contains a list of specific factors for the court to consider when hearing the application. **Section 25(2)(a)** refers to the income, earning capacity, property and other financial resources which each of the parties has or is likely to have in the foreseeable future. In terms of income and earning capacity, Finlay has a well-paid job, whereas Emilia has no current income or earning capacity. These factors suggest that a periodical payments order would be required, at least in the short term. But in *Wright v Wright* [2015] **EWCA Civ 201**, the court emphasised that a middle-aged woman is expected to seek employment/improve her earning capacity. Emilia cannot therefore expect to receive periodical payments from Finlay for the rest of her life.

In terms of property and other financial resources, the couple has a joint bank account with £10,000 in it, but the matrimonial home is registered in Finlay's sole name. This does not mean that Finlay will retain ownership of the property, as this would mean that Emilia's housing needs would not be met. **Section 25(2)(b)** requires the court to consider the spouses' financial needs, obligations and responsibilities, and the primary need for both parties is housing. It would be unfair to transfer ownership of the property to Emilia, and a settlement seems unnecessary[3] given the fact that there is £400,000 of equity in the property, which would enable both spouses to purchase a small home. It thus seems likely that the court would order the sale of the property and division of the proceeds. In *White v White* [2001] **1 AC 596**, the Court of Appeal held that equality of division of family assets should be seen as a 'yardstick' but the court may order Emilia a greater share to compensate her for the loss of earning capacity she has suffered as a result of her contribution to the marriage (see *McFarlane v McFarlane* [2006] **3 ALL ER 1**). The contributions which each of the parties has made to the welfare of the family, including any contribution by looking after the home or caring for the family, must

[2] George is an independent adult and so does not need to be considered.

[3] Explain why this is the case.

be considered under **s.25(2)(f)**. In *White v White* (above), the Court of Appeal emphasised that there should be no bias against the home-maker and child carer and no bias in favour of the breadwinner. This point was reiterated in *Miller v Miller; McFarlane v McFarlane* **[2006] 3 ALL ER 1**. **Section 25(2)(c)** directs the court to take into account 'the standard of living enjoyed by the family before the break-down of the marriage'. There are insufficient funds to enable both spouses to maintain the standard of living enjoyed prior to separation: both parties will therefore have to live in a property that is smaller than they are used to.

Section 25(2)(d) then provides that the court must have regard to 'the age of each party to the marriage and the duration of the marriage'. Finlay is 47 and may therefore work for up to 20 years. Emilia's age does not preclude her from working or retraining: in *Wright v Wright*, the 51-year-old ex-wife was expected to seek employment. The duration of the marriage means that the court will look favour-ably on Emilia's application, for the longer the marriage, the more likely the applicant will receive a substantial award. The case study does not mention any physical or mental disability that would need to be considered under **s.25(2)(e)** or whether Emilia will lose pension rights, which must be taken into account under **s.25(2)(h)** and may justify a pension-sharing order.[4]

[4]We do not know if Finlay has a pension and so it is not necessary to discuss this in detail.

In conclusion, it is likely that the court will order the sale of the matrimonial home, which will enable a substantial lump sum to be paid to Emilia. The court will also order Finlay to make periodical pay-ments to Emilia, probably for a limited period of time whilst Emilia retrains or finds employment.

b) The position if Emilia and Finlay had never married

If Emilia and Finlay had never been married, Emilia would not be in a position to apply for financial relief available to spouses under **the Matrimonial Causes Act 1973**. The division of assets is based on ownership.

The family home is registered in Finlay's sole name but Emilia may be able to claim a beneficial or equitable interest in the property. A beneficial interest will be acquired if the legal owner creates an express trust. **Section 53(1)(b)** of **the Law of Property Act 1925** requires a signed written document to create an express trust and so Finlay's oral statements regarding the property would not suffice. However, it is possible to acquire a beneficial interest in property by the creation of a resulting or constructive trust, neither of which requires writ-ten documentation. A resulting trust is created if one party provides all or some of the purchase price for a property that is registered in the name of the other. There is no evidence that Emilia contributed to the purchase price and so could not claim that a resulting trust exists. To establish a constructive trust Emilia would need to prove a common intention that they should both be beneficial owners of the property and would need to establish that she relied on this to her detriment (*Lloyds Bank v Rosset* **[1991] AC 107**). A common intention will be found if the parties expressly discussed sharing the property or if intention can be inferred from the parties' conduct.[5] In *Grant v Edwards* **[1987] 1 FLR 87**, the claimant was untruthfully told that her name would not be on the title deeds because it might cause problems with her divorce proceedings, which were pending at the time. This express discussion was sufficient to establish a common intention. In *Hammond v Mitchell* **[1992] 2 ALL ER 109**, the comment: 'don't worry about the future because when we are married [the house] will be half yours anyway and I'll always look after you' constituted evidence of common intention to share the property. However, *Curran v Collins* **[2015] EWCA Civ 404** demonstrates that it can be difficult to prove the existence of an express agreement to share the property. The comments that Finlay made regarding ownership of the family home would be sufficient to establish a common intention to share the property.

[5] There is no evidence of conduct from which intention could be inferred in the case study.

Emilia then has to demonstrate 'detrimental reliance', which requires conduct that the claimant could not reasonably be expected to have embarked upon 'unless she was to have an interest in the house' (Nourse LJ in *Grant v Edwards* **[1987]**). Carrying out manual work on the property constituted detrimental reliance by the woman in *Eves v Eves* **[1975] 3 ALL ER 768**, whilst assuming joint liability for mortgage payments did so in *Crossley v Crossley* **[2005] EWCA Civ 1581**. But non-financial contributions, such as housework and looking after the children, will not amount to reliance. It therefore seems extremely doubtful that Emilia will be able to establish a constructive trust. The lack of reliance on the conversation will also prevent Emilia from making a claim based on proprietary estoppel (*Pascoe v Turner* **[1979] 1 WLR 431**).

[6] It is important to discuss Emilia's entitlement to the joint bank account as she is unlikely to be able to claim a share of the home.

In terms of the joint bank account,[6] Emilia and Finlay have a joint interest in the whole fund even if Finlay deposited all the money (*Jones v Maynard* **[1951] Ch 572**). Emilia is therefore entitled to a share of the joint account. In addition, household items purchased for common use using funds from the account will be classed as jointly owned by Emilia and Finlay, unless there is an agreement to the contrary. Items purchased for Emilia's personal use would be considered her own, as this is normally the intention of the parties in such circumstances.

[7] Her position would be much improved if **the Cohabitants Rights Bill 2014–15** becomes law.

In conclusion,[7] Emilia will be able to claim a share of the joint bank account and some of the items purchased from its funds but will not be able to claim a beneficial interest in the family home.

LOOKING FOR EXTRA MARKS?

▓ Refer to *Wright v Wright* [2015], which emphasises that ex-wives are expected to work.

▓ Demonstrate the currency of your knowledge by referring to **the Cohabitation Rights Bill 2014–15**.

Online Resource Centre   www.oxfordtextbooks.co.uk/orc/qanda/

Go online for extra essay and problem questions, a glossary of key terms, online versions of all the answer plans and audio commentary on how selected ones were put together, and a range of podcasts which include advice on exam and coursework technique and advice for other assessment methods.

Skills for Success in Coursework Assessments

12

As explained in chapter 1, family law modules increasingly utilise in-course assignments or coursework to formally assess students. They enable the assessment of skills such as research and reflection and provide students with the opportunity to demonstrate effective time-management skills, word-processing skills and the ability to reference material in accordance with academic practice. Coursework also enables students to explore an aspect of family law in more depth than it has been covered during lectures and tutorials.

It is now unusual for a family law module on an undergraduate course to be assessed by an examination alone. Students may be required to complete an in-course assignment *and* an examination at the end of the module, or there may be no examination, as the module is assessed by coursework alone. The word count for family law assignments may range from 1,500 words, if, for example, the assignment is worth 30 per cent of the module, to 6,000 words if the module is assessed by one single piece of coursework. Clearly, the amount of research that you are expected to undertake and the depth of your answer will vary according to the word limit.

The style of coursework questions does not differ from the style of examination questions: they may take the form of essays or problems. You should therefore refer to chapter 1 for tips on tackling essay and problem questions. The questions included in this textbook could be set as examination questions or coursework questions and the suggested answers will help you to begin your assignment. However, your answer should be more in-depth than the suggested answers in this textbook, as you will have plenty of time to complete a coursework question. As explained in chapter 1, the suggested answers in this textbook are likely to be shorter than you would be expected to produce for an assignment and contain fewer academic references and references to Government reports, etc. than your lecturer expects when marking coursework. Refer to the annotations and the 'Looking for Extra Marks' sections for additional information that can be included in a coursework answer. You should also produce a longer, more in-depth conclusion than the brief ones included in this textbook and you may be discouraged from using headings.

Given the time that students usually have to complete an assignment, the lecturer will adopt a more stringent approach to the assessment. He or she will expect an in-course assignment answer to:

● begin with a clear introduction which sets out the purpose of the assignment;

● utilise a far wider range of sources than a student would cite in an examination;

- cite academic opinion throughout the answer (which is not always expected in an examination);
- provide more detail in relation to the cases cited;
- reference the information in accordance with a prescribed referencing system, for example OSCOLA (The Oxford Standard for the Citation of Legal Authorities);
- be well written and logically structured;
- contain no basic mistakes (which may be excused in an examination)—the law must be explained clearly and accurately;
- end with a conclusion that sums up your arguments.

Ensure that you seek advice from your lecturer so that you know what is acceptable and what is expected.

Research and Planning

Start your coursework early so that you have plenty of time to complete it. Do not underestimate the time that it will take to gather the relevant materials and read them. If you start early, you will tackle the assignment with more confidence.

Begin by making sure that you comprehend the basic law before attempting to explore the topic in more depth. Start with the core textbook that has been recommended by your lecturer and read the relevant chapter or chapters to ensure that you understand the key rules and cases. Good textbooks will refer you to a variety of sources related to the topic, for example journal articles, Government reports, additional cases, etc. These materials will contain references to additional sources that you may be able to utilise in your coursework. Remember, you are expected to use a wide range of primary and secondary materials when completing assignments. Family law is a dynamic, fast-changing subject, so you will need to trawl the legal databases and online resources to ensure that you have the most up-to-date material.

Plan your answer by utilising the IRAC method for problem questions and the PEA method for essays. Make sure that every point you make is supported by legislation, case law or both, and, where appropriate, an academic comment.

When planning your coursework it is acceptable to work with other students, for example to analyse and debate the issues it raises. But take care that your informal discussions do not turn into collaboration or plagiarism.

Critical Analysis and Evaluation

When answering a coursework (or examination) question it is not enough to describe the law: you need to analyse and evaluate it. In problem questions this means deconstructing the law (i.e. breaking it down and properly explaining what it means) and applying it to the scenario that you have been given. In essay questions you need to formulate an argument, often for or against a proposition made in the question itself. The sorts of issues that you will consider in an essay question are: whether the law is clear and comprehensive; whether the law fulfils its objectives; whether the law is fair; and whether the law complies with international law. In order to do this you will need to refer to a wide range of secondary sources, for example academic journal articles, Government reports and Law Commission reports.

The Word Count

Students often find it difficult to adhere to the word count set by the lecturer. However, it is important to do so, as the ability to discern relevant information and the ability to write in a concise manner are important skills, which will be rewarded by the marker. In addition, you may be penalised for exceeding the word limit. If you have exceeded the word limit it is likely that you have included unnecessary information. General information that is broadly, but not specifically relevant to the question set can be condensed or omitted. For example, if you are given a problem question on divorce where one spouse has committed adultery, it is not necessary to discuss the other four facts, if the couple has not lived apart and there is no evidence of behaviour that the petitioner cannot be expected to tolerate.

N.B. Some law schools permit students to exceed the word count by 10 per cent. You will need to check the rules that apply to the course that you are studying before embarking upon your coursework. Footnotes, tables and the bibliography do not normally contribute to the word count.

Referencing

Many law schools require students to reference information contained in the coursework in accordance with a prescribed referencing system, for example OSCOLA (The Oxford Standard for the Citation of Legal Authorities). If you properly reference the materials used in your coursework you will be adhering to academic conventions and you will avoid allegations of plagiarism.

The OSCOLA system requires students to reference primary and secondary sources cited in the coursework using numerical footnotes. You must also include a table of legislation, table of cases and a bibliography, which must be set out in accordance with the OSCOLA rules.

Proofreading

Make sure that you complete your coursework early enough to proofread it. This will enable you to check that:

● there are no spelling or grammatical errors;

● your paragraphs flow and that the overall structure of the answer is logical;

● you have referenced all primary and secondary sources correctly;

● you have not exceeded the word count, but if you have done so, you will have time to condense your answer;

● you have adopted a formal, academic style rather than a journalistic or informal style;

● you have actually answered the question set!

Submission of Coursework

Ensure that you know how and when the coursework must be submitted. You might have to submit a hardcopy to your lecturer and/or submit an electronic copy via the university's virtual learning environment. Many universities require electronic submission using a plagiarism detection tool, such as Turnitin.

Penalties will usually be imposed for late submission of coursework (unless you have extenuating circumstances) and in some cases, your work may not be marked and you may be required to re-sit the coursework. Unless there is a good reason why you cannot complete the work on time, it is usually better to submit an unfinished piece of work by the deadline, than to incur late submission penalties.

Index